Genealogy Online

Genealogy Online

Researching Your Roots

Second Edition

Elizabeth Powell Crowe

McGraw-Hill

New York   San Francisco   Washington, D.C.   Auckland   Bogotá
Caracas   Lisbon   London   Madrid   Mexico City   Milan
Montreal   New Delhi   San Juan   Singapore
Sydney   Tokyo   Toronto

McGraw-Hill

A Division of The **McGraw·Hill** *Companies*

©1996 by The McGraw-Hill Companies, Inc.

pbk   4 5 6 7 8 9 FGR/FGR 9 0 0 9 8 7

Crowe, Elizabeth Powell.
    Genealogy online : researching your roots / by Elizabeth Powell
Crowe. — 2nd ed.
       p.   cm.
    Includes index.
    ISBN 0-07-014754-X (pbk.)
    1. Genealogy—Data processing. 2. Internet (Computer network)-
-Handbooks, manuals, etc.   I. Title.
CS21.C68   1996
929'.1—dc20   96-25800
                                                           CIP

McGraw-Hill books are available at special quantity discounts to use as premiums and sales promotions, or for use in corporate training programs. For more information, please write to the Director of Special Sales, McGraw-Hill, 11 West 19th Street, New York, NY 10011. Or contact your local bookstore.

Acquisitions editor: Jennifer Holt DiGiovanna
Editorial team: Robert E. Ostrander, Executive Editor
               Kellie Hagan, Book Editor
               Jodi L. Tyler, Indexer
Production team: Katherine G. Brown, Director
               Donna K. Harlacher, Coding
               Wanda S. Ditch, Desktop Operator
               Linda L. King, Proofreading
               Toya B. Warner, Computer Artist
               Janice Ridenour, Computer Artist
Design team: Jaclyn J. Boone, Designer   014754X
               Katherine Lukaszewicz, Associate Designer   WK2

Contents

Acknowledgments

As with any book, this one was made possible by the efforts of many people besides me. First, I'd like to thank each and every person mentioned in this book, as I obviously couldn't have done it without all of you.

Very special thanks to Jeri Steele and Cliff Manis, who pointed the way out of many a dead end. Special thanks to Jennifer Holt DiGiovanna and all the staff at McGraw-Hill.

Great gratitude is due to all my family and friends, who were more than patient with me while I was writing this book. But most of all I want to thank my mother, Frances Spencer Powell, who urged and encouraged me, babysat and researched for me, traveled and travailed with me throughout the entire process—from initial idea to final galleys.

Introduction

"I've gotten more genealogy done in one year on Prodigy than I did in 20 years on my own!" my mother exclaimed. And this from a 70-year-old grandmother who claims not to know a byte from a baud. This quote, from a 30-year genealogy veteran, shows how technology has changed even this popular hobby. The mind-boggling deluge of data needed to trace one's family tree has finally found a knife to whittle it down to size: the computer.

This book will help you understand that there's a rich community of information out there—information that can help you find where those missing ancestors are lurking. Some of the sources are free, some cheap, some dear. But until you know about them, they're worthless to you. Once you know what's available, you can decide for yourself whether or not to use them.

This book won't teach you how to do genealogy, rather how to use the tools of the online world to help you do it better. Still, I feel I should at least touch on how and why we do genealogy.

 # For those new to genealogy

Genealogy is the study of ancestry, or family bloodlines. Genealogists trace lines of family ancestry and usually show their findings by means of pedigree charts, or genealogical trees. Professional genealogists' studies can be relevant to history, law, sociology, and eugenics. To an amateur, the appeal is usually more limited and personal, such as finding out about family history.

Almost any self-respecting public library, no matter how small, has a local history and genealogy section. Some even have entire floors dedicated to those subjects. The desire to make history personal is a long-standing tradition.

Most cultures have, at some time, revered their forebears, often by ancestor worship. Primitive societies, such as tribes or clans, often sought to trace clan ancestry to gods, legendary heroes, or animals. Clans thus bolstered their identity and aspired to divine protection. Lineages were originally transmitted by oral tradition, but later literate societies began to write them down. Notable early Western examples include the genealogies of the tribes of Israel (recorded in the Bible), the Greeks, and the Romans.

Genealogies assumed special importance in connection with the principle of inheritance—of power, rank, and property. Lists of hereditary kings were compiled by the ancient Sumerians, Babylonians, Egyptians, Indians, and Chinese. To this day, one reason for hiring a genealogist is to contest a will or prove the right to an inheritance.

In medieval Europe, feudal landholders kept relationship records for transferring rank and land. Concern with kinship, and thus rank, was also reflected in heraldic developments; a single coat of arms can incorporate considerable genealogical information. With the Domesday Book now being put on CD-ROM, genealogists will have access to records heretofore too expensive or too rare to use.

Today, social status depends less on pedigree, but genealogy remains of interest to many people other than scholars. The United States, for

example, has numerous genealogical societies that trace people's descent. Some of these are national, but many more are local or regional, such as the Tennessee Valley Genealogical Society or the New England Historical Society. Others are specific to certain names. Many patriotic organizations, such as the Daughters of the Confederacy, limit membership to descendants of a particular historical group.

The Mormon church has collected an extensive bank of genealogical data (official registers of births, marriages, and deaths, and related documents), probably the greatest such collection in existence. Church members use these records in order to bring their ancestors posthumously into the church.

The federal government has recently started to put much of its data, such as death records, veterans' records, and so on, in machine-readable databases, which can then be accessible via the Internet. This has genealogists everywhere excited.

Popular interest in genealogy was increased by the television miniseries based on Alex Haley's *Roots*; in researching this book, Haley traced his ancestry back to his African forebears. A major appeal of genealogy is that it provides people with a sense of continuity and of belonging, for the hobby teaches you one thing very quickly: mathematically, we all must be kin somehow. This sense of belonging extends to other genealogists, for it's almost impossible to research any family line by yourself.

A recent cover article in *CompuServe* magazine highlighted the uses of their online genealogy forum. "We get several thousand users per week on this forum," says sysop Dick Eastman. The article then proceeded to describe how the forum helped one woman find her natural father, how stories about ancestors are swapped, and the sort of informational files uploaded to the library.

Genealogy is a popular hobby (the National Genealogical Society has 9,500 members; the American Canadian Genealogical Society has 1,900) and it's also becoming a popular home business. It's a way to learn history that makes it personally meaningful, yet it's challenging

and often frustrating. Native Americans, Jews, blacks, and adoptees often run into impasses in trying to find their ancestors.

 # Where computers come in

Databases, online services, online card catalogs, and bulletin boards are changing the sense of frustration that people have often felt in the past when trying to trace their roots. And genealogists who have faced the challenges and triumphed are online, helping others.

There's no denying that the computer has changed just about everything in our lives, and the avocation and vocation of genealogical research is no exception. Further, a wonderful new resource for computers, the Internet, has come into being and is still developing— at a pace that's dizzying. This book will explore many different networks, services, and bulletin boards that can help you in your pursuit of your ancestry.

Stories about how online communities have helped people in their genealogical research abound. For instance, I received this message on the Fidonet echo:

```
By: Roger L. Cousins
To: Libbi Crowe
Re: Success Stories
```

```
Ten or twelve years ago, I was doing my research partly by mail and
partly by phone. I was searching for all of the descendants of Samuel
Cousins, who settled in Alma, Wellington County, Ontario. There were five
sons and four daughters, and since I had information on only one son, I
had a long way to go. I contacted a gentleman in Aurora Ontario who was
my fourth or fifth cousin (through number 3 son). He gave me the address
in Weston Ontario of another cousin who had "a family tree from someone
in California." I wrote to this lady, but she would not send me the
information, could not copy it, and I could not visit her.
```

```
Four or five years later, when I lived in Alberta, I interviewed a lady
about the Cousins family there, and collected family group sheets on
about 130 individuals who, as far as I could determine, were not related
to me. Last spring, when I first got onto this echo, I noticed a lot of
messages from a lady in San Diego (Mary Ferguson—thanks Mary), who seemed
to know everything. On a hunch, I asked her if there was anyone in her
local club/association named Cousins, hoping to contact the individual
```

who had supplied my cousin with the information previously mentioned.
Mary wrote back that there was no one named Cousins, but that a gentleman
named Weidenheimer had done a book and his family was connected to the
Cousins family. Could that be it? I dug out the letter from Weston, and
sure enough, the man's name was Weidenheimer! Mary sent me photocopies of
the FGS from her library, and lo! The Weidenheimer connection showed the
descendants of number 1 son, and guess what? The Alberta bunch were all
descended from him! Mary and the echo had supplied me with over 190
Cousins descendants in one fell swoop!

Sincerely,
Roger
* Origin: ? The Point Of Confusion ? Gloucester, ON (1:243/23.14)

And these letters from "snail mail," as online folks call post-office mail:

Dear Libbi,
Here are a few examples on how the net has helped me and some friends:

There were a couple of queries last fall (1992) from Lori Campbell in
California and Lynn Young in Dallas, Texas, both of whom were looking for
their Forney ancestor. I replied to both that I didn't know their
particular Forney (and we ALL are still looking), but Lynn told me of a
researcher on Prodigy (which I can't afford) and gave me her name and
address. I wrote, and received a reply from a NEW (6th) cousin in
Maryland! (Shari and I are now corresponding via U.S. mail.) I extended
one of my lines back to Kent in England about 1400, although all links
[are] not verified yet. And Lori is going to send me ALL the data she has
on the northern Forneys just as soon as she figures out how to produce a
GEDCOM with her new utility package for Roots III. (I use Brother's
Keeper.)

Then in early November, I got a posted note from Ann Stroupe in
Washington State, asking about *her* Forney ancestor. Again I had no
knowledge of that Forney, but the note was seen by a Dan Straite (also in
Washington State), who posted a note to Ann. The next net mail note I saw
from Ann had exclamation marks all over it. SHE AND DAN HAD A MATCH! So
although I could not help her at the time, SHE found a new cousin and
more information on her line. And although she has a Macintosh and I an
IBM clone, we have exchanged data on our mutual line.

Along about November, while browsing through all the messages, I noticed
a note by someone who lived in Augusta, Georgia. (I live in middle
Tennessee.) I posted her a note, told her my family had no record of my
grandparents' marriage nor of my grandmother's parents' marriage, but
knew they lived in/around Augusta, Georgia in the 1880s to 1920s. I gave
her names and what dates I had, which was not much. In a few days she
replied, giving me the date and place of BOTH marriages, the county, book
number, page number, place to write for copies, and how much each county

asked in costs. I wrote and received a certified copy of both certificates for a mere $6. So ninety years or more after the fact, my uncle in Huntsville, Alabama now has a copy of his mother's and his grandmother's marriage certificate. Without the national genealogy echo, we would still be wondering.

I saw a note one day from a researcher in North Carolina, offering to look up specific information in his local libraries. Since my family was somewhat prominent in NC for some time, I asked for him to get me copies of a couple of things, plus any and all information he might find on Forney, and sent him some money to cover copy costs. I received a LARGE package from him in a few weeks, just CHOCK FULL of information! Here are some results from just that one message:

1) I was able to add the names and dates of all 19 children of my great-great-great-grandfather's 2nd marriage to my files, and am now hunting for their descendants.
2) I added all eleven children of my 5x great-granduncle, plus most of his descendants up to about 1900.
3) I now have copies of several wills, land deeds, etc. that I would never have been able to get otherwise. (Being local, John knew where to look; I didn't.)
4) From a copy of a local magazine he loaned me, I got the names and addresses of a dozen or so researchers interested in the same surnames that are on my list.

Now I know about three new cousins and two new Revolutionary War ancestors, and have information from one of the new cousins that links us to the Scottish and English royal family.

I saw a note one day from someone in Florida looking for information about his ancestor, who was supposed to have served in the Revolutionary War. As I had just seen a big three-volume set of genealogical abstracts taken from Revolutionary War pension files in my local library, the next trip I checked the book but was unable to find his ancestor. I posted a note to tell him where I had looked, and that I did not find his ancestor. A month or so later I put out a query looking for a certain marriage in Alabama, or so I thought at the time. Garland [the man in Fla.] replied that he could not find that marriage, but that he had found some information on some other members of MY family in HIS local library. (He had been watching the echo, and knew what other surnames I was looking for.) I asked would he mind looking a little deeper, and he has since sent me copies of several write-ups of some prominent members of the Alabama branch of the family, AND has posted a couple of notes to some other folks (who I didn't know were on the echo) trying to help me find that particular elusive marriage. Garland has not asked me to send him any money to pay for any of this yet.

I responded to a note from Richard Murphy (in Florida) expressing interest in any information on the Middleton family. Well, it's not my direct line, but I have an out-of-print book with some information on one of the descendants, so I told him what I had and offered to send him a

GEDCOM. In a couple of days, when I had split off that line from the rest of my database, I mailed him a disk (cost less than $1). I cautioned him that I had not verified ALL of the information on the disk. I quote some lines from his latest message to me:

"I knew that there was connection with some lines, just did not have the start . . . The info you sent me was just like a door that had been sealed shut and all of a sudden was opening up. Much of what you sent was correct. AND verified . . . Thanks for the response."

Richard now has a GOOD chance of connecting his Middleton line with the English royal family, thanks in part to the genealogy echo.

So there you have a few examples. The value of the net to me is immense, and well worth the yearly subscription price I pay my local BBS. Although there is information in a lot of libraries, obviously not ALL information is in ALL libraries (except maybe the Library of Congress, but I have at least one book that I don't think THAT library has). I might be very interested in a book that I know is in the Memphis, Tennessee library, for example, but NOT available through interlibrary loan, ask a friend on the net to check the index for a particular surname when he/she has time, and he/she will respond to my query. Often, fellow net participants will copy stuff for me, and all they generally ask is that I reimburse them the 25 cents per page that the library charges for photocopies, plus postage. That's only fair; after all, nothing worth having is ever really free. I have checked census data for total strangers, browsed through microfilm looking for a will, and learned a great deal about genealogy research in general, simply by helping other people on the net.

I am of the opinion, for what it's worth, that any serious genealogical researcher today (and certainly in the future) who does not make use of the net is leaving untouched a resource far more valuable than almost any other I have seen to date. It allows researchers to investigate, with the help of friends on the net, the information in other libraries to which they might not otherwise EVER be able to get at. All you have to do to see that in action is to monitor the messages for a month or two. Researchers not only here, but in Germany, Denmark, Italy, Australia, and Canada to name only a few, have in the past offered to do specific (and the key word here is SPECIFIC) research for others who could not afford to actually visit the places in question. Sure, there are a lot of seemingly lazy people who ask questions that can be answered by any good encyclopedia, but maybe THEY don't have access to ANY encyclopedia. Or maybe they cannot afford to travel to the nearest big library that would have a good genealogy reference section. One of the best for one of my lines is over 150 miles away, and I don't know if they're open on Saturdays (the Tennessee Archives isn't), even supposing I could afford to drive over for a day, which I can't. So my only access to the information in this library is via U.S. mail (slow) or a friend on the net. And it's generally the friends I've made on the net who have helped me most.

Elizabeth Ferguson of Kingston Springs, TN

And here's an example from James R. Bridges of New York:

The Genealogy Fidonet echo conference, sponsored by the National Genealogical Society, has given me major help on several different occasions.

Shortly after logging on in 1990, I noticed someone else was logging on with the same surname as my second great grandmother's maiden name—Lucy Sissom. I decided to inquire if he knew anything about her. It turns out he not only knew about her, but also about her parents and her grandparents. He sent me several pages of a book, written by a cousin of his, which traced this line of Sissoms. I, in turn, was able to bring him down to the present on this line. It is only through this contact that I have ever seen anything on this Sissom line of mine. Also because of the material he sent me, I have recently been able to make the connection with a number of cousins in Illinois.

The second major help occurred when I was referred to a book, obtainable through LDS [Mormon church] microfilm at their family history centers, entitled "the William Hyde of Norwich Genealogy," written in 1864. While I had been able to ascertain each of the direct ancestors carried in this book independently, the book gave me a wealth of surrounding information. It gave me the names of all siblings and their spouses, and even better it provided in many occasions a geographical history of the family line in question, most of which I had lacked. Without the conference, I seriously doubt if I would have stumbled across this book.

Also through this conference, I was contacted by a fellow Darrow researcher. Through numerous telephone calls, he helped me considerably, providing me with a copy of some bible records, etc. of my fourth great grandfather. Some time later, another BBSer and I exchanged numerous messages on the Darrow surname, finally resulting in a massive exchange of information between us on this line. The other researcher had compiled a book of Darrow descendants, with a good amount of information from me. Of course, I received a complementary copy of the book. It was through this second researcher that I was able to ascertain that indeed Clarence S. Darrow, of the Scopes Monkey Trial fame, and I were related, being fourth cousins removed a number of times. This was the answer to a question I first wondered about when I started this hobby, as I knew from a family history I had been given that my great great grandmother Bridges was a Darrow.

Another early help was on the ancestors of Sarah Way, who married John Lord. Here, a user from Pennsylvania pointed me in the direction of the Way Genealogy, compiled in 1989 by Harry Abel Way. Although the BBSer sent me the relevant information, I chose to purchase the genealogy as well, so that I might have a full accounting of the family. That direction from the BBSer gave me something on the order of four more generations of Way ancestors. As in the Hyde genealogy, I seriously doubt if I would have stumbled upon the book without the BBS information. Within the past year, another BBSer did much research for me (going

through vital records in Marblehead, Massachusetts and providing me with
the name and address of the Marblehead Historical Society) on lines
related to the Peach line. Essentially, she helped me go back several
generations on a number of wives' lines. Again this was a contact
achieved only through the BBS.

Last but certainly not least, this past summer I was directed to contact
a non-BBSing lady in Kansas by another BBSer. This lady was able to
extend several different lines back from my 6th great grandmother (1700s)
to the 1400s. Again, without the initial contact by BBS, I would not have
known where to go nor where to find this lady. She, incidentally, not
only sent me her common lineage, but she also sent photocopies of many of
her source documents as well.

So yes, BBSing has helped me considerably. It has helped me in my own
research, while at the same time I have also been able to help others in
similar ways. Sometimes the help is minimal, and at other times it is
great. There are certainly dry spells, but then something heats up again.

This is what is happening, right now, online around the world. How
did this come about?

 # Some conceptual background

Genealogists have had publications to turn to for many years. From
local/regional publications such as the Tennessee Valley Genealogical
Society's *Valley Leaves* to the venerated *Genealogical Helper*, a
wealth of information has been printed to help genealogists find
others working on the same ancestral lines, publish interesting tidbits,
and help each other with vexing research problems.

For not quite so long, but for some time now, they have also had
computers and genealogical database programs to help them track,
organize, analyze, and share their genealogical information. For a
while there was a dearth of such programs, then a widening choice of
formats, and then finally some semblance of a standard in the
GEDCOM. Everyone was plugging away, gathering and storing
information. They all had more information than they could use, some
of it germane to their own lineages and some of it not, but it was
surely useful to someone, so why throw it away?

So here were all these collections of data and all these users wanting to share that data. Now how could they transfer it, for example, from a CP/M to a DOS-based machine to a Mac?

In other fields, people were faced with the same problems. Astronomers, teachers, and the military were all doing the same thing genealogists were on different subjects. Electronic mail systems (e-mail), bulletin board systems (BBSs), and the Internet came into being to solve the problem of getting data from one place to another using phone lines and protocols, regardless of the machinery and proprietary software involved.

Electronic mail

Electronic mail systems are simply a way to send text from one place to another, just as regular mail does. Through a variety of different programs, that text can be private messages, public postings of articles, text files, graphics, even sounds.

But please take that "private messages" phrase with a grain of salt. I'll make this point several times in this book: posting something to a list, echo, or board means that many, many people will read it. Posting something to a certain person at his or her e-mail address means you and that person will read it, but so will the people who run the system to which you posted the text. As of this writing, no law or court case has established that electronic mail is as private as first-class mail. One or two court cases, indeed, have held the opposite; when something is posted to a company-owned, company-run, electronic mail system, the text is considered the property of the company.

An e-mail system might be a part of the Internet, a bulletin board, or a pay-per-use commercial service; it might even be part of a combination of these. Or it might stand alone, as a company-run e-mail service does. You need to check out any e-mail service you use, as well as its costs and distribution, carefully.

 # Bulletin boards

A bulletin board, as the name implies, is a place to post messages and information that anyone with access to that board is free to read and retrieve. Most bulletin boards have several functions, including games, but the two most genealogists will want to know about are messages (or mail) and files.

To continue the image, imagine a big cork bulletin board with messages tacked to it. On many systems, the messages are allowed to stay for only a few days or weeks; then they're replaced with new ones. The old ones are either filed or just thrown away, depending on the system operator's (sysop's) preference. Picture in your mind several of these boards, each one devoted to a specific topic. On a typical BBS, there are many of these.

Next to these boards are corresponding file cabinets. In the drawers are libraries of files, generally longer than the messages. They might even be collections of certain threads of messages, if a topic was interesting and informative enough. (A *thread*, in e-mail parlance, is a series of messages on a topic from several different people. Typically such a discussion lasts only a few days, and the issue is resolved in a few dozen messages. There are, however, exceptions!)

In the file cabinets concerning genealogy, you'll find programs, help files, ahentafels and tiny tafels, GEDCOMs, and so on. You can go in the file drawer and get a copy for your own computer, or you can leave one from your computer for others to see and use. Generally, you cannot modify the files you find there.

 # Networks and echos

Now let's look back at the cork bulletin board, the messages, for a minute. Each one is signed. Beside the person's name, the signature might include an address, the names that person researches (perhaps in what states or countries), and the origin of the message. On some bulletin boards they'll all be local. On some, they'll be from all over. In

the latter case, the bulletin board is associated with an echo or a BBS network. Here's my Internet signature, for example:

```
Elizabeth Powell Crowe (Libbi)
etravel@delphi.com
Searching POWELL, SPENCER, BEEMAN, MINER, CRIPPEN, ABBOTT
Ask me about TVGS and SG&HS
```

These networks are called Fidonet, RIME, ILINK, and so on. To send messages to someone on one of these echos, you must use a bulletin board on that echo. Then when you post a message, you flag it as either local or echo. If it's echoed, then the BBS you used will get and receive messages from all the other BBSs connected to the same echo or network.

In general usage, *network* refers to the overall exchange regardless of subject matter and *echo* refers to a specific subject category on that network. However, sometimes you'll see the terms used interchangeably, which is a sloppy practice. Occasionally, files are also sent this way.

At least one of these echos, Fidonet, is "gatewayed" to the Internet. That means that if you use the proper addressing scheme, you can send a message from a Fidonet BBS through a computer somewhere to an Internet address. It's trickier than it sounds, but quite useful once you get the knack.

These networks are not unlike the Internet in purpose. But when you get to the Internet, the functions and services are unimaginably expanded, and ever-changing.

A quick look at this book

This book will give you a basic education of the online world, but please be aware that what is written here was current as of 1996. Since that time, commercial online services, BBSs, and the Internet will have added, expanded, revised, and changed what they offer, as well as how and when they offer it. The only constant in the online

world for the last five years has been change, and at an exponential rate. So be prepared for adventures!

✳ Chapter 1: What you need

You have to have the proper hardware and software to begin this journey. This chapter will also point out the latest in browsers and review the current situation with packet-switching networks, from the consumer's point of view. It contains a very short description of ISDN and its associated costs. Attitudes and etiquette, and the various standardized forms of genealogical information, are also covered.

✳ Chapter 2: Local BBSs and their networks

The concept of the local bulletin board system and message networks are discussed in this chapter, with examples of good genealogical boards to visit. The system operators of these boards talk about their boards, and give you the latest information on their systems.

✳ Chapter 3: Fidonet

This chapter reviews the lively genealogical discussion groups on Fidonet, Ilink, and other BBS message networks, and tells you how to find a local board that carries them.

✳ Chapter 4: The Usenet newsgroups

Soon after the first edition of *Genealogy Online* came out, two major changes in the Usenet world came about. First, the structure of genealogical discussions on the Usenet were split from the catch-all soc.roots to several subcategories covering software, regions, how-to, and other topics. Second, CompuServe, America Online, GEnie, and Prodigy all began offering Usenet newsgroups as part of their services. The first change, with an explanation of news readers, will be covered in this chapter. I'll also provide instructions on how to subscribe to Usenet newsgroups on each of the major online services.

✳ Chapter 5: Roots-L and other mail lists

The simplest way to use the Internet, mail lists offer you conversation, research contacts, and more, delivered to your electronic door. You'll learn how mail lists are conducted and get specific detail on Roots-L.

✳ **Chapter 6: FTP, gopher, and the World Wide Web**
Gophers, FTP sites, and the World Wide Web can help you not only find where things are, but make contact with other genealogists. You'll read about specific WWW sites and learn about the software to use the Web.

✳ **Chapter 7: The National Genealogical Society BBS**
The first and oldest BBS dedicated to genealogy, the NGS board has more messages daily than almost any other genealogy board.

✳ **Chapter 8: Everton Publisher's BBS**
This bulletin board offers several online databases of genealogical information, some of which you can search for free.

✳ **Chapter 9: America Online's genealogy areas**
AOL offers online courses, messages, files, and full Internet access. Many people use AOL as their first online experience because the software is so easy to use!

✳ **Chapter 10: Delphi's custom forums**
Where there was one, there are now two: Searching for Roots (general) and Irish Genealogy. Delphi, still all text, is very active in genealogy, and this service offers Usenet and World Wide Web browsing. The service is still one of the best ways to read Usenet offline.

✳ **Chapter 11: CompuServe's Roots Forum and WWW page**
The oldest and most complete Genealogy forum on a commercial online service, the Roots Forum offers genealogists many files and messages, plus a weekly newsletter on the latest in genealogical research. In addition, CIS now has full Internet access.

✳ **Chapter 12: GEnie's Genealogy RoundTable**
GEnie has finally seen the GUI light. This is one of the most friendly, helpful online communities.

✳ **Chapter 13: Microsoft Network's Genealogy Forum**
This very new service added genealogy as one of their first hobbies' area. Find out how you can help it grow!

✳ **Chapter 14: Prodigy's Genealogy BBS and column**

Prodigy now offers some offline features, as well as full Internet access. The bulletin board is still one of the most active.

✳ **Chapter 15: The Church of Jesus Christ of Latter-Day Saints**

Though they aren't yet available by modem, the CD-ROMs of LDS genealogical data are available at almost every LDS library in the world. This chapter will give you a quick review of how to use this resource.

✳ **Chapter 16: Online library card catalogs**

You can find out what books are available at many libraries across the world and the country. Here's how.

✳ **Chapter 17: The Library of Congress online**

Available through telnet, FTP, WWW, and commercial services such as AOL, this is an invaluable resource.

✳ **Appendix A: The GenServ project**

This system is the best way to research actual GEDCOM databases online. This appendix looks at the current system and shows you how to use it.

✳ **Appendix B: Tiny tafel matching system**

A Fidonet service, this is a searchable database of contact information for genealogists and the family lines they're researching. The database covers many different BBSs.

1

What you need

T O take you to the online communities, you'll need, so to speak, a car and some road maps. You might also need to know the customs of the place and the dialect spoken there. Finally, you'll need to take something to share. These things are what this chapter is about.

⇨ Modem (the car)

The car you'll take on this electronic road is your modem. To the average user, this is a box that sits on your computer or a card in an expansion slot that's connected to a phone line and your computer. Note that telephone lines have very little electrical resistance. If lightning strikes a telephone wire outside near your home, the electricity can travel right into your home's phone lines. The stories you've heard about people who are killed while talking on the phone in a thunderstorm are true. Therefore, if you have a modem you should always disconnect it from the wall during a thunderstorm. If you don't, your modem, computer, and even printer could be irreparably damaged by a lightning strike. Installing a surge protector on your phone lines wouldn't hurt, but it's no substitute for unplugging during electrical storms.

A modem converts the data of your computer system into sounds, which are sent out on a phone line (or a cable physically connecting two computers) to another computer. That's modulation. The other computer, with its modem, translates these sounds back into computer-readable signals. That's demodulation. The modulator/demodulator, called a *modem*, makes it possible for computers to "talk to each other."

Unfortunately, phone lines in much of the country were never made to carry this sort of signal, and some of them have a hard time doing it at a reasonable speed. So standards of translation came into being to help phone lines carry this data faster and faster. The bad news is that, unlike fax machines, which all use a standard way of sending data to one another, modems come in a plethora of standards. And speeds. (How fast a modem can transmit data is commonly called its *baud rate* and is measured in *bits per second*, or *bps*.) There are also

a variety of compression methods (more about that in a minute) and error correction. Let's look at how all of this came about.

A little history

In the beginning, modems had switches to enable them to talk to different systems, and you had to mess with the switches to set stop bits, parity, and so on. And you often needed to change them in order to dial different destinations, which could be a real pain.

Then Hayes created modems with a set of software commands to control these settings without requiring you to touch the switches. This set of commands became the Hayes standard, which led other modem manufacturers to emulate Hayes and produce Hayes-compatible modems.

If errors in transmission were introduced by noisy phone lines, then telecommunications software took care of it. If the data was compressed for faster transmission, decompression software took care of it (programs such as StuffIt for Macintosh, PKZip for PCs, and uuencode for UNIX systems).

Then manufacturers began designing modems with compression and error correction built into their wiring. This helped with the transmission of data, but it meant that both modems had to be using the same kind of compression and error detection. The standards wars went on for a while, but have settled somewhat, into names like V.32.

I started out with a little old 300-bps Hayes Smart Modem in 1982, and I now find that the speed and variety of modems available today can be quite confusing. Many articles and even books are out there to help you choose from today's models, so I won't go into detail here. You have to decide what you want based on these three criteria:

Cost The older, slower models can be found in second-hand shops, flea markets, etc. The fastest, fanciest ones can set you back several hundred dollars. Just remember that, on almost every online service or system you'll use, time is money. Spending a little more up front might very well save you money over the life of the modem.

Speed Get at least a 9,600-bps modem. Currently, the fastest modem is a 28,800, and the prices on these are dropping rapidly. Many systems won't let you log on at less than 2,400 bps because they want as many users as possible to get on, get what they want, and get off again. Other places might let you on, but will charge by the minute. Uploading or downloading a large file of genealogical data will be painfully slow and painfully expensive at less than 9,600 bps.

Compression standard The highest-speed modems use compression to push more data through the phone line at a time. The methods to do this vary, and two modems that are communicating must use the same method (or standard) or nothing constructive will happen. The most-often used compression method is V.42bis, with the very close runner-up being MNP. Some modems do both, which is useful if you use many different services and systems. Buy a dual-standard modem if you can afford it.

Communications software (the engine)

What makes a modem work is your communications software, which can be likened to the engine in a car, your modem being the car. There are two basic types: serial communications programs and TCP/IP stacks. The first is just fine for dialing into bulletin board systems and some commercial online services. This kind of program is most commonly bundled with a modem or another software package.

TCP/IP is the standard communications format for the Internet. Because so many of the commercial online systems are now offering Internet connectivity, the software you get with a CompuServe or America Online membership is probably TCP/IP now. Windows 95 with the Plus! package has a TCP/IP stack built into it, and there are versions for DOS, Macintosh, and many other platforms.

Serial programs

There's a diverse selection of programs for standard serial communications. Many modems and some applications, such as Windows 3.1 and GeoWorks, come with a communications package, and it's usually enough to get you started. But sooner or later you'll want more than a stripped-down, basic program. Before you can effectively choose one, however, you must learn and understand the several functions of communications software packages.

First and most important is which modems the program supports. Most commercial communications programs come with more than 100 configurations, and you can count on most popular models being included. If your modem isn't listed, chances are that your modem and program will work with one of the generic configurations; you just might not get to use all your modem's bells and whistles. But if you've purchased a just-released model, especially on the high-performance end, make sure it's supported by the program you have in mind. Be especially careful with the Hayes program's SmartCom; it provides configurations for only Hayes modems.

The supported file-transfer protocols are also important. At first glance this seems easy, because it's a rare program that doesn't come with all the major transfer protocols (XModem, ZModem, and YModem) and many different flavors for that matter (batch, G, etc). Though XModem is probably the most typically used protocol, especially on the systems you'll explore in this book, I personally prefer ZModem. It allows you to resume an interrupted file transfer instead of starting again, a blessing if you're uploading and downloading large files on unreliable phone lines. YModem's advantage is that it allows you to batch-send a number of files in sequence.

Advanced versions of protocols might interest you as you become more experienced in computer communications. A shareware one, HSLink, allows you to send and receive at the same time, as long as the other system is also running HSLink. Two commercial programs, Crosstalk and HyperAccess, both available for Windows, have their own proprietary transfer protocols. If you use this program on both

ends, you can generally expect fast downloads and uploads with few errors. CompuServe Information Manager prefers to use the CompuServe B protocol.

A typical serial communications program will have a capture feature and a scroll-back buffer. The first allows you to save every character and keystroke to a file as you proceed with a session. This is useful for scripting, which I'll explain in a moment. The second allows you to use the Page Up and Page Down keys to see what's happened so far, but the buffer isn't usually written to disk for later reference. You should check how large a screen buffer the program offers. For many online sessions on the Internet and with some bulletin boards, it's useful to scroll back to see something that has already moved off the screen.

If you have a multitasking environment, look at the communications program's resource handling. Does the program adjust its share of processor time depending on whether it's running in the foreground or background? If not, you'll have annoying interruptions when transferring files in the background and working in the foreground.

Many modems today also come with a fax function. If yours has this, you'll need a communications program that can send and receive faxes. However, some of these programs hog the serial port, something that can be annoying if you have the fax program in memory and need to call an online service. Procomm Plus is one of these. If you use a multitasking environment, you'll have to close PCPlus to use CompuServe Information Manager.

Now let's talk about scripts. A good example is shown in chapter 10 of this book. This is one feature of data communications programs that's developing rapidly, and while many features are useful, others seem to be there just to impress you. Be certain the program offers a scripting language you can live with. Learning any of these scripting languages takes considerable time, so many users rely instead on scripts written by others, editing them to suit their needs. Also bear in mind that, in general, the more commands the more powerful the scripting language, but the harder it is to learn and understand.

The best thing to do is look for a program that comes with a library of predefined scripts for operations such as logging onto the most

popular online services and setting the program and modem to answer mode in order to receive calls. When you log onto popular online services such as CompuServe, Delphi, or GEnie, you might find that the forums there have member-written scripts for you to download. Check how many scripts are available on the software company's bulletin boards, too. These scripts are generally set up to let you provide your user name and password the first time you use the script, and from then on the script carries out your session automatically.

If you plan to write your own scripts, having a capture-to-file feature is a big help because you can record your first session and turn it into a script for future use. It's also nice if the program offers a built-in script editor because it's faster and easier to open script files using a built-in editor from the communications program itself. The editor often includes extras such as help screens, which list the available script commands, and step-through debuggers for locating problems, which make writing scripts easier. Determine whether the program will let you import scripts from other communications programs or platforms. This can save you some work if you're switching from one program to another, or even from DOS to Windows.

A feature that has become almost standard is a "phone book" for storing the name, number, speed, and modem setting for your favorite places to call. This should be easy to set up, edit, and sort according to your current whim: alphabetically, by phone number, by entry last dialed, whatever.

Another feature to consider is queuing. If you call a lot of bulletin boards or commercial online services, particularly if you experience busy signals repeatedly, you'll want to make sure the program can queue calls. This feature has the program continually dial the numbers until it's able to connect with one of them. Queuing saves you the tiresome task of cycling through the calls manually.

You might also want to be able to have multiple sessions open at the same time. (A *session* is a configuration file within the program's phone book for placing a call to a certain service or bulletin board, including name, phone number, modem speed, and the appropriate modem parameters.) Multiple sessions mean you can open a new session without closing a previous one, especially helpful if the

preceding session was busy and you want to retry it. A session that remains open also serves as a reminder to try the call again. Some programs even let you run multiple sessions simultaneously, say one on a modem and another through a direct connection or network gateway. Many businesses find this handy, but a genealogist probably won't need it.

Many genealogists will want a program that gives them remote access. If you're interested in calling your home computer from a library or a convention to download or upload files, you'll want to look at the communications program's remote-access features. Can you assign a password so you can log on from a remote location? Can anyone else log on without your permission or can you lock people out? Once logged on, can you allow or deny access to directories on your hard drive? Can you set the program to call you back to continue the session? This feature would be worthwhile if it's a toll call, but would be most useful if you regularly call in from the same phone number, since the call-back number has to be preset on the host computer before you leave home.

Also, if you plan to communicate via modem, one on one, with other genealogists regularly, you'll want to look at the chat utilities. These allow users on both ends to carry on a typed conversation. While any communications program lets you type messages back and forth in the terminal window, chat utilities separate your typing and the other person's typing into two windows, making it much easier to follow the conversation. This is most useful when you're running a BBS yourself, but if you and another genealogist are exchanging tiny tafels directly, chatting might be helpful.

Lastly, if you get serious about this way of researching genealogy, you might want network support. Many homes now have more than one computer, and some people like to connect them. If you plan to share a network modem or modems, you'll need a program with network support. You can use several programs to access modem pools with NetWare's NASI protocol, while other programs support NetBIOS networks. Match your communications program to your network program if you plan to set up something like this.

By all means consider the commercial communications programs, and read the ads and reviews. But also look into the many fine shareware programs: Telix, CILink, and so on. They're usually good buys, have good support for registered users, are powerful programs, and have most of the features discussed here. Ask at your local computer users' group to find out about these, or sign on to a local bulletin board and ask the sysop for a recommendation.

Whichever communications program you choose, you can fine-tune your engine, er, communications software for error-free, high-speed file transfers. Look for a chip called the UART, located inside your computer near your main processor. It's both a transmitter and a receiver. Your universal asynchronous receiver and transmitter (UART) simplifies terminal, printer, and computer interfaces by being fully programmable, including the bps, number of data bits, number of start bits, number of stop bits, type of parity, manipulation of output handshaking lines, and sending of input handshaking lines. If a UART is too old, it can't keep up with the new modems when it tries to speak "modemese," or RS232 protocol. If you need help with this, you can read technical manuals or ask your local computer shop.

If your modem can operate at 9,600 bps or higher, be sure your serial port uses a UART 16550 chip; if was made in the last three years, it probably does. If it doesn't, you can buy an I/O board that has one for as little as $40. And use the communications program to turn off the software flow control for connections at 9,600 bps or faster. Xon/Xoff uses characters inserted in transmitted data to instruct the modem to pause when the transmitted data exceeds the capacity of the receiving modem's buffers. Unfortunately, this method really slows down high-speed transfers. Set the program to use RTS/CTS, a hardware-based flow control, and let the modem decide how fast it can take it.

You can use other engines besides your main communications program. Many of the commercial services have front-end software, which is a communications and script program to connect to their service. CompuServe Information Manager, Aladdin, D-Lite, and so on can make your sessions on these pay-by-the-minute services faster and less painful. Some of the front-end software have the features I've

mentioned, and you can use some of them as very limited, general-purpose communications software to log onto other systems.

 # TCP/IP stacks

There are many communication programs that allow you to communicate with the Internet, on all platforms from PC and Macintosh to VAX and UNIX. However, one catch is that you usually have to get on the Internet to download the latest (often in a final test form called *beta*) or the cheapest. Don't despair, though; there are ways around this.

First, if you get onto a local BBS you'll often find older but reliable TCP/IP programs for many platforms, with names such as Trumpet. Those will be enough to get you online to start downloading newer ones. Second, consider an Internet connection package. These run from $19 to over $100, depending on how much software and documentation is included. Netscape Navigator, for about $30 for PC and Macs, is an excellent package that gives you not only the TCP/IP but also several programs you need to use the Internet effectively. Internet the Easy Way from GT Interactive Software and InterAp from California Software, Inc. are two more packages that offer a full suite of Internet applications to help you get started. Many times such packages come with a trial subscription to an Internet service provider (ISP).

Which brings me to the third way to get Internet software before you're on the Internet: Find a good Internet service provider. The best ones will include a package of software, manuals, and hand-holding to get you started.

 # Choosing an ISP

Why go the direct route? Although commercial online services like America Online and Delphi offer lots of non-Internet goodies, dedicated Internet providers can offer a cheaper, faster, and more comprehensive entrance to the Internet. For example, AOL's Internet offerings are slow, sometimes clunky, and not well integrated, and

Delphi features lots of Internet services, but they're all text-based. With a dedicated Internet provider, you can use a graphical front end like Mosaic or Netscape, access every Internet service in existence via 28,800-bps or faster lines, and pay as little as $20 a month.

But, like choosing a mate, you should know what you want before you start looking. Your choice isn't final, of course, but you don't want to hopscotch from one to another. So go into this knowing that Internet providers are as different as dog breeds. All of them will get you onto the Net, but access speeds, services, software, and other goodies will vary. Before you lay down any cash, ask yourself some basic questions:

> ➤ What services do I need?
> ➤ How often do I need them?
> ➤ How fast do I need them?
> ➤ How many hassles am I willing to put up with to save money?
> ➤ How much am I willing to pay?

Just keep in mind that there are trade-offs no matter what provider you end up choosing. For example, you might find there's a price break for slower and less direct connections. And you might find that some companies consider support extremely expensive to provide, so if you sign up with a full service provider it will cost a bit more. You might save money by choosing only what you need, but in the end you'll probably find you need the whole shebang. While some users are happy with just the basics, to find all the genealogical treasures out there, you'll need more features, such as a Web browser to fetch sound, pictures, and animation. So you'll need a provider who can offer a high-speed connection.

When it comes to services, you should insist on the whole shebang: e-mail, telnet, Usenet newsgroups, FTP, gopher, and more—in short, everything the Internet has to offer. Even if the ISP service is austere, you should get at least a little support with that, too.

All the commercial online services now offer Internet access, and for your first online forays they're probably your best bet. Once you're

online with CompuServe, America Online, or a similar service, however, you might decide you want an Internet service provider instead. To find one, before you sign off the commercial online service use a Web browser to go to the following address:

```
http://www.commerce.net/directories/products/isp/isp.html
```

You can choose to search either by area code or by region. Use this list to find a local Internet service provider or a remote one that offers access via a local number. Make a list of two or three and contact them. These are the questions you should ask, and the answers you're looking for:

Do you offer 14.4 Kbps and faster access? The answer should be yes. The faster the better, because the genealogical information out there is pretty hefty.

Will I get a busy signal if I call during prime time in the evening? (In other words, how many high-speed lines does the provider have, and how many customers usually log on during prime time?) The answer should be that you can get on any time you want. They should have enough lines or enough ISDN capability to handle their current customer base. Make sure you test them on their answer; dial them up just after supper!

Do you offer anything else besides Internet access, such as BBS echos and file collections? The answer should be yes; Internet access alone can get old fast.

Can I use a graphical third-party front end like Netscape to access your system, and do you provide this software? Both answers should be yes. If the first answer is no, then you have to deal with a text-oriented UNIX system, and the provider should supply a written manual. If there's no manual or menu system, this should be a really cheap service.

Which message readers can I use with Usenet newsgroups? The answer should be a client that runs on your machine that they can provide you. If the answer is rn or nn, beware! These are arcane text-based UNIX news readers, a real pain to use. User-friendly Windows

and Mac-based readers like Free Agent are better; new browsers such as Mosaic and Netscape include news readers as part of the program.

What's the capacity of private e-mail boxes? The answer should be at least 100K of space. Bigger is better. If you subscribe to even a few genealogical mail lists and newsgroups, your mailbox could be stuffed quickly. If your mailbox is limited to 100 messages, you might miss important mail.

Will my connection be SLIP or PPP? PPP is better; it's newer, faster, and more reliable than SLIP, but if SLIP is all you can get, take it.

Do you provide access to all Usenet newsgroups, or just a selection? The answer should be all. This is very important for some of the more arcane genealogical ones.

When do you schedule downtime for maintenance? How heavily loaded is the system? Good luck getting straight answers to either question. The sysop should at least reassure you that downtimes will be announced in advance. For the real answer, nose around Internet discussion areas and ask users of the service for the real poop.

Do you have points of presence (POPs) across the country, so if I'm on the road I can still reach you with a local (or toll-free) call? Hope the answer is yes, but reality might dictate that you get Internet accounts from two different providers: one for home, and one for the road.

How do you charge? A flat monthly fee for unlimited connect time is the ideal answer. Second best: a flat fee with a generous allotment of online time and a low hourly fee ($1 to $3) for use beyond that allotment. Beware of hourly-based connect charges, which can add up in a hurry.

According to Michael Fraase, author of *The Internet Tour Guide*, an excellent book/disk set to get you started on the Internet, really smart ISPs offer a complete manual, training classes, and online news featuring phone number changes, service enhancements, and other information of interest to users.

With prices ranging from $10 a month for telnet access to $260 a month for an always-open direct line, there's something out there for everyone. The trick is knowing what you want, asking tough questions of prospective Internet providers, and finding a company that will give you what you need. Don't forget to compare the answers to these questions with the commercial online services, and to check up on how prices have changed every few months.

 # Inoculations

No journey is without risk. Whenever you enter the realm of file transfer, the dreaded microorganism, the computer virus, might be lurking. A virus is a program hidden on a disk or within an executable file that can damage your data or your computer in some way. Some simply display a message. Others will wipe out your entire hard drive. I strongly recommend that you inoculate yourself and your computer before using this mode of electronic travel. Programs to detect and remove viruses are available on BBSs, in your computer store, and on various online services. Some are shareware and others more costly, but if the program ever deletes a virus before it harms your system, it's worth the price.

As a general rule, when you download ask the sysop specifically if all files on the system are checked for viruses. If not, reconsider downloading from there. If someone mails or hands you a diskette, always run a virus checker on the disk before you do anything else. Once a virus has infected your hard disk, getting it off can be a headache. And run the virus checker on your hard drive at least twice a month, just to be certain. This should be part of your regular tune-up and maintenance.

 # Navigation systems (road maps)

Okay, let's assume you have your motor running. Now you'll need some road maps. There are two I want to draw to your attention: Internet Roadmap and Hytelnet.

⇨ Internet Roadmap

My mother (now pushing 70) wanted to know about the ins and outs of the Internet, and she wanted to also have a "cheat sheet" by her side in case she couldn't remember the difference between an FTP site and a gopher. As luck would have it, Patrick Douglas Crispen of the University of Alabama was about to start the third round of his e-mail correspondence course on the Internet, called Internet Roadmap. This excellent series of lessons is in clear, concise language, with definitions and examples for each concept. Your homework in the course is to carry out the steps he outlines in each lesson. In no time, Mother was off and running from Web site to WAIS, happily downloading this and that; if she forgot how to do something, she simply referred to the printed copies she had made of the lessons.

This book can't cover every detail of learning the Internet, but the Internet Roadmap course does. Crispen has had such success, he's allowed other people to post the full course at various sites on the Web, so there are copies of it in gophers and FTP sites; there's even a version in Japanese. If you're already on AT&T, America Online, CompuServe, or Delphi, use the Internet browser to go to:

```
http://ua1vm.ua.edu/~crispen/roadmap.html
```

which is the Internet Roadmap's home page. Unfortunately, as of this writing the workshop's distribution list is no longer accepting subscriptions. However, you can still get the workshop lessons e-mailed to you, in either individual files or in one-week blocks.

If you have a small e-mail box or if you want to retrieve only a particular lesson, you can send an e-mail letter to:

```
LISTSERV@UA1VM.UA.EDU
```

with the command:

```
GET filename filetype F=MAIL
```

in the body of your letter, replacing *filename* and *filetype* with the appropriate name and type of the lesson you want. What is a filename and filetype? Well, look at the following chart:

Filename	Type	Description
MAP01	LESSON	Welcome
MAP02	LESSON	Listserv file server commands

The filename appears in the first column and the filetype appears in the second column. So the filename and filetype for the welcome message would be MAP01 LESSON, and the filename and filetype for the listserv file server commands lesson would be MAP02 LESSON. So to get lesson 2, you'd send e-mail to:

```
LISTSERV@UA1VM.UA.EDU
```

with the command:

```
GET MAP02 LESSON F=MAIL
```

in the body of your e-mail letter. After you send your letter off, a computer at the University of Alabama will process your letter and—usually within 24 hours—e-mail you the lesson(s) you requested! Here's a complete list of the various lessons in the course:

Week	Filename	Type	Description
1	MAP01	LESSON	Welcome
	MAP02	LESSON	Listserv file server commands
2	MAP03	LESSON	Levels of Internet connectivity
	MAP04	LESSON	E-mail
	MAP05	LESSON	Listservs
	MAP06	LESSON	Other mail servers
	MAP07	LESSON	Netiquette
3	MAP08	LESSON	Usenet
	MAP09	LESSON	Spamming and urban legends
	MAP10	LESSON	Internet security
	MAP11	LESSON	Telnet (part one)
	MAP12	LESSON	Telnet (part two)

Week	Filename	Type	Description
4	MAP13	LESSON	FTP (part one)
	MAP14	LESSON	FTP (part two)
	MAP15	LESSON	FTP mail
	MAP16	LESSON	FTP file compression
	QUIZ1Q	LESSON	Pop quiz
	MAP17	LESSON	Archie
	MAP17B	LESSON	FTP sites
	QUIZ1A	LESSON	Pop quiz answers
5	MAP18	LESSON	Gopher (part one)
	MAP19	LESSON	Gopher (part two)
	MAP20	LESSON	Bookmarks and booklists
	MAP21	LESSON	Veronica
	MAP22	LESSON	Gopher mail
6	MAP23	LESSON	WWW (part one)
	MAP24	LESSON	WWW (part two)
	QUIZ2Q	LESSON	Pop quiz
	MAP25	LESSON	Address searches and Finger
	NEAT	LESSON	Map extra: neat stuff to check out
	ADVERT	LESSON	Map extra: advertising on the Internet
	MAP26	LESSON	IRC/MUDs/MOOs and other "talkers"
	SMITH	LESSON	Guest lecture: Richard Smith
	QUIZ2A	LESSON	Pop quiz answers
	MAP27	LESSON	The future . . .

Now you don't have to get each lesson individually; you can get the lessons in one-week blocks. Send an e-mail message to:

```
LISTSERV@UA1VM.UA.EDU
```

with the body of the message being:

```
GET WEEK# PACKAGE F=MAIL
```

replacing the # with the week of the block you want to retrieve. For example, to get all the week-2 files e-mailed to you, all you have to do is send the message:

```
GET WEEK2 PACKAGE F=MAIL
```

Because Crispen has carefully constructed his course, you should request the first week of lessons first, then the second week, and so on. And you should get only one week's lessons at a time. The reason for the first is to study and understand each lesson before you go on; the reason for the second is that asking for them all at once will place a great deal of strain on the University of Alabama's system. If too many people do that, UA might have to take the course off its machine.

⇨ Hytelnet

Hytelnet (the latest as of this writing is version 6.9) was designed to assist users in reaching all the Internet-accessible libraries, freenets, BBSs, and other information sites by telnet, and is a text-based program. There are versions for UMS, VMS, Windows, and Macintosh, too. You can link up to a version on the Internet, or have a copy of it on your own system. I recommend the latter because if you have a copy of Hytelnet installed on your own system, you can easily add your favorite sites to its extensive list. I downloaded a copy from Delphi; there's also a Web page with the different versions at:

```
http://www.lights.com/hytelnet/
```

Many other sites also have copies. Earl Fogel of the University of Saskatchewan has written a UNIX version of Hytelnet that's available via anonymous FTP from ftp.usask.ca. You can ask him about it by writing e-mail to him at fogel@herald.usask.ca. Charles Burchill of the University of Manitoba has written a Macintosh version of Hytelnet; his e-mail address is burchil@ccu.umanitoba.ca. The program is also distributed as shareware. If you find it to be of use, send $20 to the author by regular mail:

Peter Scott
324 8th Street East
Saskatoon, Saskatchewan Canada S7H 0P5

For the DOS version, you change directory (CD) to the directory where you've placed the program, type HR, and hit Enter to install the program in memory. Once loaded, hit Ctrl–Backspace to activate the program. To leave the program temporarily, hit Esc. To remove it from memory, hit Alt–T while in the program.

Call up Hytelnet before you load your communications program. It will stay in the background until you need to find a telnet address. To use it, hold the Ctrl key down and depress the Backspace key (Ctrl–Backspace). When you do, you'll get the screen shown in Fig. 1-1 (although the appearance will change slightly depending on the platform, the text will read the same).

Figure 1-1

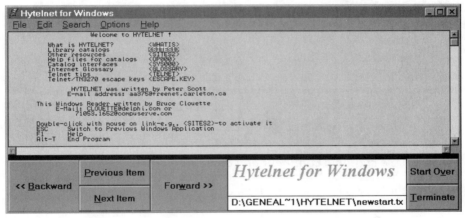

The opening screen of Hytelnet, one road map for the Internet.

Hytelnet's main use for genealogists is to find libraries to telnet to on the Internet (chapter 5 will discuss how to do that). Hytelnet is useful in many ways; not only does it allow you to find the exact telnet addresses of hundreds of libraries, but it has help screens from the online public-access catalog (OPAC) program you'll encounter there, as well as the opening screen in some cases. Throughout Hytelnet, whenever you see something in angle brackets, such as <OP013>, it refers to another text file with information.

Let's step through Hytelnet to find the University of Alabama in Huntsville OPAC. From the opening screen in Fig. 1-1, you'd choose

Library Catalogs. (Position the cursor on the selection, then press either Enter or the right arrow key. Moving the left arrow will take you back one screen.) This will give you the screen that asks you to choose a region of the world. From this screen, highlight The Americas and press Enter. (The text within the angle brackets on the screen refers to the text file that will be called up.) From the next screen, choose the selection United States, and you'll get the screen in Fig. 1-2, where the sorting is now by type of library.

Figure 1-2

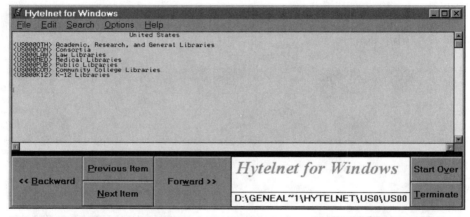

When you've chosen a continent and country, your choices are sorted into types of libraries. The University of Alabama in Huntsville will be under the first choice: Academic, Research, and General Libraries.

University of Alabama in Huntsville will be under the first choice: Academic, Research, and General Libraries. So highlight that choice. You now have an overwhelming number of choices. By hitting Page Down, you can page through them. In the Windows version, use the Search menu item at the top to find the word *Huntsville*, and you'll see something like the screen shown in Fig. 1-3. Now highlight University of Alabama, Huntsville and you'll get the screen in Fig. 1-4.

This screen tells you the address to use to telnet there, the first command you'll want to use, the type of OPAC used there, and how to exit. The screen also tells you that this site has a PALS catalog; for an explanation of how that catalog works, highlight the <OP013> and press Enter. This new screen will tell you the most commonly used

Figure 1-3

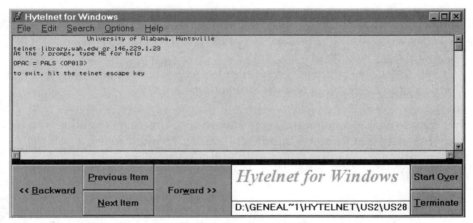

In the extensive list of libraries, here's the one you're looking for. In this Windows version, use the Search menu item at the top to find Huntsville.

Figure 1-4

With just a few keystrokes, you have specific information on how to get to that card catalog. Use your telnet program and follow the instructions.

commands for the OPAC system. Press the Print Screen key to print it out, in order to have it handy when you sign on. Using your telnet program, you can connect as shown in Fig. 1-5. It's that easy.

When you've read the information you want in Hytelnet, you can either hit the Esc key to return the program to the background or hit Alt–T to remove it from memory altogether. (Keep in mind that

Figure 1-5

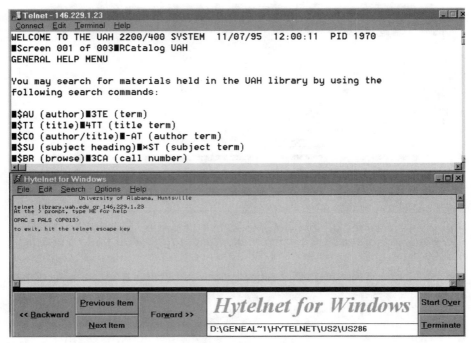

Connected to UAH with Hytelnet's directions.

HR.EXE should be unloaded from memory in the reverse order that it was installed. That means that if you loaded HR.EXE before you loaded another program, then unload it after you unload that program.)

If you find something you want to remember but it isn't listed in Hytelnet, it's easy to customize the program. You can change an existing file (the ones noted in the brackets). Suppose, for example, you want to add some details to the file for the Cleveland Public Library <US010> in the \HYTELNET\US0 subdirectory. Just read that file into your favorite word processor, edit it, and save it as a pure ASCII file. (If you use WordPerfect, for example, save it with the Text In/Out function, not F10; for WordStar, open it as a nondocument file.)

Or you can add a new file. First write it with your word processor and be sure to save it as pure ASCII. Then add it to the appropriate directory, e.g., \AT0 or \CA0. When adding the new file, be sure to surround its name with the hypertext link characters (the angle brackets), for example <SITES1>.

Hytelnet has much, much more information than just libraries, and it's worth the registration fee if you're going to spend much time exploring the Internet looking for files and programs.

Other road maps

As mentioned, many of the commercial services have front-end programs to help you navigate their systems. They also often have, at additional cost, hardcopy manuals that can help the beginner. Usually, however, by the time you learn what's in the manual, the service has changed things around! Still, if you find yourself using, say, Delphi regularly, you'll want to get the user's manual to minimize your online charges.

The average BBS will have a help file that you can download. Some of these list only the one-letter commands and what they do. Others, however, draw maps of what's where to help you find your way around. If your local genealogical BBS has neither, use your communication program's capture feature to build yourself a manual for that system. I'll discuss other road maps in chapter 6, which describes Internet services such as the Web.

Now that you have your road map, you need a way to exchange messages with your compatriots out there. The least painful way to do that is with mail-reading software (also called *offline readers*).

Mail-reading software

Reading mail is the biggest part of online life. Whether you're using a local BBS, Delphi, or the Internet, a mail reader makes life much easier. If you send and receive e-mail from a number of online services, you need an electronic Labrador retriever that can fetch your messages from anywhere: commercial online services, BBSs, and the

Internet. Here I'll describe four basic types: general-purpose, BBS-oriented, Internet-oriented, and front ends for specific online services. There will be some overlap; some programs such as QmodemPro come with features of all four types.

General-purpose programs

E-Mail Connection, RFD Mail, and RoboComm are three general-purpose mail-reading programs. I'll describe RFD mail since it's representative of this type of software.

RFD Mail is a Windows-based communications program that grabs your e-mail from a number of services: CompuServe, GEnie, MCI Mail, World Unix, The Direct Connection, and even TCP/IP networks. You can also add BBSs and other text-based services to RFD's list by writing scripts. When you first install RFD, you supply your name and password for each service, the numbers to dial, and other parameters. If you go by different names on different systems, you can store these "e-mail signatures" as well. Built-in binary file-transfer features let you upload and download files attached to messages. Once everything is recorded, click an icon and RFD will trot off to get the mail. RFD gathers all your mail in one place, and makes reading and answering messages a one-click job. There's a single electronic address book for all the services you use, and the program also keeps track of what service a message came from. The only downside is that RFD Mail calls only systems that use ASCII characters (it turns off any ANSI environment), so you can't use it with Prodigy or America Online. But this is a quibble. As one satisfied customer wrote, "RFD mail pays for itself in about three months in reduced charges."

BBS-oriented programs

For BBSs, investigate programs that use the QWK format. More than 75 percent of the BBS software out there, including PCBoard, RBBS, Remote Access, and Wildcat BBS, uses the QWK packet format. If you're new to the online world, you're probably scratching your head at that last paragraph, so here are some definitions:

QWK is a program/format for retrieving a lot of messages at once, quickly, to be read later after you've logged off. The BBS selects the messages you want according to what you input. It gathers them all into one file, then compresses them with a program such as PKZip, ARC, or StuffIt. That file is then downloaded to you and you sign off.

It's assumed that you have the program to uncompress the file on your machine. Your mail reader will use that program, then let you look at all the messages, one by one, answer the ones you want, delete whatever you don't want, and so on.

Many programs allow you to sort the messages several different ways: by date, subject, sender, or receiver. Some have what's called a "twit filter," a feature that excludes messages from a certain name if you've found that person to be offensive or otherwise unhelpful. A mail reader will usually save and compress your answers, including any changes in your preferred subject categories of messages, and then upload the answer file to the board the next time you sign on. This saves you time and, on certain systems, money. It frees up your phone line while you read and answer messages. Best of all, it organizes things!

My favorite BBS mail QWK reader is Off-line Xpress because it comes with an editor, a great interface, and even a spell checker. (There are other popular ones, such as Blue Wave, and you should certainly give them a try.) OLX, as it's called, is now included in Mustang Software Inc.'s QmodemPro communications software. This is an outstanding, feature-packed communications program that was shareware and is now commercial, although there are still thousands of copies of the shareware version out there on BBSs. OLX is now a module of the communications program. Messages prepared in OLX can be sent by fax, CompuServe, MCI Mail, or a BBS that uses .QWK mail doors. QmodemPro can even function as a BBS host. Another nice feature is that the whole QModemPro package requires only two megabytes of disk space.

Internet-oriented programs

There are two very good Internet mail programs, with free versions that new users should consider.

✳ **Eudora**

Eudora is a mail program named for author Eudora Welty, and it's as simple and powerful as her stories. If all you need is simple mail management, either Eudora Pro or its free version called Eudora Light will take care of it with ease. If you lack a TCP/IP stack or Winsock software, you can use the one supplied in the Eudora Pro package. If you don't have a service provider, you can automatically sign up for the portal service (a national ISP) as you install Eudora Pro; if you do have a provider, simply enter the mail server's address (a painless task) and log on.

After you've logged on to your mail server, sending and receiving messages are one click away. You can log off to read your mail and then log on to post your replies, using Eudora Pro's spelling checker to help prevent embarrassing mistakes. Eudora also lets you set up a timer for retrieves: anywhere from every few seconds to once a day. Eudora Pro and Eudora Light both offer configuration options stored in one easy-to-navigate Settings window; you can, for example, set the program so it won't retrieve messages larger than, say, 20K.

Eudora Light puts all received mail in the New box and lets you sort the messages into other boxes by hand, but Eudora Pro lets you filter messages as they come in, route them to specific mailboxes, and sort messages by various criteria. You can also search all message headers and bodies for text strings in both versions. The Macintosh and Windows versions of Eudora Pro are nearly identical in capabilities, except the Mac version lacks support for multiple mailboxes. Eudora Light also works perfectly under Windows 95. On either platform, Eudora is so simple to install and configure that you'll be sending and collecting e-mail less than 30 minutes after opening the box.

To get Eudora Pro, call Qualcomm Inc. at 800-238-3672 or 619-658-1292. The list price is currently $89. To get the slightly less functional Eudora Light, check you local BBS or log onto:

`http://cwsapps.texas.net/smail.html#eudora`

to download it. The price of Eudora Light is to send the author a postcard!

✳ **Pegasus**

Pegasus Mail has all the features of Eudora Light and more. Because it has so many more features, it's a little harder to learn at first, but once you get the hang of it, Pegasus Mail is just wonderful. It's an extremely intuitive, great-looking mail program with integrated address books and mailing lists.

Extensive drag-and-drop capabilities also help to make Pegasus Mail easy to use. You can attach or include a file in a message with Pegasus Mail, but there are so many wonderful options for how to do that, you might have to do it a few times to get the hang of it. Pegasus also includes a spelling checker, advanced filtering controls for incoming messages, and a feature that lets you minimize Pegasus and have it check the mail at regular intervals and play a sound file when it finds new mail. Most functions are one click on the menu bar, and you can change your setting easily from the Configuration menu. One of the best features of Pegasus Mail is how wonderful it is to use offline; all you have to do is connect in order to post and retrieve. And when you send or reply to a message, you can send a copy to both the recipient and yourself or just to the recipient, and you can review or delete queued mail. The price is nice too . . . it's free!

To download Pegasus Mail, use FTP to get it from either of the following two addresses:

```
risc.ua.edu/pub/network/pegasus or ftp.let.rug.nl/pub/pmail
```

or if you're on CompuServe, you can get it from the NOVUSER area or via gopher from ftp.cuslm.ca.

⇨ Front ends

Other shareware front ends for the commercial online information services can help you read your mail offline. Be aware, however, that for the commercial services you won't often find a mail reader with QWK or any other compression technique. Still, they save you money by performing the commands faster than you can type.

One of the vintage programs for using CIS is Support Group Inc's TAPCIS, which takes multiple passes at the CompuServe Information Service. TAPCIS has no menus and is only a text-based interface, but many people feel it saves them hundreds of dollars a year in online costs. Ozarks West Software's OzCIS offers a more graphical interface and more powerful capabilities, such as suspending an automated session so you can enter your commands manually. WinCIS offers a Microsoft Windows interface for CIS, which is gaining popularity fast; its emphasis is on doing much of your activities offline. In contrast, CIS's product WinCIM, or the CompuServe Information Manager for Windows, is better suited to interactive online mode, guiding you through the CIS labyrinth but conducting much of the business while the meter is ticking. Pro-Master, from Gateway Software Inc., is a terminate-and-stay-resident (TSR) program that lets you automate navigation through Prodigy menus; another one is Pro-Util by Royston Development. Delphi users can use D-Lite, which is described in detail in chapter 8, or Rainbow, which was released in July 1994.

A word about cost

As this book progresses through several services, networks, and echos, I'll do my best to note the fares and fees involved. At first, this way of gathering genealogical information will seem expensive, especially when you're on the learning curve of the programs and services. But when you find a source that has helped you as much as the examples in the Introduction, when you're proficient enough to send and receive files and messages with little or no pain, when you find important information in a place you could never visit yourself, or when you realize you've formed a close friendship with someone you've never laid eyes on, it will perhaps seem a bargain.

Still, it's important for you to learn your software well. Study the examples in this book before you sign on, study your road maps and manuals, and be ready for surprises. Then you'll be making the most of your online dollar.

There's another way to get the most of your online dollar. To get to CompuServe, Delphi, and so on, you dial a certain number, usually

local, to connect to some place nonlocal, even foreign. This isn't done with mirrors. It's done with packet-switching networks, which are also known as *public data networks* or *PDNs*.

The point of these systems is cost. At the time I'm writing this, the best deal you can get from AT&T on long-distance calls is around 11 cents a minute ($6.60 an hour). These PDNs allow you to connect via modem (not voice) for as low as a dollar an hour.

This is a quickly growing industry, and entire books are being written to guide you to the best buys as more and more people start offering these services. But let me list some of the companies who have been in business a while:

 # CPN

CompuServe's Packet Network is how to dial up CompuServe using a local number. But CIS isn't the only place you can go on CPN, and you don't have to be a member to dial other services. For information on where you can dial, call 1-800-848-8199 (voice) and ask.

 # Tymnet

Originally for our friends in the United Kingdom to reach across the ocean, this company has recently forayed into the North American continent. For information and local access numbers, call 800-937-2862 or 215-666-1770 (voice). To look up access numbers by modem, dial a local access number, hit the Enter key, type A, and enter information at the "please log in" prompt.

 # SprintNet

SprintNet has two programs to help you connect from a local phone number: DataCall Plus offers global dial-up access to host computers, using the SprintNet data network for asynchronous and X.25 applications up to 14.4 Kbps with end-to-end error protection. DataCall (SM) give you 800 access numbers to SprintNet. Each 800

number provides access to the SprintNet network at speeds of up to 14.4 kilobits per second from every local exchange in the continental U.S. Call 1-800-817-7755 for information.

 # ISDN

The modem isn't the only way to connect to all these services, nor is it the fastest. The alternative, ISDN, is so cutting edge and expensive that I hesitate to mention it, but in the interest of completeness I feel I must. This will be a very short introduction; if you want to try to jump into ISDN, you'll have to read much more than this brief section before you'll be ready.

The phone companies currently marketing ISDN (integrated services digital networks) to their customers would like you to believe that faster is better and that's all there is to it. ISDN is a new kind of connection that has three channels—A, B, and Data—to carry your signals. Phone companies have been promising for years that ISDN would replace our old (and reliable) analog phone lines. With an ISDN line hooked up to your PC, phone, fax, and what have you, you can send and receive just about any kind of data—voice, documents, graphics, sound, and the full-motion video necessary for movies or teleconferencing—over the line at speeds up to 64,000 bps.

Another selling point is versatility. With the right equipment and software on your end, a single ISDN line can support two phone numbers. In effect, you could get a video phone call from Grandma on one line and transmit a report to your company on the other. ISDN also lets your phone be a little smarter, because the "ring" sent down an ISDN line could tell your phone who's calling, the type of call (data or speech), the number dialed, and so on. Your intelligent phone could analyze this information and act appropriately. For example, you could program your phone to answer calls from certain numbers only or to answer specific calls on specific lines, such as all fax calls on line two.

Unfortunately, ISDN isn't cheap, and there are times when it seems like a solution in search of a problem. Although you'd treat an ISDN line like your old analog phone line—you'd be billed for long-distance charges, could have call waiting, and so on—it comes with a passel of complications. Cost, for one thing.

Although an ISDN line costs as little as $20 a month in California, it's considerably more expensive in the east. And installation runs about $200. An ISDN line would eliminate the need for a modem; after all, a modulator/demodulator is designed to turn digital data into analog and back again, and ISDN is all digital. But hooking your PC up to an ISDN line would require a special adapter that can cost up to $1,000 or more, depending on the application. And using your existing fax machine, telephone, and so on requires buying bridging devices and still more software. The alternative is to buy all-new, ISDN-smart equipment.

Another consideration is that the ISDN system is powered by your household current, not the phone company's. If the power to your ISDN system goes out, you're unreachable. This is why many businesses that have jumped on the ISDN bandwagon also buy a separate power source for their ISDN system—and keep an old analog line around, just in case of thunderstorms, brownouts, and earthquakes.

The price tag for your local telephone company is also pretty steep, and no doubt some of that cost will find its way onto your monthly bill. For starters, all the "switches" in your phone company's central office have to be replaced with digital switches that can recognize ISDN. The new switches also have to be within 3½ miles of your house. So the cost on both sides of the ISDN connection is high.

As a result, communities that have adopted ISDN have become like isolated islands in a distant atoll. But the "baby Bells" have been selling ISDN hard the last year or two, so many major cities in the U.S. have it, as well as smaller communities such as Chapel Hill, North Carolina and Huntsville, Alabama. The web of ISDN communities is growing, so sending and receiving data at blinding speeds from point A to point B across country might be possible fairly soon. But not just yet.

Criticizing ISDN is easy; after all, adopting it involves more than a few leaps of faith. And a lot of companies you'd expect to be taking the ISDN leap—such as commercial online services—haven't budged. You're lucky if you can find an Internet service provider who has an ISDN link. But ISDN might be coming soon to a town near you.

The idea of high-speed, multi-channel phone lines is appealing. But like most cutting-edge technologies that don't offer immediate, quantum gains in productivity, ISDN won't make serious inroads until it's as ubiquitous, invisible, and cheap as cable TV—that is, when ISDN support is built into PCs, phones, and faxes, and can be accessed via a plug in the wall. Personally, I'm waiting until then.

 # Attitudes and etiquette

I've already noted that the online world has definite communities, and none are friendlier and more helpful than the genealogical ones. Nevertheless, as with any community, there are customs and etiquette (often called *netiquette*) you're expected to follow. Some of these you should know before you sign on.

One good idea is to lurk first and read a list or echo without posting messages yourself. It's sort of like sitting in the corner at a party without introducing yourself, except it's not considered rude online; in some places you're expected to lurk until you get the feel of the place. Read the messages for a while; find out who's interested in what. If the board or service has a help or information file, read it well; understand what's allowed and not allowed with this particular group. Then introduce yourself with your first message.

When you post a query, which should be your second message, never make the subject line (called the *title* in some places) something vague and general such as "query" or "searching my family." Some people choose what messages to download based on the subject line; if yours isn't specific enough it might not get read at all. Your subject line should have the surnames mentioned in the messages, such as "Spencer, Powell, Crippen, Beeman." If it's a general information request, don't use "general information" as your subject line, but rather "is the IGI on CD-ROM?" or similar specific phrase. Respect people's time (and lack thereof) by being quite clear about the subject matter in your title.

If you can avoid it, don't ask electronically what can be more easily, efficiently, and quickly done over the phone or at your own library. Sometimes your local sources won't have an answer that to others

seems simple; in that case, ask. But you might get flamed (I'll deal with that in a minute).

Another commonly accepted practice is to target your messages. When posting a message, you have a choice of how wide the distribution will be on most systems; sometimes you can flag it to a subcategory, as on CompuServe and Prodigy. In other places, you can aim it to go only to those who read a certain subject, as on Fidonet, or only to those who use a certain BBS. Or it can go over the whole Internet. Choose wisely, for the same reasons you want to use descriptive titles. It's considered bad form to post a message to the wrong subject heading on BBSs; certain groups have rules about what can be posted and how it must be worded. You might inadvertently break some rules by posting it to the wrong heading. And post a message only once, especially to groups where all the messages are stored somewhere. This doesn't mean you can't repeat a query once in a while; just don't do it so often that you become annoying. This is an obvious courtesy to those trying to control the traffic. It's also considered tacky to test out a system with a message like "this is a test" to a forum. The software works. Trust it.

Many people store a signature, which serves the same purpose as a return address label. This should be a pure ASCII file with the details of how to reach you, which is inserted at the end of a message. Try not to make yours overly long and complicated, but do try to update it often as it helps someone contacting you directly. (Surnames in the signature are discouraged on the Internet, due to the archiving of the messages.) In addition, you can add a "tagline," some pithy or humorous statement of ten words or less. Some examples are:

```
I'm in shape . . . round's a shape isn't it?
If this were an actual tagline, it would be funny.
It's only a hobby . . . only a hobby . . .
Libbi's Law: You cannot do just one thing . . .
```

These are used just as signatures are. Again, they're fine if not overdone. Lurk a while to see whether taglines are accepted before using them in a certain group. Note: Don't take seriously or execute any code mentioned in a tagline, like "<Ctrl><Alt><Del> to read the next message." On the Internet a most vicious code has appeared in taglines, one that a Bourne shell would eventually interpret as RM * (a

command to remove all files on the current disk, like DEL *.*), and there are no recovery tools like Norton on UNIX. Sadly, vandalism has followed us into the virtual world.

Sooner or later, you'll see a message you want to answer. Great! But remember that there are customs to be followed in this case, too. First, look at the top of the message. Several lines will tell you who posted the message, from where and when, and how it traveled. This is the header. Use it to direct your answer.

Be as brief as possible. Everyone is busy. Postings on some networks are huge in number. With so many going so far, only the most important bytes of information should be included. Also remember that somewhere, someone down the line is paying a long-distance phone charge to send your postings on. The briefer the article, the more likely it is that people will take the time to read it.

When you see something you want to answer, comment on, or discuss, it's traditional to summarize the message in the following format:

```
Joe Usenetter said in the title or subject line:
>what he said, with one arrow for each quoted line.
>>two arrows for information Joe quoted.
My answer to this is:
```

and so on. Some mail readers will take care of quoting the original for you. This way, if someone didn't see the beginning of the message, he or she can take the time to look up the original or take your word for the direct quote. However, don't directly quote the whole article! Only truly pertinent parts, at most four or five lines, should be repeated.

Use e-mail to answer a question posted at large. Instead of posting an article that everyone reads, post a mail response only to the person who asked the question. Also, check to be sure no follow-ups have already been posted; someone might have already given "your" answer. The questioner is then expected to post all the answers received in an edited, summarized form. Editing means stripping the headers and signatures, combining duplicate responses, and briefly quoting only the original question.

As mentioned earlier, you might get "flamed." This is when someone sends an insulting or offensive message. It's almost always a personal attack in response to an opinion on an issue. If you're flamed, the best, easiest, and safest thing to do is ignore the flaming message. Forget it. Put the sender on your twit filter and go on. The optimum course of action is not to start or get involved in a flame war.

If you must flame, listen to Cliff Manis, the guy who helps run the Roots-L list on the Internet. The following exchange started when someone insulted a new user for sending a file request to the mail list:

```
>David, lighten up will you? You have to understand that the whole
>Internet community is growing faster than anyone can possibly
>keep up.
>Flames don't help AT ALL! A gentle reminder (and I bet Cliff sent
>one to the person you are flaming) is much better than a baseball
>bat.
>Bill
```

```
Yes, I did send about four short words, DIRECT to that person, with the
address of where to send it the next time. The baseball bat idea doesn't
work here, home runs don't count at all. Bunts are more effective.
```

```
PATIENCE is a VIRTURE - Don't ever forget it !
```

```
On this net and mailing list I and we get many, many opportunities to
exercise it.
```

```
Sometimes this job doesn't pay enough, especially since there is none.
```

```
Anyone wishing to do a FLAME, please EMAIL it direct to me and not the
net and I will read it, but we don't need them on the net. The new
subscribers are trying to learn, and some of the more seasoned
subscribers use a wrong address from time to time, but 'so what'.......
```

```
enough said, back to genealogy....
Thanks..cliff
```

```
Cliff Manis K4ZTF  Researching: MANIS / MANES Family History
My USMAIL Address: P.O. Box 33937, San Antonio, Texas 78265-3937
Take the time to read the documentation, you will be surprised
and learn!
INTERNET: Cliff.Manis@csf.com Genealogy: ROOTS-L Mailing List
Administrator
```

Rule #1, indeed, could be stated as "Never forget that the person on the other side is human." You're using machines to upload and download, so your interaction with the online world at first might seem pretty dry and impersonal. But the whole point of online communication is to connect people. Don't treat the people out there as machines. Remember they have feelings.

Also be aware how your postings reflect on you. Never write anything you wouldn't say at a party or in a crowded room. Those postings are all that many, many people will know about you. And you never know who's out there reading. The world is in constant motion today; no matter where they are right now, people online might someday be clients, work with you, or meet you in other circumstances. And they could remember your postings. In the end, you can't really hide behind the modem.

And let me repeat my warning about the privacy of e-mail. It all depends on your and the other guy's system administrator. Generally, yes, something posted to someone's e-mail box will be seen only by you two. But system operators have been held responsible for what goes over their boards and networks, so they have good reason to spot-check messages. Be aware of that.

Also keep in mind that humor and sarcasm are best used cautiously. Subtle humor, especially satire, is hard to get across with no facial expressions, body language, or hand signals. Really well-done sarcasm so closely resembles the attitude it belittles that it's sometimes taken for a genuine attitude when delivered only in written form. So it's polite to clearly label all humor. How? Well, some conventions are (tilt your head to the left):

:-) or :-]	A smiley face
:-D or HAHAHA	A laugh
;-)	A wink
LOL	Laughing out loud
ROTF	Rolling on the floor

Other expressions besides humor are:

:-o	Surprise
:-/ or :-\	Frustrated or puzzled
:-P	Sticking out your tongue
:-(or :-[	A frown
IMHO	In my humble opinion
TAFN	That's all for now
TTYL	Talk to you later

(See the glossary for a more complete list.) It might seem silly, but these symbols can help prevent misunderstandings. And if you're tempted to become incensed over something you've read, remember that some people consider themselves above using these silly symbols. Don't "flame" people unless you're sure they're serious.

Also be aware that in many cases a network or echo stretches across oceans and borders. Don't criticize someone's spelling or grammar; that person might be using English as a second language.

Be careful about copyrights and licenses, and cite appropriate references. Copyright law is complicated and no clear-cut case has defined the use of copyright in electronic versions of text. Further, no one "owns" some of these networks. You could be personally guilty of plagiarism unless copyright laws and rules are carefully followed. Posting licensed software anywhere is another good way to get flamed, if not sued.

It's also important to cite references. If you give statistics, quotes, or a legal citation to support your position, you'll be much more believable if you give full credit to the source.

Finally, on the subject of rights, be aware that because of the powerful editing programs that come with mail readers, it's possible to post a message from one network to another, either in its original form or altered in some way. For this reason, some nets have a rule against posting something from another net; it's very possible to accidentally or deliberately misquote a message with the originator's signature still attached. Be sure you're quoting accurately and that the forum or network you're using allows quotes from other sources.

 # Ahentafels, tiny tafels, and GEDCOMs

One of the reasons to get involved in the online genealogy world is to share the information you have, as well as find information you don't have. To do that, standards have been set up for transmitting that information: ahentafels, tiny tafels, and GEDCOMs. They're all designed to put information in a standard format. The last two are readable by many different genealogical database programs, and many utilities have been written to translate information from one to another.

Ahentafels

Ahentafels are not big tiny tafels. The word means *ancestor table* in German, and the format is more than a century old. It lists all known ancestors of an individual, and includes the full name of each ancestor as well as dates and places of birth, marriage, and death. It organizes this information along a strict numbering scheme.

Once you get used to ahentafels, it becomes very easy to read them, moving up and down from parent to child and back again. The numbering scheme is the key to it all. Consider this typical pedigree chart:

```
                                          8.  great grandfather
                        4. paternal grandfather |
                        |                 9.  great grandmother
            2. father   |
            |           |                 10. great grandfather
            |           5. paternal grandmother |
            |                 11. great grandmother
1. person   |
            |
            |                 12. great grandfather
            |           6. maternal grandfather |
            |           |                 13. great grandmother
            3. mother   |
                        |                 14. great grandfather
                        7. maternal grandmother |
                                          15. great grandfather
```

Study the numbers in this chart. Every person listed has a number, and there's a mathematical relationship between parents and children. The number of a father is always double that of his child's. The number of the mother is always double that of her child's plus one. The number of a child is always one half that of its parent's number (ignoring any remainder). In this example, the father of person #6 is #12, the mother of #6 is #13, and the child of #13 is #6. In ahentafel format, the chart reads like this:

```
1. person
2. father
3. mother
4. paternal grandfather
5. paternal grandmother
6. maternal grandfather
7. maternal grandmother
8. great grandfather
9. great grandmother
10. great grandfather
11. great grandmother
12. great grandfather
13. great grandmother
14. great grandfather
15. great grandmother
```

Notice that the numbers are exactly the same as in the pedigree chart. The rules of father = 2 × child, mother = 2 × child + 1, child = parent ÷ 2 ignore remainder, etc., remain the same. This is an ahentafel chart. In practice, ahentafels are rarely uploaded as text files, but it's one way to show what you do know about your tree, quickly and in few characters. Just clearly state that it's an ahentafel.

Tiny tafels

Despite the similar name, a tiny tafel (TT) is a different animal. It provides a standard way of describing a family database so the information can be scanned visually or by computer. It was described in an article entitled "Tiny-Tafel for Database Scope Indexing" by Paul Andereck in the April-May-June 1986 issue (vol. 5, number 4) of *Genealogical Computing*.

The concept of TTs was adopted by CommSoft first in their popular program, Roots-II, and later in Roots-III. It has since been adapted by other genealogical programs, such as Brother's Keeper and GED2TT.

A TT makes no attempt to include the details that are contained in an ahentafel. All data fields are of fixed length, with the obvious exceptions of the surnames and optional places. A TT lists only surnames of interest (with Soundex) plus the locations and dates of the beginning and end of that surname. Tiny tafels make no provision for first names, births, marriages, deaths, or multiple locations.

The format of the tiny tafel is rigidly controlled. Here's the specification as released by CommSoft:

```
Header:
Column  Description
1       Header type
2       Space delimiter
3 - n   Text (n < 38) (n + 1) Carriage Return
Defined types:
Header
Type    Description                                Remarks
N       Name of person having custody of data      Mandatory first record
A       Address data                               0 to 5 address lines
                                                    Optional
T       Telephone number including area code       Optional
S       Communication Service/telephone number     0 to 5 service lines
        (MCI, ITT, ONT, RCA, ESL, CIS, SOU, etc,   Optional
        e.g., CIS/77123,512)
B       Bulletin Board/telephone number            Optional
C       Communications nnnn/X/P                     Optional
           nnnn = maximum baud rate
           X = O(riginate only), A(nswer only), B(oth)
           P = Protocol (Xmodem, Kermit, etc.)
D       Diskette format d/f/c                       Optional
           d = diameter (3, 5, 8)
           f = format MS-DOS, Apple II, etc.
           c = capacity, KB
F       File format                                 Free-form, optional
        ROOTS II, ROOTS/M, PAF Version 1, etc.
R       Remark                                      Free-form, optional
Z       Number of data items with optional text     Required last item
           In the COMMSOFT Tiny Tafel, the name of the database, the version
           of the database, and any special switches used when the Tiny Tafel
           was generated are shown on the Z line. The definitions of the
           special switches are shown below.

           D
```

DATEFILLDISABLED. Tiny Tafel normally suppresses the output of data for which the birth dates necessary to establish each line of output are missing. When this switch is on, The Tiny Tafel generator has estimated missing dates. The Tiny Tafel program applies a 30-year-per-generation offset wherever it needs to reconstruct missing dates.

N

NOGROUPING. Tiny Tafel normally "groups" output lines that have a common ancestor into a single line containing the most recent birth date. Descendants marked with an interest level greater than zero, however, will have their own line of output (see below for definition of interest level). Alternatively, when this switch is enabled, one line of output is created for every ultimate descendant (individual without children).

M

MULTIPLENAMES. Tiny Tafel normally lists a surname derived from the descendant end of each line. Specifying this option lists all unique spellings of each surname (up to five) separated by commas.

P

PLACENAMES. Tiny Tafel will include place names for family lines when this switch is enabled. Place names will be the most significant 14 to 16 characters of the birth field. When this option is enabled, the place of birth of the ultimate ancestor and the place of birth of the ultimate descendant of a line of output, respectively, are added to the end of the line.

S

SINGLEITEMS. Tiny Tafel normally suppresses lines of output that correspond to a single individual (that is, in which the ancestry and descendant dates are the same). This switch includes single-person items in the output.

#I

INTERESTLEVEL. Tiny Tafel normally includes all family lines meeting the above conditions no matter what its interest level. An interest level may be specified to limit the lines included to those having an interest level equal to or greater than the number specified. For example, with the interest level set to 1, all lines which have an ancestor or descendant interest level of 1 or higher will be listed.

Tiny Tafel Data:

Col	Description
1 through 4	Soundex Code (note 1)
5	Space delimiter
6 through 9	Earliest ancestor birth year
10	Interest flag, ancestor end of family line (note 2)

```
11 through 14      Latest descendant birth year
15                 Interest flag, descendant end of family line (note 2)
16 through 16+     SL Surname string area (SL = total surname length)
                   (note 3) above + PL  Place name area (PL = total place
                   name length) (note 4) above + 1  Carriage return
```

NOTES:

1. The Soundex code for any given line is obtained from the end of the line that has the highest interest level. If interest level is the same at each end, however, the name at the ancestor end will be used. If the application of these rules yield a surname that cannot be converted to Soundex, however, the program will attempt to obtain a Soundex code from the other end of the line.

2. Interest flag:
```
   [space] No interest (level 0)
   .       Low interest (level 1)
   :       Moderate interest (level 2)
   *       Highest interest (level 3)
```

3. Up to five surnames can be accommodated for one line where surname has changed in that line. If more than five surnames are found in a line, only the latest five will be shown. The inclusion of additional surnames is enabled by the M switch.

4. Place names for the birth of the earliest ancestor and the latest descendant may be included by using the P switch. If a place name is not provided for the individual whose birth year is shown, the field will be blank. The place for the ancestor is preceded by a backslash (\) and for the descendant by a slash (/).

Terminator:

W Date Tiny Tafel file was generated, DD MMM YYYY format.

That's how you build one manually. Most genealogical software packages now have a function to create and accept either a TT or GEDCOM, or both, from your information in the database. Always be certain a downloaded GEDCOM or TT has verified information before you load it into your database, because taking it back out isn't fun.

The best way to use tiny tafels is to compare and contrast them with as many others as you can. Thus the Tiny Tafel Matching System was born. It's a copyrighted software program from CommSoft, Inc., and is on many BBSs, which have to be on The National Genealogy Conference (Fidonet) to carry the program. You have to be a qualified

user of a BBS and submit your own TT file to be allowed to use TTMS to the fullest. Your file can have more than one tafel in it.

To find a TTMS near you, call the CommSoft BBS at 707-838-6373, register as a user, and look at the Files section under genealogy-related files. You can also get a description of the system there. Or call Brian Mavrogeorge's board Roots(SF!) at 415-584-0697. He also has an eight-page article about the system. Send him an e-mail message to ask for a copy, at the following address:

```
brian.mavrogeorge@p0.f30.n125.z1.fidonet.org
```

The TTMS system has three main functions:

> ➤ Collecting and maintaining a local database of TTs

> ➤ Presenting "instant" matches on the local database

> ➤ Allowing batch searches of all other databases on the NGS

In this context, "instant" means while you sit waiting at your keyboard, hooked onto the BBS, which could take some time, with you and your line tied up. For this reason, some BBSs will limit the time of day you can try this. A batch search means that your query is sent out on the NGS and, in a few hours or days, you'll receive messages about other TTs that match yours. Then you can contact the persons who submitted the data.

Anyone who can sign onto a BBS can look for instant matches, but you have to submit a TT file of your own to do a batch search. The searches can be limited by dates, Soundex, interest level, and so on to make the hits more meaningful.

Your TTs should be machine-generated (by Brother's Keeper, for example) to avoid formatting errors. Keep the TT as concise as possible and submit to only one board; for the batch system to be most efficient, redundancies have to be minimal. And be sure to experiment with the date overlap features to keep the reports short. As you find new information, you can replace your old TT file with new information; this is especially important if your address changes.

⇨ GEDCOMs

In February 1987, The Church of Jesus Christ of Latter-Day Saints (the Mormon church) approved a standard way of transferring data between various types of genealogy software, including its own Personal Ancestral File, or PAF. The standard has been adopted by most major genealogical database programs, including MacGene, Roots, Family Roots, Family Ties, Brother's Keeper, and so on. It's a combination of tags for data and pointers to related data.

If data from one database doesn't fit exactly into the new one, even with GEDCOM's format, the program will often save the extraneous data to a special file. A good program can use this data to help you sort and search for whether it has what you're looking for. Which is why so many people upload GEDCOMs to BBSs; perhaps someone somewhere can use the data. But, as GEDCOMs tend to be large, many BBSs have a policy against uploading them. Instead, you upload a message that you're willing to exchange for the price of the disk, or some other arrangement.

As a practical matter, it's often easier to turn a GEDCOM into a TT for uploading, although some details won't go through. Then you can exchange GEDCOMs when someone's TT matches yours at some point.

So now you're ready to go. Let's look at some specific systems.

Local BBSs and
their networks

I F your town has a local genealogical organization, chances are you also have at least one electronic bulletin board system with at least some genealogy on it. You might even have access to one devoted to genealogy. And while some BBSs stand alone, sending and receiving messages and files from only local sources, others are connected to networks.

A bulletin board network is based on the same principles as other computer networks, from local-area networks (LANs), which can be as small as connecting the two computers in your home, to the Internet, which is so big it's hard to imagine. In a network, two or more computers share and exchange data and programs through cables, phone wires, and other means. They can do this either with interruptions now and then or constantly, with no interruptions in the connection. Most BBS nets pass mail and files among themselves at a set time each night. They do this by having each participating BBS calling the hub BBS, which passes the information on to the next hub, possibly through a backbone (a set of connections comprising the main channels of communication across a network, through which the heaviest traffic travels), and finally to all the various local BBSs. This way you can call your local BBS, leave a message for a new-found fourth cousin in Utah, and receive a reply in usually less than two days.

Now this procedure of course means that several people have to pay long-distance phone charges. Most BBS sysops use the highest-speed modems available for the mail runs, and the reason the calls are at night is to get the cheapest rate. Still, the costs do add up. If your local sysop has a subscription or support fee, you really should consider contributing. Most sysops do this because they love it, but if they go broke for the love of their hobby, you've lost your connection.

 # Be prepared

There are some dangers out there, as mentioned previously. This is a good time for a cautionary tale.

Every BBS, commercial system, or network requires you to have a password that only you know. One person, who shall remain nameless (because he really did know better than to do this), used exactly the same password on every system he signed onto. From CompuServe to Fred's Pretty Good BBS and everything in between, he used precisely the same series of characters to identify himself as the proper user of that account at that online place.

To be friendly, he also left his ID number on some of these systems he used in messages on BBSs, so folks he met online could meet him in another place, so to speak. It was sort of like saying "Meet me at the corner pub, and ask for Charlie."

But unfortunately, some BBSs have users whose morals and discretion are not what they should be. And sysops are all-powerful on their own BBSs; they can look up any information deposited on their boards, even passwords. And some people are good at cracking security systems and can pretend to be the sysop.

Well, someone less than ethical decided to try that online ID number left in a message with the password from the BBS's "secret" file, just to see if it worked. It did. Everywhere Charlie had an account. Pretty soon old Charlie found himself paying for other people's joyrides on some of the more expensive online services.

Learn from his costly mistake; your password should be unique on every system. It should never be something easy to guess such as your maiden name or your birthday. It should not even make much sense to anyone but you. And to make it truly secure, which is the whole point of a password anyway, combine numbers, letters, and punctuation marks. No one could guess the password !m55d19y3#, even trying every word in a 40,000-word dictionary.

Because it's not easy to remember 12 different passwords, some people keep a 3 × 5 card or a sheet of paper with their various passwords posted by the computer. It works. But this is where the scripting function of your communications program can come in handy. If you record your first session on a board, you'll have a record of what password you created there. Then, using the scripting language, you can write a script with that system's phone number,

your online name, the password for that account, and any other commands you want carried out every time. The thing to be cautious about here is restricting access to your computer communications scripts, in case the kids decide to use your computer.

Finally, once you get the hang of it, look for some navigators to make BBS life easier. For example, RoboComm will automate your access to computer bulletin boards that run PCBoard and Wildcat! software. You can set up RoboComm to call a list of BBSs. For each board you call, you create an "agenda of things to do," which it does, and faster than you can type. To do this, though, you need to be very familiar with each of the boards in order to write the script for the agenda. Setting up RoboComm is tedious and time-consuming, but once it's done, your BBS chores are a breeze.

There are also offline mail readers with telecommunications programs in them, such as Speed Read. For information, contact:

Parsons Consulting (RoboComm)
5020 S. Lake Shore Dr., Suite 3301
Chicago, IL 60615
BBS: 312-752-1258
Online filename: ROBOxx-A.ZIP, ROBOxx-B.ZIP

J. E. Smith (Speed Read)
344 Observatory Dr.
Birmingham, AL 35206
$25
Online filename: SPEEDxxx.ZIP

Some examples

Let's look at a few examples of local BBSs, in alphabetical order:

Cat Eye BBS

✳ West Virginia
(304) 592-3390

Sue Moore began her board in 1992, she says, "Because we didn't like a lot of the boards we called and thought there was a need for one

Figure 2-1

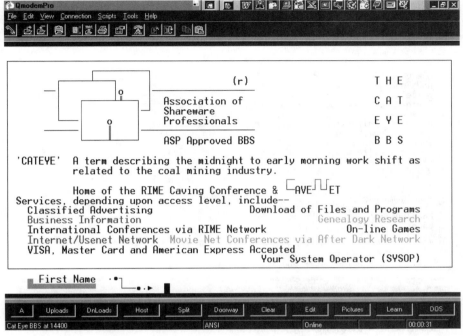

The opening screen of Cat Eye explains the name.

in the West Virginia area." So, with PCBoard software and two phone lines at 14,400 bps, they were up and running. The opening screen is shown in Fig. 2-1.

Moore is proud of her caving, genealogy, and other conferences, but she would like to improve the genealogy area. "We are growing bigger all the time," she says. "We try to carry all the genealogy programs we can find. We also are building a good deposit of other people's works for the VA, MD, PA, NC, WV, NJ, and KY area."

Everyone can call free for 15 minutes a day. The rates are $45.00 for the first year, and $35 a year after that for 1 hour of long distance or 45 minutes of local per day.

The Files area, reached by the command F from the main menu, has several genealogical files in area 49, as you can see in Fig. 2-2. At any prompt, enter a ? and you'll get a help file, as shown in Fig. 2-3.

Figure 2-2

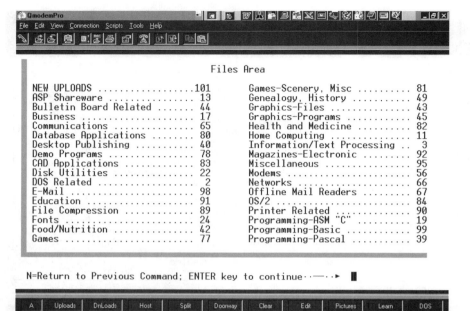

Files area 49 has genealogical files, and new ones are added regularly.

Figure 2-3

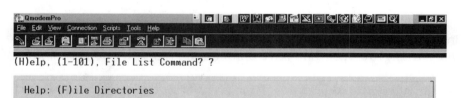

You can access help files on Cat Eye by typing a ? at any prompt.

You can also search the files from the main menu with the Z command, for example, Z SPENCER 49.

From the Main Board (the main menu), shown in Fig. 2-4, you can choose to read messages from the message commands while online or use the DOOR command to go to the offline mail area. You'll also find reviews of genealogy and history books in the West Virginia message areas. This board has a generic QWK mail and a Rosemail door. Both are good choices. On either one, if you try a download without first telling it your preferred protocol, compression technique, and so forth, you'll get an error message. You can also type QWK from the main menu to download mail once you've set your parameters. All these are improvements since the first edition of this book.

Figure 2-4

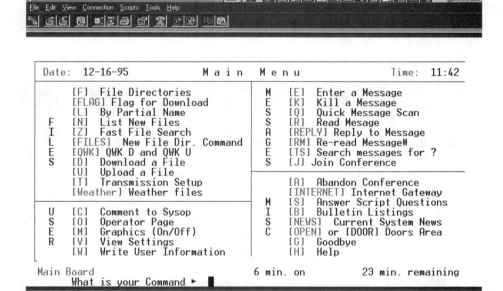

Cat Eye's main board organizes the offerings, which include Internet services such as telnet and FTP.

But Moore didn't stop there. She was instrumental in founding Software Valley Inc., a nonprofit organization to help bring technology to rural West Virginia. The company has a bulletin board system, called Software Valley Information Systems, or SVIS, also running PC Board. Because it's nonprofit, when you call the toll-free numbers you're severely limited in time: seven minutes per day. So you pretty much have to download messages and get off when you call in on one of the two 800 numbers:

➤ 800-SOFTVAL

➤ 800-SVISWVA (WVA only)

They also have regular dial-in numbers: 304-592-2682 and 304-592-2723 for U.S. Robotics 28.8 modems. These don't have daily time limits. What's really neat is that if you have telnet you can also use the board this way: telnet 198.77.8.11 or svis.org, type in your user ID and password, and you're in. The bulletin board looks very similar in a telnet session as it does in a regular session, as you can see in Fig. 2-5. This allows members who are travelers and rural

Figure 2-5

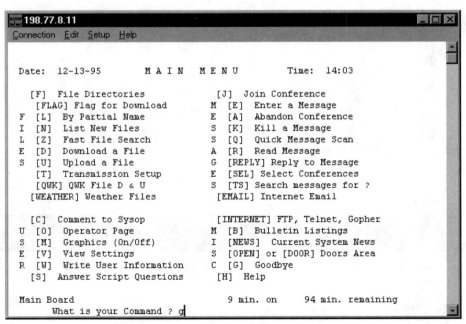

A telnet session to Cat Eye is all text, but convenient.

users to gain access to valuable genealogical information, including Internet mailing lists, Usenet genealogical discussion groups, genealogical data files available for download from the BBS, a gopher, and an FTP server. Like Cat Eye, this board carries the RIME message echo, which has a genealogy subject group. This is a good example of a general board with genealogy on it.

⇨ Instant Relatives

✻ Salt Lake City, Utah
801-466-5374

A genealogist, bulletin board enthusiast, and full-time software engineer, Larry Maddocks combined his two favorite hobbies with his work when he started his Instant Relatives board in 1991. His goal is to eventually have the most user-friendly online research help for the genealogist.

"I hope to someday make it easy for genealogists to share research," he says. "It's not as turnkey as I'd like it to be yet, but I'm still working on it. My goal is to help people, to make my genealogy bulletin board as easy as Prodigy."

Currently running his business out of his home, Maddocks has worked professionally on programs for genealogists at the Church of Jesus Christ of Latter-Day Saints' main office, as well as on GEDFIX and other shareware genealogy programs, and is currently working on a genealogy program for Windows. His BBS is how he's tinkering with his grand scheme for online research; he hopes to write a program that will match GEDCOMs throughout a network, letting people know in a matter of minutes who else might be interested in their lines.

"There's a tiny tafel matching system out there, but it took me a long time to figure it out, and I'm a professional programmer," Maddocks says, "so I can imagine how hard it is for a beginning genealogist! What I like best is helping people with their research. I like the messages, really connecting to people. What most people enjoy is the interaction. What bothers most sysops is people who log on, get the latest files, and leave. We're in this to interact with people."

Maddocks is still refining and redefining how his software looks, but let's take a quick tour of the system as it was in early 1994. The main menu gives you several choices in a typical PCBoard setup (see Fig. 2-6). The best feature about this board is the genealogical database program in the door (Fig. 2-7).

Figure 2-6

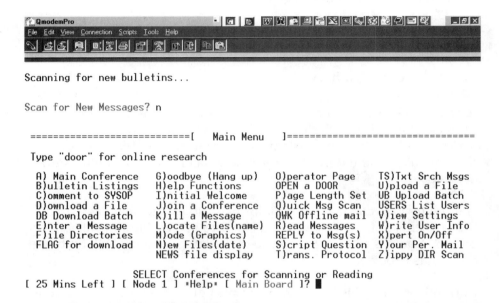

Instant Relatives is still one of the most popular genealogy BBSs. The main menu is a typical setup for this type of bulletin board software.

One program is his Instant Relatives, shown in Fig. 2-8. This program allows you to create a genealogy query and find out who has information on your line. You can fill out all the fields, entering name, sex, date, and so on, but the search looks at only the Soundex code of the surname. If you get matches that don't exactly match the name you entered, it's because you're seeing all the names that match the Soundex.

Figure 2-7

```
                    SELECT Conferences for Scanning or Reading
[ 32 Mins Left ] [ Node 1 ] *Help* [ Main Board ]? door
Please type in the number of the program you wish to run.

1.  *INSTAREL* Instant Relatives!  Search names from uploaded GEDCOM files.
2.  *DEPOSIT* Deposit Leftover Time and Bytes!
3.  *ILLINOIS* Illinois Marriages,  from early years to 1825. For subscribers.
4.
5.             (On-line chess.)
6.  *TENN*     Tennessee Marriages 1801 to 1825. For Everyone.
7.  *ALABAMA* Alabama Marriages,  from early years to 1825. For subscribers.
8.  *MISSOURI* Missouri Marriages, from early years to 1825. For subscribers.
9.  *KENTUCKY* Kentucky Marriages, from early years to 1800. For subscribers.
10. *VERMONT* Vermont Census, 1790. For subscribers.
11. *RHODE*    Rhode Island Census, 1790. For subscribers.
12. *GEORGIA* Georgia Marriages,  from early years to 1800. For subscribers.
13. *MISS*     Mississippi Marriages, from early years to 1825. For subscribers
14. *VIRGINIA* Virginia Marriages,  from early years to 1800. For subscribers.

Enter the DOOR # to Open (Enter)=none?
Temporary Sysop privileges granted this call


[ █
```

Instant Relative's doors (programs to run on the BBS) include several genealogical database searches.

Figure 2-8

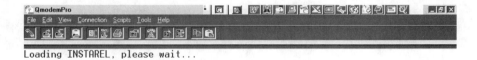

```
Loading INSTAREL, please wait...

Dear Libbi,                      12-16-95

Well, it took forever, but I found the bug.  Now I'm working on a
nicer report screen, and other features.

This program will allow you to create a genealogy query and
find out who may have information on your same line.

You can fill out all the fields, but the search only looks at the
soundex code of the surname. If you wonder why you get matches that
don't exactly match the name you entered, it is because you are seeing
all the names that match the soundex.

If you would like to help make this a better service by providing
databases, GEDCOM files, equipment, or cash, please leave me a comment
after you quit from this query area.

Good luck!

Larry Maddocks
[       ENTER            ]? █
```

The Instant Relatives door that Maddocks invented is one of the most popular features of his board.

There are other programs in the door that allow you to create a query
on several different kinds of information, sorted by state: cemeteries,
marriage records, and more. When you've tried it out, your comments
to the sysop are welcome, as are additional databases. Once your
query is entered, the program searches for surnames in the database
that might match (see Fig. 2-9).

Figure 2-9

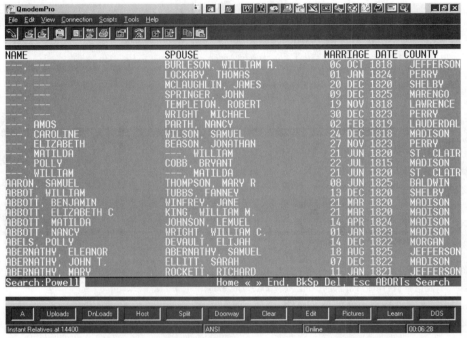

The Instant Relatives door found my Powell surname quickly.

Another friendly touch on this board is that, as soon as you're a
registered user, you'll find several messages waiting for you. They're
sent to all users, and have some useful information. Logging off is
simple; on all PCBoard systems the command is G for goodbye.

As of this writing, Maddocks offers more time to users who donate
$25 a year to help defray costs, although he doesn't require anyone to
pay. His Files area is extensive, and he encourages uploading
GEDCOMs.

KC GeneSplicer

✳ **Kansas City, KS**
913-648-6979

The opening screen of KC GeneSplicer (Fig. 2-10) is clear about the mission of this board. This board is by, about, and for genealogists.

Figure 2-10

Kansas City GeneSplicer is a popular genealogy-only board, with considerable Native American information.

This is a colorful, active board, allowing you to use the Remote Access BBS software with hotkeys. (When a BBS system responds to one-keystroke commands without requiring you to hit the Enter or Return key, that option is called a *hotkey*. Some BBS software enables it with no option to turn it off; others let you set your user configuration to choose it or not. This board has the hotkeys set on, in an effort to keep things easy.)

"I will be changing things from time to time," says sysop Steve Everley (don't forget the last e!), "however, the general look will not change much. I have tried to keep it as simple as possible for people. Since I run a genealogy-only BBS, no games, etc., I find that it is fairly easy to keep it simple. I want the new person in the BBS world to have an easy way to find things."

From the main menu (Fig. 2-11) you can choose from many areas. All are open to you, but subscribers get more time per day. You can be a free user or a subscriber on Everley's board; daily time credit is also given for file uploads. It's a complicated formula that allows you to pay for actual usage, but averages out to about 15 minutes a day for one year or one hour a day for three months—all for about $5.

Figure 2-11

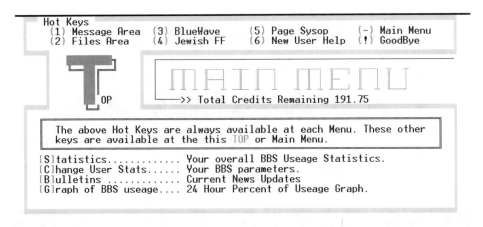

Select (21 min): ▮

The main menu of KC GeneSplicer has hotkeys (single-stroke commands) to take you to the most popular functions.

"I carry echos from three different networks: FidoNet, IGA_net, and Native Net," Everley says. "This makes about 40 different echos available to the users with a good range of subjects."

As several of the board's introductory screens explain, not all of the echos are available to the new user. "I generally don't give access to the BBS without having some contact with the people who call, either voice or my NEWUSER.APP, which is a simple information sheet that

can be filled out and sent in. If people do not feel like contributing to the General Funds account then I feel the amount of time they should have should be limited to 30 minutes. Then if you wish to contribute I will grant more access time. I feel that this is fair since I make three long-distance calls every day to bring in mail and files. People who use the system should share in some of the expenses incurred. It costs me about 50–70 dollars a month right now in telephone bills," he says.

An important feature is his emphasis on the more difficult genealogy problems: African-American, Native American, and off the continent. The main menu is simple and direct, without a lot of clutter. From any menu, the ! will log you off, although it asks you twice whether you mean it.

Blue Wave Mail Reader is a mail door. You must configure the mail door before you even try to use it, or it won't download to you. Of course, you want to choose the echos first, as shown in Fig. 2-12. You could string together choices, for instance typing in 12 13 69 109 as your preferred conferences, then go on to the next screen.

Figure 2-12

Area	Status	Description of Message Area
1	All	GENESPLICER_LOCAL
2	All	LOCAL_SYSOP
201		ABQ_GENE
202		IGA_ABGSC
203		ADOPTEES
204		ANAG
205		AAGENE
206		AUG_GEN
207		IGA_AUS.GEN
208		IGA_ACADIAN.GEN
209		CAROLINA_GEN
210		CHICORA_GEN
211		CIVIL_WAR
213		IGA_GEN_EVENTS
215		FM-GENEALOGIE
216		IGA_FRENCH.GEN
217		GENDATA
218		GENREPLY

Area #(s) or More [Y,n]? ▮

Choose from the several dozen available message topics, then download a packet of messages to read offline later.

The nice thing about Blue Wave (and by the way, it's a shareware program that allows you to read the mail on your end, and also contains a door for the BBS end) is that you can choose keywords for

the selections. If you're interested in Spencers and Ohio, you can set the keyword function on and have it retrieve only messages with those two keywords. Be aware, however, that in this case it's an OR search, not an AND search, so you could get messages with one but not the other term.

After you've selected your conferences (echos), you can choose (D) to download the package, as shown in Fig. 2-13. It's quick and easy. KC GeneSplicer is a good board for the heartland of U.S. genealogy, and worth a visit.

Figure 2-13

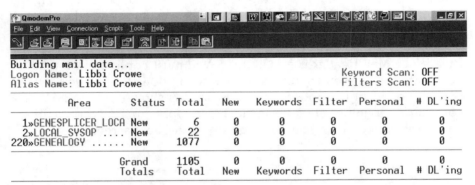

Get in the habit of downloading messages from BBSs like KC GeneSplicer; it saves time and long-distance charges!

Pot of Gold

❋ **Huntsville, Alabama**
205-650-0998

Pot of Gold has been sponsored by the Huntsville Computer Club, Inc. since June 1989. Mike Cothran is the sysop; the cosysop is his wife, Marie McCormack, who is also in charge of memberships. "We currently have over 380 users. Our average user age is 40; we're one of those sedate boards," Marie says. Some time back, Marie says, the club wanted the BBS to offer something that area BBSs were lacking. That subject turned out to be genealogy. Now they carry one of the most complete genealogy message areas I've seen.

The board runs the latest VBBS software and has lines for up to 28.8. The nice thing about VBBS software is that the QWK door is built right in; a ! command at the main menu takes you right into the mail download area.

POG is a "real names only" board; your member ID is a number associated with your full name. When you first log on, after pressing Enter to bypass the redundant language choice, enter NEW and follow the screen prompts to create your account. Once you have an established account, you can enter your user number rather than your name; it's shorter and there's less chance for error. If you live in Huntsville the board will call you back to verify your information, but if you live out of town you must ask the sysop to upgrade you to general public access. Be sure to read your "welcome new user" e-mail message; this has Mike's voice phone number, and a voice call is the fastest way to get upgraded.

The general public can get access to Pot of Gold 30 minutes per day, read-only access to genealogy message bases and full access to the genealogy file area. About 50 percent of the remaining (nongenealogy) file areas are invisible to users with public access accounts.

The only way to obtain full access is to join the Huntsville Computer Club, Inc., a nonprofit organization. Dues are $25 annually for an individual membership or $35 annually for a family membership. This

type of account entitles the user to one hour daily on the BBS (with family membership, each family member gets one hour per day), full read/write access to all message bases, access to all file bases, e-mail privileges on all networks POG carries (including an Internet e-mail box), a copy of the Club's monthly 32-page publication, *The Journal*, which is full of how-to computer articles, both online and offline subjects.

"It also gets you the ear of the sysop," Marie says with a smile," who will arrange additional time if needed, or subscribe to another mail list if he's asked nicely. We have several members in other states already, so long-distance members are nothing unusual for us. They might not make it to the Christmas luncheon as regularly as the locals, but we think just as much of them."

The networks on POG include all FIDO genealogy conferences, with the exception of JEWISHGEN, which is gated in through Internet anyway. POG also has the entire soc.genealogy hierarchy with the exception of the fairly new soc.genealogy.australia+nz, the Master Genealogist mail list, and Orangeburgh German-Swiss Genealogical Society mail list. "We do not currently subscribe to Roots-L, and due to the amount of traffic on it we don't plan to. We do these two mail lists because they are low traffic, highly specialized, and of particular interest to a couple of our club members," Marie says.

⇨ Roots & Branches

* **Billerica, MA**
508-670-9053

Mark Esplin began Roots & Branches about three years ago when a local users' group meeting got him excited about combining online communication with genealogical research. So he asked a lot of people a lot of questions until he was able to set up his own BBS. He loves getting to know people and helping others with their genealogical research.

He feels his board's best feature is that it's all genealogy, and he hopes to improve his Internet connection soon. His files include GEDCOMs, TTs, and a wide range of software to help the

Figure 2-14

```
[U]ser Utilities
[C]omment to SysOp

<29 min left> Command: M




                 M E S S A G E   A R E A S   M E N U

[1] General (Local)
[2] Genealogy Echo
[3] Genealogy Software
[4] Tiny Tafels only
[5] Tiny Tafels Replies
[6] WGW  Who's Got What Database Swap

[L]ocality Genealogy Echoes
[O]ther Echoes

[P]revious Menu
[T]op Menu

<28 min left> Command: █
```

The main menu of Roots & Branches includes M for Message Area.

telegenealogist. Type M from the main menu (see Fig. 2-14) to get to the message area. The board is free to users, although he will accept donations. He typically has around 200 regular callers at a time, about 50 percent of them local.

"My advice to the beginner is to stick with the BBS and don't get discouraged. They are all hard to learn at first, and it takes a while to get the hang of it," Esplin says. "Take advantage of the messaging capabilities of any board you visit. That's where the action is."

An important point is that when you're a new caller, not yet registered and verified, you can neither upload nor download to R&B. The bulletins contain information ranging from local genealogical meetings to computer and BBS how-tos; be sure to read them in one of your first calls.

Esplin says mealtimes are the best time to log onto his board, as that's when traffic slows somewhat. He has a QWK mail door on his board, which also makes it easy to use. This is a fun board, and the emphasis on genealogy is a plus.

 # Genealogy (SF) of San Francisco

✳ San Francisco, CA
415-584-0697

Brian Mavrogeorge has put together a simple BBS for genealogy only, and it works quite well. The unadorned opening menu is shown in Fig. 2-15. Your choices are all just a single keystroke away; this board uses hotkeys.

Figure 2-15

```
Thank you for using The Blue Wave Mail Door
Now Returning to Genealogy(SF) San Francisco 415-584-0697 HST...



MAIN:
Message section  File section    Goodbye (logoff  Need Help?
Statistics       Yell at sysop   Change setup     History
ListUsers        ?HELP           JFF searches     TMS searches
Blue Wave Mail
Select:
```

Genealogy (SF) of San Francisco isn't big on fancy graphics, but it has loads of goodies.

The membership list at the time this was written was small, under 200 people, and mainly from the Bay Area of California, though there were a few people from other states. The folks there are very active, though.

One of the nice features of this board is that Mavrogeorge uses Gary Mokotoff's database, Jewish Family Finder Search. Here you type in the surname, city, and country and find the names of other researchers looking for the same lines. A great boon to someone searching this particularly difficult type of genealogy!

He also participates in the Tiny Tafel matching system: Choose T from the main menu and M from the TTS menu. If you have a report waiting for you, the menu will change and give you options for scanning, downloading, and deleting your report. If you don't have a report waiting for you and type TM, the system will still ask you questions as if you had requested a matching report. Simply use Q to exit the questionnaire; input the name, dates, and how closely to match them (to allow variation in spelling, for example) and you'll be given a list to choose from. Of course, uploading your own TT is the best thing to do; that way you give as well as take.

The Files area, shown in Fig. 2-16, has loads of goodies: vital statistics files from the U.S. and UK, Mavrogeorge's own excellent

Figure 2-16

Genealogy (SF) of San Francisco's Files area has an assortment of useful text and data.

articles on genealogical research, GEDCOM files uploaded by members, and software for genealogy and general purposes.

The quick mail package on this board is the very popular Blue Wave, shown in Fig. 2-17. With the Blue Wave mail door, you can use filters (I don't want messages with this word) and keywords (I do want messages with this word) and select your favorite conferences. Mavrogeorge's selection is as good as any local BBS I've found: African-American, several European, and the National Genealogy echo from Fidonet.

Figure 2-17

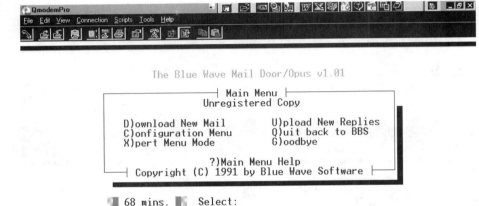

Blue Wave, a popular program for sending and receiving message packets, is the mail door on Genealogy (SF).

You're on your own

This is just a small sampling of the fine local bulletin board systems that carry genealogy, either in part or as their entire reason for existence. More are being created all the time. They aren't limited to the United States, either, though I limited myself to the continental U.S. for this chapter. Because of the variety of BBS nets, you can send mail to and from almost any board in the world, and also sign onto them yourself. You need to search around and find a network or two on a board or two that suit you.

There are several ways to do this. First, ask at your local genealogy meeting or computer users' group meeting about what local BBSs are available, especially ones with genealogy on them. Sign on and look at the messages. Almost every message has a tagline with something about the origin of the message, usually the name of the board and the phone number. Collect enough genealogy messages and you'll soon have quite a list of numbers to try.

For strictly Fidonet genealogy boards, I'll look later at the National Genealogical Society's board, on which Richard Pence keeps a wonderful list of BBSs that carry those echos. It's updated every month, so I made no attempt to reproduce it here when you can get a much more current version quite easily.

Finally, look in genealogy magazines and journals. Many BBSs advertise there as well as in general computer magazines such as *Computer Shopper*.

Fidonet

F IDONET has been around for almost as long as bulletin boards. A network system for BBSs, the program was designed to connect individual PCs, Macintoshes, and other breeds of computers, allowing free-form communication.

Fidonet has always been a distinct kind of wide-area network. The hardware matters somewhat, of course, but the basis of Fidonet is software, which was written because hobbyists and software authors needed utilities to automatically share files, messages, and e-mail among various BBSs.

The first Fidonet software was written by two guys living on opposite coasts: Ken Kaplan and Tom Jennings. The idea was to have a good program for hobbyists who wanted to run a local BBS. These authors required an easy way to swap updates across the continent. The best idea seemed to be to have the computers and modems do it at night, when rates were cheap. (This was before public data networks.) So the programs were set up to "fetch" the needed data. Legend, in the form of Thom Henderson, has it that this program was concocted from three different programs. The comment "that's a real mongrel" was made and so the name was born. Soon what was a software program to run BBSs became an automated wide-area network program as well.

Of course, they weren't the only ones who needed this capability, and it seemed the logical next step was to permit the traffic of private e-mail messages, called *net mail*, between the sysops of various boards along the way. So the program grew to include routing through hubs, leaving off and picking up messages, either private or public, and then continuing the routine down the line. Thus we now have echo mail, or the ability to have a message on a local BBS echoed across several, or even thousands, of boards.

It got so big that, according to Thom Henderson, the users decided they needed a framework to manage the system. Thus the Fidonet Association was born.

"But," says Henderson, who was the last chairman of the last board of directors of this group, "it was shut down. The members decided they liked to be more loose-knit than that." Henderson, author of the ARC programs, says that the organization was just too formal for the

sysops on Fidonet. Deep in their hearts, the Fidonet sysops were basically anarchists.

 # How Fidonet works

In Fidonet terms, you have nodes and hosts, which are almost synonymous. A node is a site made of hosts. Where you're sitting is a host. Someone can remotely log onto a host. So your local BBS can be a host or a node. The dictionary defines *node* as a point of concentration, a central point. (The people who invented a lot of these network terms were biologists, so a lot of the terms are from biology.) Messages are *echoed* from node to node.

Echo mail is the term on Fidonet for a conference or forum. With echo mail, you're talking to the net at large. With access through a local BBS, you can leave a message to people all over the world. If you leave a message for Fidonet, you assign it to a certain interest group, say Southeast. That night, the BBS operator has his computer dial a regional hub and upload all messages. The hub knows where the packet came from and will send it to all other BBSs in the region according to which BBS accepts messages on which topics. It also sends it to a national hub, which sends it to every national hub plus every regional hub except the one it received the packet from. The regional hubs also distribute according to what echos the BBS asks for. So echo mail can go anywhere. The backbone knows where it came from, and it bundles and sends messages everywhere except where they came from.

Unless the BBS sysop charges a fee for signing on (some do, some don't, some charge by the message) this looks "free" to the user. Yet someone, somewhere is paying that long-distance phone charge. It could be the BBS sysop, who pays the hub sysop, or the university sponsoring a hub, or even your tax dollars if you've used a gate to the Internet. This is why it's so important to stay on the topic of the group to which your message is posted. There are French-only message echos, and they don't want their time and long-distance calls wasted on messages in German or English. Similarly, echos specifically for Native American or Jewish genealogy don't need

messages about the Civil War unless it's about, for example, a Cherokee or a rabbi involved in that conflict.

The personality of the echo depends on the moderator. Each echo is required to have at least one moderator, and while this is often a BBS sysop, it isn't always. The moderator is required to check that messages are on topic and will often chastise senders who don't adhere to the rule. The moderators don't, however, censor messages.

Be aware that you basically have no privacy on Fidonet, even if a message is sent as "private." There's no encoding; the only security is you accepting or not accepting a certain echo's messages.

Fidonet is for the amateur, in the sense of people who do something just for the love of it, whether it pays anything or not. The Fidonet folks love BBSs for their own sake. As with all amateur efforts, it's hard to keep track of it. Some 10,000 BBSs are on the net, and each might claim up to 500 users. But that doesn't really tell you how many people are on the net, Henderson says.

"People who call BBSs call a lot of BBSs," Henderson says. "And some call, register, and disappear. Others are regular users, but of the online files, not the message system. So, on the net, you might have 20,000 people." But that's at any given time. BBSs come and go with dizzying regularity, and members of a defunct BBS have to find another board on the net before they can get back on the echo mail line.

The sense of community, Henderson says, comes from the message system. It's very big in Europe and Australia, he says, where people love to carry on conversations in written form. Fidonet, while growing, is not doubling every year as it used to, Henderson notes. Still, it's hard to keep up with who's on and who's gone.

Asked what Fidonet's biggest advantage is, and Henderson says, "It's free. You pay your phone bill, or a subscription to the local board sometimes to help with his phone bill, and you're in touch with the world, with people on the leading edge. Fidonet people were the first to use protocols, the first to use top-of-the-line modems, the first to figure out how to squeeze every last bit of data into each packet down the line. You know some of these guys go to vendor's shows, and talk

about device drivers to support 9,600+ bps. The manufacturer rep says, 'But DOS doesn't do that.' And the sysop is saying, 'Oh, yes it does, if you know how. I do it all the time.' They know how to replace standard UARTs with something that'll go 38,000 bps or better. They'll do what they can to let the users download 1 megabyte in 10 minutes."

Asked what the biggest disadvantage is, Henderson says, "It's free. The sysops can be wonderful, but some can be not nice to deal with for the average user. A lot of them feel their boards are a public service, and try to help the average user. Others feel it's their own baby, and 'I'll do it the way I want to.' To these guys the users are at best unimportant and at worst a nuisance. Remember, these guys are tied into 1,000 other boards, and they sometimes feel they don't need the local user so much."

Many genealogy-only boards have sysops that are thrilled to have new members, though. So shop around your hometown and find a local Fidonet board. One way is to log onto CompuServe at the Roots forum, download the latest list of bulletin boards, and look for a Fidonet connection. Another way is to hang out at a local users' group and ask for a local Fidonet node. Then, after determining which flavor of sysop you have here (the helpful, public-service flavor or the "it's my party and I'll do what I want to" flavor), jump in on the Fidonet echo mail.

Fido friends

You can soon learn how to send a message to the other users of your BBS and the local area Fidonet. Generally, one keystroke will send your message to everyone who gets that echo on the entire network.

And it's just the beginning. For Fido has connections to the rest of the world, thanks to people like Tim Pozar. He wrote UFGATE, a program to help e-mail move from one system to another, more specifically from the Internet to Fidonet. Several other programs exist to hook up other nets, but his is the most commonly used.

UFGATE runs on IBM PC/XT/AT and PS/2 machines or compatibles. UFGATE will also work with MS-DOS or PC-DOS machines that aren't 100% IBM PC hardware compatible with an appropriate FOSSIL (a communications device driver). You can even use it with PC Pursuit.

The package allows you to import and export UUCP messages, and will automatically delete old Usenet newsgroup messages. UFGATE will also handle mail and newsgroups that have been either 12- or 16-bit compressed. Message formatting, like automatically appending individual signature files, is supported. Detailed debugging is available, so setup is easier than it used to be.

The best part is that UFGATE is free to noncommercial, nonsupported users. If you're interested in support, which includes updates for a year, the Late Night Software telephone support service, and a hard copy of the manual, you're asked to pay $35. If you're a commercial site, you can get the support and the manual for $195. Support is available to all users via the UFGATE echo on Fidonet.

You can download the UFGATE package from the Late Night Software BBS at 415-695-0759. They have a USR dual standard (HST/v.32) modem. The time to transfer the file (UFGATE.ARC) is 10 minutes at 9,600 bps, or about 40 minutes at 2,400 bps.

UFGATE is also available via an anonymous FTP from zeus.ieee.org. I'll cover how to do that in chapter 5. You want to get ufg_103.arc from the directory /pub/fidonet/ufgate.1

 # How to use Fidonet addresses

When you address a message on Fidonet, it looks like this: 1:105/302.0. Usually the 1: (North America, which includes the U.S., Canada, and Mexico) and .0 are left off, but they're there by default. (Europe is 2: and the Pacific Basin is 3:.) The address 1:105/302.0 can be translated as Zone 1, Net 105, FidoNode 302, Point 0.

To make that an Internet address, you reverse the order and put a letter in front of the numbers. According to Pozar, "That has two purposes. It makes it easier to parse out in case of errors, and there's a rule that you can't begin an Internet domain address with a number."

So the Fidonet address becomes p0.f302.n105.z1. But that's not all. You must add the Fidonet domain of .fidonet.org to the end of that, cut off the p0 (it is, again, a default) and you have f302.n105 .z1.fidonet.org—the "fully qualified domain name" of a Fido node.

Now, if the node in question has several points to it (that is, several different machines answering to the same Fidonet address), you don't chop off the p#. The Fidonet address 1:105/4.3 (zone 1, net 105, node 4 point 3), for example, would be written as p3.f4.n105.z1 .fidonet.org (there's a point number other than 0, so you have to keep it in). If the address were in Europe or the Pacific Basin, the z1 would become z2 or z3, respectively.

So once you have the basics of addressing down, you can send this message to your nearest Fidonet/Internet gate. The local sysop should know, or be able to find out, where that is. At this point, hope fervently that you've chosen the helpful, friendly flavor of sysop.

Out in front

Fidonet generally sets the pace for other BBS nets. There are over 1,400 Fidonet echos, or topic areas. Many active and interesting genealogy echos are worth looking for on your local bulletin board systems. The echos are as amorphous as the number of boards on the net, and this list is probably already out of date:

ADOPTEES Adoptees Information Exchange is the place for adoptees and birth parents to go for help and suggestions in their search. The echo discusses legislation affecting adoptees, birth parents, and adoptive parents. Organizations and agencies offering help for adoptees and birth parents are also discussed. This echo gets

about 150 messages a week and is moderated by Michael Kirst, Dave Warwick, and Bob Heide.

AAGENE An abbreviation for African-American Genealogy, this echo focuses on the genealogy of African-Americans in the United States and Canada. The primary moderator and originator of the echo is Mike Wade. It originates from 1:376/140.0 at fidonet.org, and has a volume of about 100 messages per month. The moderators are Mike Wade and David Hamiter.

CAROLINA_GEN This is a general conference for Genealogy hobbyists who are interested in the south-eastern states of North and South Carolina. Those with ancestors from this general area are urged to send queries through this echo to get response from others doing research in the same general area. Moderator approval is required for gating into networks other than Fidonet. The echo has about 30 messages per day and is moderated by Foxy Ferguson.

CHICORA_GEN This echo originates from Carolina Cousin BBS (1:376/140), located in Columbia, South Carolina, and addresses the genealogy of the Carolinas and Georgia from 1650 to 1865. In other words, it focuses on the colonial period to the end of the Civil War. The echo gets about 500 messages per month and the moderators are David Hamiter, Gene Jeffries, and Van Hoyle.

GEN4SALE Otherwise known as the Genealogy for Sale echo, this was created to give genealogists a place to buy, sell, or trade any goods or services related to genealogy. It originates from 1:376/140.0 and gets about 100 messages a month. The moderators are David Hamiter and Brent Holcomb.

GENDATA Otherwise known as the Tiny Tafel database, this echo is a method of circulating one form of genealogy information. These messages are in a predetermined format and are called Tiny Tafels. Discussion of these Tiny Tafels is now permitted within the echo. Anything not related directly to Tiny Tafels is automatically deleted. The TT messages in this echo are archived and distributed via the Genealogy Software Distribution System on a semiregular basis for use on any Fidonet BBS, and are intended for use by amateur genealogists doing their own research. The messages sent to this echo are repeated

to the BBS networks GTnet RBBSnet and Familynet. It gets about 40 messages a week, and the moderators (John Grove and Michael Kirst) have to approve your message before it goes on.

GENEALOGY The National Genealogical conference is the "main" genealogy message echo. Here you'll find people exchanging information and data concerning all aspects of genealogy. This conference is primarily oriented toward U.S. and Canadian research, and includes queries, requests for help, product/software announcements, and exchange of information between researchers. It gets about 400 messages a day and is distributed worldwide. The moderators are Don Wilson, Richard Pence, and Frank Williams.

GENEALOGY.CDN The Canadian Genealogy echo covers topics of discussion including Canadian ancestry, genealogical societies, Canadian genealogical meetings and announcements, and exchanges of data and information. The moderator is Ken Quinn.

GENEALOGY.EUR This is the Fidonet tag for the International Genealogy and Family History echo. The echo is for discussing anything related to genealogy and family history anywhere in the world, except locally within the U.S. Discussion of immigration to or emigration from the U.S., however, is acceptable. It gets approximately 30 messages a day and the moderator is Steve Hayes.

GENREPLY This is the echo for users to post reply messages for Tiny Tafels that were posted in the GENDATA echo. Tiny Tafel generation software might also be discussed in this echo. Messages posted here are copied to the WGA_Net. This echo gets about 25 messages a week and is moderated by Michael Kirst and John Grove.

GENSOFT The Genealogy Software echo is all about genealogy programs, no matter what the platform. Come here to discuss genealogy software, hardware, utilities, reviews, announcements from suppliers, and help with problems. The distribution is worldwide and the echo gets about 15 messages a day. The moderators are Frank Williams and Richard Pence.

ITALIANO.GEN This is the Fidonet Italian Genealogy conference. Here you'll find discussion of the genealogy and family history of

Italian-speaking people throughout the world. This list is in English and Italian; it posts about 200 messages a week. The moderators are Rudy Lacchin and Debbi McKay.

JEWISHGEN This is the Jewish Genealogy conference, moderated by Susan King.

SC_GENEALOGY This is an echo for South Carolina genealogy. The echo focuses on the genealogy in the state of South Carolina; you have to ask moderators Gene Jeffries and David Hamiter to join. It gets about 100 messages a month.

SE_GENEALOGY This is about genealogy in the southeastern United States: TN, VA, WV, KY, GA, AL, FL, TX, LA, MS, MO, SC, NC, AR, and MD. People with ancestors in this general area are urged to send queries through the echo to get prompt response from others who are doing research in the same general area and are more than willing to assist others with the research needed. About 50 messages are posted a day; the moderator is Hershel Kreis.

SPANISH.GEN This is the place for questions and answers about genealogical research on Spanish surnames. Most of the 50 messages a week are in Spanish, but English and other languages are allowed. The moderators are John Grove, Miny Dittmer, and Fleet Teachout.

TENN_GEN This is an open discussion for all individuals interested in researching their family history and tracing ancestors who lived in or emigrated through the state of Tennessee. It gets about 50 messages a month and is moderated by Foxy Ferguson.

WGW This is the "who's got what" (WGW) message area, for posting queries and input to the WGW database. The WGW database is a directory of who possesses what genealogy-related research material. About 50 messages a week pass through here; the moderator is Jack Williams.

CIVIL_WAR The Civil War History echo isn't strictly genealogy, but as the discussion is on historical aspects of the American Civil War, its

causes and effects, battles, tactics, the people—military and civilian—and so on, sometimes you can find interesting tidbits to show you where to research next. It's a busy forum, with 350 messages a week, and is moderated by Al Thorley and Frank Coleman.

This list is, of course, subject to change, as anarchy still rules on Fidonet. Some will be added and some might fade away. The last chapter in this book looks at some pretty typical genealogy boards; most of them will carry some or all the genealogy echos. If one you like isn't carrying one, talk to the sysop about it.

Finding a Fidonet board

This part is easy; almost any BBS that has networked messages at all has Fidonet. The trick is finding one with genealogy echos, all or as many as match your interests. As mentioned in chapter 2, first use word of mouth. Ask at the local genealogy meetings and seminars, "Who has a BBS with the genealogy echos on it?" and give those local ones a try.

If that doesn't work, dial up the National Genealogical Society BBS Genealogy One at 703-528-2612, and get the zipped text file GBBS*xxxx*.ZIP. GBBS* is maintained and copyrighted Richard Cleaveland, with acknowledgment to Richard Pence for his design guidance. The *xxxx* in the filename will be replaced by the month and year of the latest list. The December 1996 file, for example, should be GBBS9612.ZIP. Download the latest one, unzip it, and you'll have an ASCII text file called GBBS*xxxx*.TXT, readable by any word processor, of over 1,000 worldwide BBS systems carrying at least some of the Fidonet genealogy echos. Open it in your favorite word-processing program and search for your area code (see Fig. 3-1).

Figure 3-1

```
AL Gunther       Thunder Mountain BB 205-582-4719   Ge...........  1:18/233
AL Huntsville    The American BBS    205-851-6220   ....Da.......  1:373/4
AL Huntsville    Pot of Gold         205-650-0998   GeSoDaEuSeMw.. 1:373/5
AL Huntsville    The Trading Post    205-828-1944   Ge....EuSe.... 1:373/6
AL Huntsville    PC Help Desk BBS    205-882-6167   Ge...........  1:373/7
AL Huntsville    Post Offis          205-650-5777   Ge......SeMw.. 1:373/20
AL Huntsville    Power Windows! BBS  205-881-8619   GeSo....SeMw.. 1:373/27
AL Millbrook     King James Bible BB 205-285-5948   ........Se.... 1:375/1611
AL Mobile        Genealogy Today     334-478-6533   Ge......Se.... 1:3625/445
AL Mobile        The World According 334-633-5875   Ge......Se.... 1:3625/462
AL Mobile        The Data Connection 334-602-0917   Ge......Se.... 1:3625/465
AL Mobile        Di's Online Cafe    334-661-8945   Ge......Se.... 1:3625/470
AL Montgomery    StarScan (sm)       334-279-7313   GeSoDaEuSe.... 1:375/1
AL Moulton       Cyclone BBS         205-974-5123   ........Se.... 1:3607/3
AL Pleasant Gro  Family SmorgasBoard 205-744-0943   Ge....EuSeMw.. 1:3602/77
AL Tuscaloosa    OptiNet BBS         205-556-2436   ........Se.... 1:3606/10
AR Benton        The Fishin' Hole    501-794-4072   Ge...........  1:3821/102
AR Bentonville   The Chicken Coop    501-273-0152   Ge...........  1:19/18
AR Conway        Global Gateways     501-329-2939   ......Eu......  1:399/3
AR Conway        Conway PC Users Gro 501-329-7227   ..So..........  1:399/4
AR Farmington    The Fast Micro Conn 501-267-2662   Ge...........  1:391/1500
AR Fayetteville  The Fortran Fortres 501-582-3579   Ge...........  1:391/1410
AR Fort Smith    Jackalope Junction  501-785-5381   Ge......SeMw.. 1:3822/1
AR Fort Smith    AOPCUG BBS          501-452-5417   Ge......Se.... 1:3822/2
AR Fort Smith    Beyond Insanity BBS 501-782-1367   Ge....EuSe.... 1:3822/12
AR Jonesboro     Hard Times BBS      501-935-3402   Ge...........  1:389/9
AR Little Rock   Thunderbolt BBS     501-568-4915   ..........Mw.. GT:35/5
AR Paragould     Phantasia 2000      501-236-9813   Ge......Se.... 1:389/5
```

The GBBS list is available from the NGS bulletin board system. It's worth a quick call!

⇨ Ancestry BBS (461-382-9061)

An important board for any Fidonet genealogist to visit is the Ancestry Board in Sebring, Florida (see Fig. 3-2). It's one of the cornerstone systems in the Genealogy Software Distribution System.

"It tickles me to death to see callers from Sweden, France, Belgium, etc. on the system. One very odd fact is I'm not a genealogist. I simply provide a tool for those who are," John Grove, its founder and currently one of the sysops, says happily.

Ancestry is a site of the Genealogical Software Distribution System, or GSDS. GSDS is the Fidonet file distribution network carried on a satellite and available to any Fidonet bulletin board system. GSDS distributes files the way messages are distributed by echo mail. It was

Figure 3-2

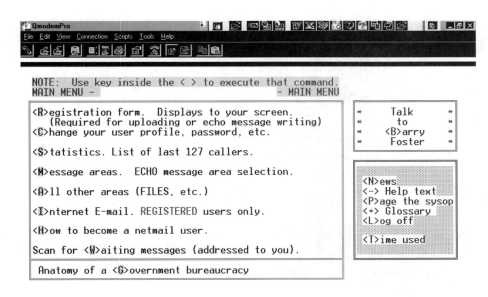

Ancestry BBS' main menu.

started by Debbie McKay in Virginia Beach and has become an essential part of Fidonet. To get there, from the main menu press A for all other areas, and from the secondary menu press F for file areas. The GSDS files are selection 3. Then you'll see the screen in Fig. 3-3.

The files are specific genealogies, how-to articles, programs, and text files too long for messages. Two of the most popular shareware genealogy programs, The Family Edge and Brother's Keeper, are distributed this way, as well as Mike St. Clair's PAF Review, a monthly update of PAF add-on utilities. This last one, by the way, is must-read material if you use PAF; it's full of ways to make your life easier using that program.

"Hundreds of textual files pass through the system. These files contain extracts of census records, etc. and are invaluable tools for researchers," Grove explains. "They can obtain these files from any

Figure 3-3

```
Select File Area
              [ 1] GSDS program files (area 1)
              [ 2] GSDS program files (area 2)
              [ 3] GSDS text files (area 1)
              [ 4] GSDS text files (area 2)
              [ 5] GSDS PAF utility files (area 1)
              [ 6] GSDS PAF utility files (area 2)
              [ 7] GSDS program demo files (area 1)
              [ 8] GSDS program demo files (area 2)
              [ 9] GSDS Jewish genealogy info (area 1)
              [10] GSDS Jewish genealogy info (area 2)
              [11] Bronscan prepared files for BBSs. (area 1)
              [12] Bronscan prepared files for BBSs. (area 2)



Cursor keys = Move highlite bar          0-9 = Enter file area #
S = Search files by name or keyword   <Enter> = Select file area
N = New files by date                       ? = Help, <Esc> = Exit
```

The GSDS programs files on Ancestry BBS.

Fidonet system that chooses to make them available. Since they're carried via satellite, they need only a downlink. In addition to the text files, programs from most all of the software authors find their way into the world via GSDS. Support for these programs can usually be found on the Genealogy Software echo conference. We are very careful about who can originate the files into GSDS. This is a process called *hatching* and we have a very limited number of locations allowed to do so."

Grove, a retired IBM employee, is the North American coordinator of the network. "The position is basically supervisory," he says. "I arrange feeds for systems that ask for them, place files into distribution, fix pathing problems, and try to maintain some semblance of order among the systems. There are three more like me, one in England and one in Australia, who fill the same position I do. We also have an international coordinator (I had been asked to take over that position but had to decline for health reasons at the time). Several years ago, the sysops who originated the network dropped out for various reasons. Since then the network has grown beyond anyone's dreams. With the new satellite links online, our user base has grown tenfold."

He spends from 30 minutes to 8 hours a day on the board, depending on the amount of traffic, but on an average it's about one hour a day. The BBS was begun in the fall of 1988.

"I worked in the Miami, Fla. office [of IBM] for 24 years, moving to Ft. Myers, Fla. when the opportunity arose. Miami had gotten far too large and crowded for me. We had purchased property in the Sebring, Fla. area many years ago in preparation for retirement. When the move presented itself, my wife and I decided we would go ahead and build in Sebring and I would commute on weekends. It's about half as far between Sebring and Ft. Myers than Sebring and Miami. I lived in a 30-foot travel trailer during the week and came "home" on weekends. While in my new location, I called a local BBS and found out there was a genealogy echo conference available. My wife had been doing genealogy since about 1980 and I thought she would be interested. She was. I had been a sysop, although not in Fidonet, since 1981. I thought it best if I just started a new BBS in the Sebring area and brought in those areas she wanted most. The fall of '88 saw Ancestry TBBS online for the first time. Being as remote as this area is, I never expected to draw many users. My regular caller list is up to 440 users from all over the world now," he says.

The system uses TBBS software from eSoft Corp., a multiline system that can run as many as 64 phone lines on one CPU. Ancestry runs on a fast 386 computer with 4 megabytes of main memory and 760 megabytes of hard drive, state of the art for 1988.

With two phone lines, the first rolls to the second on busy signals. The numbers are 813-382-9061 and 813-471-0552. Both lines are high-speed U.S. Robotics modems, but only 0552 has V.32bis and V.42bis capability; 9061 is simply HST.

"I like [being sysop] because it's one way I can let folks share in some of the good fortune I've had over the years. Don't get me wrong; I'm far removed from being a liberal individual. That doesn't keep me from liking to help people if I can. I started, and still maintain, three echo conferences within Fidonet as well," he says. "Referring to the BBS itself, I think its simplicity and ease of use are its strong points. First-time callers regularly remark that it's one of the nicest systems they have ever called. I can only take them at their word."

Ancestry's most outstanding feature, according to Grove, is that easy navigating, unintimidating interface. "The software can't be touched for ability, ease of use, ability to customize the configuration, etc. Each and every screen you see while online has been designed by yours truly and implemented via the software. There are no two TBBS systems alike unless owned and operated by the same person. Each and every one looks just like its sysop wants it to look. I chose not to use any fancy graphics as it tends to severely slow down the operation."

"Genealogy seems to be growing in this area as new folks move down from 'the frozen north.' Janis, my wife, was just elected the president of the Highlands County Genealogical Society (approximately 100 members strong). They use the system as kind of a home base. We're converting more and more people to computerized genealogy. When they find out what a computer can do for them, they fall right in. I teach computer usage to them once per month in the winter. The system is also home to The Sparks Family association. I have Sparks ancestors and have a full index of the *Sparks Quarterly* available for reading," he says.

When I asked him what was best about genealogy online in general, he said, "I'll answer by asking you a question: Where else can you obtain as much knowledge/assistance/friends as you can when using the various conferences? This medium puts users in contact around the world. Information is exchanged, leads given and found, programs made available, technical assistance given, and all for (usually) a local phone call."

His plans for the future include updating the hardware to '90s technology, increasing to 16 lines, all on high-speed modems, and perhaps starting a sponsorship program to finance those and ongoing costs.

There's only one restriction on use: In order to be able to write messages in the echos or upload files to the system, you must register. There's a simple registration form available from the master menu, which you print, fill out, and mail in. But you don't even have to fill out a questionnaire when you first log on, and downloading is open to everyone if you just want to pick up files or messages.

 # Fidonet rules

The Introduction covered many of the rules you need to remember in Fidonet. Because of the enormous traffic Fidonet carries, it's most important for you to follow these:

➤ Stay on topic.

➤ Post to the correct topic echo.

➤ Quote only what is necessary.

➤ Include your name in each message, and how you can be reached.

➤ Don't waste time on flames.

➤ Support your local sysop.

Fidonet is second in size and influence only to the Internet, of which the Usenet is a part. Which is where we'll go for the next two chapters.

The Usenet newsgroups

ALL the news that's fit for bits! That's what goes across the Usenet (an Internet service) every day. But as a telegenealogist, you probably aren't very concerned about soc.star.trek or comp.amiga. You want to know about the soc.genealogy groups and how they work. Still and all, you have to understand something about Usenet as a whole to begin to use the parts that have to do with genealogy, which is just one part of the immense network.

Gene Spafford, a kind and wise man at Purdue University, regularly posts several files about Usenet to misc.news. If you find them on your local board, especially one called WHATIS_U.ZIP, be sure to read them. But for now I'll try to give you some pointers.

⇨ Complicated, but useful

The first thing to understand about Usenet is that it's hard to understand. Don't be discouraged about that. It has been said that many Usenet flame wars arise because the users don't comprehend the nature of the network. And these flames, of necessity, come from people who are actually using Usenet. Imagine, then, how hard it is for those unfamiliar with Usenet to understand it! On the other hand, it should be comforting to the novice that so many people are successfully using Usenet without fully understanding it.

One reason is that Usenet is a part of the Internet, and for some people it's the only part they use. Yet it isn't the Internet, any more than Boston is Massachusetts. Usenet could be described as a set of programs to send specific messages to specific groups. It isn't an organization per se, nor is it in any one place.

It's comprised of articles sent by e-mail, all sorted into hundreds and hundreds of *newsgroups*, which are sort of like magazines, sort of like late-night dorm discussions, and sort of like a symposium. Usenet's flavor depends on the newsgroups you subscribe to. A moderated newsgroup has a referee who decides what messages get to go on that newsgroup. An unmoderated one isn't edited in any way, except you'll get flamed (insulted) if you post a message off the proper topic. There are eight major categories of newsgroups:

ALT Alternative topics

COMP Computer-science-related topics

SCI Science not related to computers

NEWS Network software topics of interest to system administrators

REC Recreation

SOC Social interaction and hobbies

TALK To talk to others

MISC Miscellaneous items

Tom Czarnik, who is an administrator of FTP on the Internet, says, "And let's make a distinction between the Internet and Usenet. The Internet has come to mean the sum of the regional nets, while Usenet is a system for the exchange of newsgroups, mostly via UUCP." UUCP is a program that runs under a system called UNIX.

No person or group has control of Usenet as a whole. No one person authorizes who gets news feeds, which articles are propagated where, who can post articles, or anything else. These things are handled one newsgroup at a time. You won't find a Usenet Incorporated or even a Usenet users' group. This means that, although the freedom of expression and association are almost absolute, Usenet is not a democracy. It's an anarchy, that is, something with little or no control except as exerted by the social pressures of those participating.

As a result, sometimes Usenet isn't fair—in part because it's hard to get everyone to agree to what's fair, and in part because it's hard to stop people from proving themselves foolish.

Usenet history

Usenet got started, according to legend, in 1979, when a group at Duke University in North Carolina wanted to exchange data on research with some other universities. This group was in on the ground floor of the development of UNIX, an operating system. This myth holds that UNIX is a pun on a preceding program called MULTICS. Get it? MULT, meaning more than one, vs. UNI, meaning one (D. M. Ritchie, "The Evolution of the UNIX Time-Sharing System" in *Tech. J.* (October 1984, vol. 63, no. 8, pt. 2, pp. 1577–1580). Anyway, soon they had written programs in UNIX to allow them to exchange data and analysis back and forth to other universities running the same programs.

They began to send each other messages to discuss hardware, problems, industry gossip, and how to fix certain bugs. Then messages started about current events. And jokes. And dreams. And chatting about their hobbies.

Then they began routing the more interesting stuff through an automated program. This program's duty was calling other UNIX sites while people slept, dropping off packets of data and programs and messages, picking up others destined for other places, and calling another site. More than 5,000 articles a day are routed this way today. And, of course, having so much information to route meant that some sort of categorization became necessary. So messages were labeled according to their "news group" and people signed up for them the same way you subscribe to a newspaper.

Meanwhile, nonuniversity types who also ran UNIX got in on the newsgroup loop from colleges, research centers, high-tech corporations, and government agencies. Now there are public-access sites and commercial connections. In fact, there are more business than educational connections. A list of free Usenet sites is available from Phil Eschallier, in the pubnet.nixpub newsgroup. Since he updates it every month, any list printed here would be outdated before the book went to press.

Because all of this happens by and large on a volunteer basis, you must understand that access to Usenet is not a right. (Although someone in Dallas recently filed a court case claiming it was just that! He kept stirring up flames on Middle-East politics and UTD pulled his student account. He was suing to get it back based on free speech. The case was unresolved as of this writing.)

Usenet is not a public utility, at least not yet; there's no government monopoly and little or no government control. Some Usenet sites are publicly funded or subsidized, but most of them aren't. Lots of universities are connected, and often the hard work of keeping Usenet going is done on campus, but it's not an academic network.

And although many people are connected through and because of their work, Usenet is not to be used for advertising. Commercials are tolerated only when they're infrequent, informative, low-key, and preferably in direct response to a specific question. The only exception is the .biz groups, where advertisements are accepted.

Usenet is not a strictly U.S. network. Many, many correspondents are from around the globe, so be tolerant of grammar and spelling. The heaviest concentrations of Usenet sites outside the U.S. are in Canada, Europe, Australia, and Japan.

Prices

To read any Usenet newsgroup, you need some sort of Internet mail connection. America Online, AT&T Interchange, BIX, CompuServe, Delphi, EZMailBox, Microsoft Network, Portal, PSI, The Well, and many other commercial services offer Usenet connections. Many local BBSs, like the ones described in chapter 2, are getting Usenet connections. There are Usenet-only connections, too. One is UUNet. UUNet isn't free, but it's affordable. One way to hook up is to subscribe by writing to:

UUNet Communications Services
3110 Fairview Park Dr., Suite 570
Falls Church, VA 22042
703-876-5050 voice

703-876-5059 fax
Net domain address: info@uunet.uu.net

Freenets are a good source of Usenet feeds, if there's one in your local dialing area. The original one is the Cleveland freenet (telnet freenet-in-a.cwru.edu). This is like National Public Radio adapted to the online experience. As of February 1992, *Communications Week* reported that 10 were in operation across the U.S. For additional information on NPTN and freenet activities or programs, you can contact:

Dr. Tom Grundner
President, NPTN
Box 1987
Cleveland, Ohio 44106
aa001@cleveland.freeneg.edu (Internet)
72135,1536 (CompuServe)

Supported by volunteers, corporations, and sometimes quasi-governmental agencies, freenets are for everything from support to hobby groups. AIDS information and guinea pig raising, community events and private friendships abound on these.

Usenet by e-mail

This isn't an advisable way to go if you can avoid it at all; it's just plain inconvenient for you and for other users of the Internet. Most of the Usenet newsgroups get more than 100 messages a day, and the process of sorting, downloading, and deleting them will be a burden not only on you, but on the Internet itself. But if, as on some BBS, your only access to the Internet is via e-mail, you can get newsgroups that way.

The first way is to find a newsgroup that's mirrored to a mail list (see chapter 5). Lists of such newsgroups are posted in regular messages called "list of active newsgroups" or "mailing lists available in Usenet." These are posted in a newsgroup called news.lists about once a month.

The second might be called the Blanche Dubois method: depend on the kindness of others. Find a Usenet site administrator who's willing

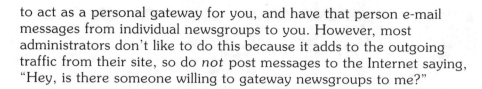

to act as a personal gateway for you, and have that person e-mail messages from individual newsgroups to you. However, most administrators don't like to do this because it adds to the outgoing traffic from their site, so do *not* post messages to the Internet saying, "Hey, is there someone willing to gateway newsgroups to me?"

There are two freely available services that allow you to access newsgroups by e-mail. One is the Stanford Netnews Filtering Service, which lets you use mail messages to search Usenet newsgroups for postings that contain keywords of interest to you. You can even subscribe to it and receive a daily list of newsgroup postings that match your search criteria. Send mail to:

```
netnews@db.stanford.edu
```

with "help" in the body of the note for full details. A similar program in Europe is the K. U. Leuven listserv in Belgium. This allows you to receive a set of newsgroups by e-mail. Send a message to:

```
listserv@cc1.kuleuven.ac.be
```

containing the single line "/nnhelp" in the body of the message. As with other freely offered services on the Net, please do not abuse or overload them, or they'll likely disappear.

 # The software

In the "old days" (the first edition of this book), you had to learn disagreeable, arcane UNIX commands and use unfriendly UNIX news readers to obtain the wonders of the Usenet. Times have changed. There are now a variety of news readers for any platform, be it Windows, Mac, UNIX, X Window, whatever. The online commercial services have all integrated news readers into their front-end software, and the most popular Web browsers (see chapter 6) have too.

Figure 4-1 shows Free Agent, a Windows news reader readily available on most BBSs, online services, and the Web. After the program is installed in Windows, you have to tell the news reader what kind of

Figure 4-1

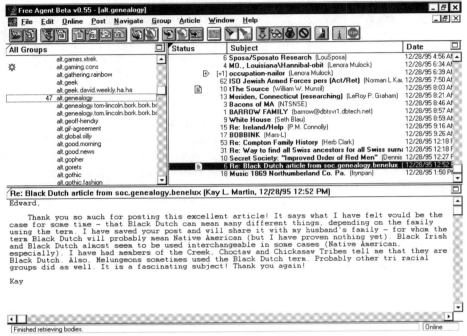

Most Usenet news readers today are graphical, with lots of choices. In News Agent, the three panes show the current list of newsgroups (upper left), the titles of the current messages in the highlighted group (upper right), and the text and header of a specific message (lower pane).

server you have. If you have an Internet service provider, the technical support people there will tell you what it is.

News Agent's layout is very typical. Three panes of the window show you information on the latest Usenet site, and the upper left pane shows the names of the newsgroups. This can be set to all newsgroups, or only the ones to which you've subscribed (that is, told the program you want to read regularly). A nice feature of this reader is that under Edit you can search this list of all newsgroups for genealogy. Simply click in the box next to the name to subscribe. Then you can select to view only the names of the newsgroups to which you've subscribed; the rest won't appear until you decide to look at the whole list again.

The upper right pane contains information about the current messages (*articles* in Usenet parlance) in the newsgroup that's highlighted in the upper left pane. Double-click on one of these lines to bring up the message itself in the lower pane. You can sort by date, sender, or subject line, another nice feature. You can reply and post simply by clicking on icons on the toolbar at top. Some news readers even have built-in spell checkers!

Although I don't own a Mac and so couldn't test it, three different sites on the Web recommended John Norstad's NewsWatcher for the Macintosh platform. NewsWatcher does everything you'd want a news reader to do, except filtering by keywords, but there's an add-on called Value Added NewsWatcher if you need filtering. The program is updated and improved so often that you'll sometimes find a new version every week.

Reading newsgroups with a Web browser (see chapter 6) isn't always so easy. Netscape Navigator's layout is very much like News Agent's, and thus is as easy. Internet Explorer, on the other hand, has three screens—a long list of the newsgroups, a list of messages in a specific newsgroup (as shown in Fig. 4-2), and an individual message—and you have to flip back and forth among those windows. Not as much fun. Even less fun are the old text-based, UNIX news readers. Sometimes, though, that's all you can go with.

A sample Usenet session

Let's say you want to read a day's worth of soc.roots messages on Usenet. Remember, your connection determines how you proceed, but let's pretend your Usenet connection is on Delphi. After signing on, type go internet usenet from the main menu and you'll be presented with the menu in Fig. 4-3. Choose 2 and then soc.roots, and you'll be presented with the following prompt:

```
1639 messages have been posted in the last 14 days; You've read 1627.
Select which messages: Unread, All, Date or ?> [unread]
```

The choices are to select U or A, type in a certain date, or simply press Enter to read from the beginning. With the great majority of

Figure 4-2

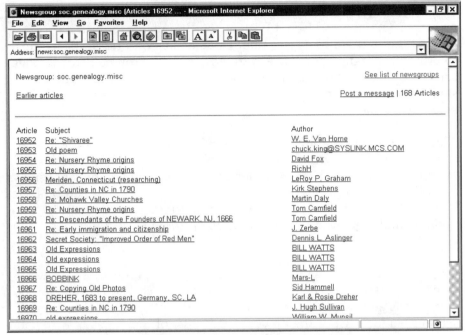

Many Web browsers have built-in Usenet news-reading functions, but they're rarely so intuitively designed as dedicated news readers. In MicroSoft's Internet Explorer, first you search a long list of newsgroup names in one window, then peruse a list of messages in the next window, then read a message in a third window, using the < button to back up to the list of messages or the list of groups. Better than a UNIX reader, at least.

Usenet readers, I've found that the oldest messages are presented first and the newest messages are on the bottom. Also, the message often scrolls by quickly; if you need to pause, type Ctrl–S (hold down the Ctrl key and hit the S key) and continue scrolling with Ctrl–Q. Other command choices are shown in Table 4-1.

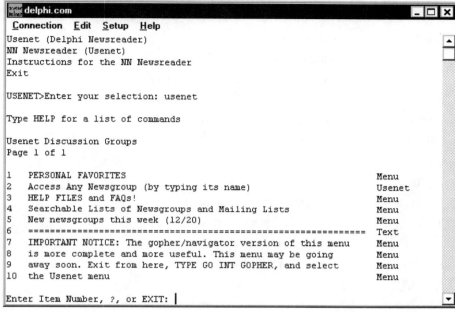

Figure 4-3

The Usenet menu on a UNIX system. If you know you want to read soc.genealogy.misc, choose 2, Access Any Newsgroup (by typing its name) and then type in soc.genealogy.misc.

Simply pressing the Enter key will give you a list of messages, as shown in Fig. 4-4. If the subject line looks interesting, type in that number and the message will scroll by. You can reply to the message, capture it with your text buffer for later reference, or simply keep pressing Return to read more messages. Typing Ctrl–Z or EXIT will take you back to the Usenet menu on this system.

I'll provide information on reading newsgroups with commercial online services in the appropriate chapter for each service.

Okay, enough about the big picture. Let's look at soc.roots specifically.

Table 4-1

Usenet commands

Command	Description
[RETURN]	Read next message.
ADD	Start a new thread with a new subject.
ADD *filename*	Start a new thread with the message from a workspace file.
BACK	Return to list of discussion topics.
ORIGINAL	Read message to which current message replies.
Ctrl–Z	Return to thread list (same as DIRECTORY).
CURRENT	Reread current message.
DIRECTORY	Display a list of discussion threads.
EXIT	Leave discussion group reader.
FILE	Copy this message to your workspace.
FORWARD	Send a copy of this message via e-mail.
GROUP	Go to next discussion group on discussion group menu.
HEADER	Display the complete header for the current message.
HELP	Show this screen.
LAST	Reread previous message.
MAIL REPLY	Send private reply via e-mail.
MARK	Mark all messages so they don't show up as unread.
MARK GROUP	Mark all messages and go to next discussion group.
NEXT THREAD	Skip to next discussion thread (subject).
ORIGINAL	Read message to which current message replies.
PREV	Read first message in the previous thread.
QUIT	Same as BACK.
READ NEXT	Read next message (same as [RETURN]).
REPLY	Post a reply within the bulletin board.
SAVE	Save this discussion group in your Personal Favorites area.
TOP	Go back to first message in current thread.

Figure 4-4

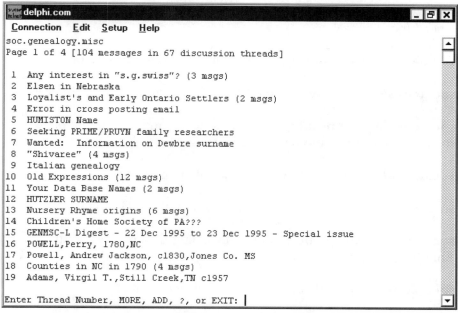

```
delphi.com                                                    _ □ X
 Connection   Edit   Setup   Help
soc.genealogy.misc                                               ▲
Page 1 of 4 [104 messages in 67 discussion threads]

 1   Any interest in "s.g.swiss"? (3 msgs)
 2   Elsen in Nebraska
 3   Loyalist's and Early Ontario Settlers (2 msgs)
 4   Error in cross posting email
 5   HUMISTON Name
 6   Seeking PRIME/PRUYN family researchers
 7   Wanted:  Information on Dewbre surname
 8   "Shivaree" (4 msgs)
 9   Italian genealogy
10   Old Expressions (12 msgs)
11   Your Data Base Names (2 msgs)
12   HUTZLER SURNAME
13   Nursery Rhyme origins (6 msgs)
14   Children's Home Society of PA???
15   GENMSC-L Digest - 22 Dec 1995 to 23 Dec 1995 - Special issue
16   POWELL,Perry, 1780,NC
17   Powell, Andrew Jackson, c1830,Jones Co. MS
18   Counties in NC in 1790 (4 msgs)
19   Adams, Virgil T.,Still Creek,TN c1957

Enter Thread Number, MORE, ADD, ?, or EXIT: |                     ▼
```

A sample menu of soc.genealogy.misc messages. Older messages appear first on most UNIX news readers; type the number of the one you want to read. Once you're reading messages, you can return to the list menu with Ctrl–Z, or continue reading them in sequence by pressing Enter.

Signing on to the genealogy newsgroups

There used to be one online genealogy Usenet newsgroup for genealogy, soc.roots. But it became unwieldy to try to discuss novices' questions, software, history, specific regions, specific family name queries, and the joy we get from our hobby all in one newsgroup. After much discussion, soul searching, argument, pleading, and finally reconciliation, there's now an embarrassment of riches in genealogical newsgroups:

alt.genealogy An older genealogy group; still a very general one, but not much trafficked

alt.culture.cajun Cajun history, genealogy, culture, and events

99

soc.genealogy.african For those tracing roots of African-Americans and other African genealogies

soc.genealogy.australia + nz Australia and New Zealand only

soc.genealogy.benelux Luxembourg, Belgium, and the Netherlands

soc.genealogy.computing Programs, bugs, and how-tos; mostly software, but also some hardware discussions

soc.genealogy.french France only, mainly in French

soc.genealogy.german Germany only, mainly in German

soc.genealogy.hispanic Spanish, including Central and South America; many messages in Spanish

soc.genealogy.jewish Judaic genealogy, moderated

soc.genealogy.marketplace Buying, selling, and trading books, programs, seminars, etc. related to genealogy

soc.genealogy.medieval Ancient genealogy, mostly European

soc.genealogy.methods How-tos, what works, tips and tricks in genealogy; moderated

soc.genealogy.misc What became of soc.roots

soc.genealogy.nordic Scandinavian genealogy

soc.genealogy.surnames Specific surname queries only. Answers are posted by private e-mail to the posters; moderated

soc.genealogy.uk + ireland The United Kingdom and Ireland only

Of course, there are several groups in the soc.history hierarchy that discuss areas touching on issues genealogists face: records, sources, and so on. Two of these groups, soc.genealogy.misc and soc. genealogy.uk+ireland, post regular frequently-asked questions files

(FAQs) to their own newsgroups and to the newsgroup soc.answers about once a month. You can post messages containing the following kinds of information to these newsgroups:

> ➤ Your own family history information and requests for others to help you find information. Tiny tafels are often posted for this.

> ➤ Information on upcoming genealogical meetings, workshops, symposiums, reunions, etc.

> ➤ Reviews, criticisms, and comments for software or hardware you've used in connection with genealogy/family history.

> ➤ Telling others about book shops around the world that contain books or information about this subject.

> ➤ Almost any message about genealogy in general.

Remember, what you send is posted as you sent it, unless it's to a moderated group such as soc.genealogy.surnames, where all messages must pass the moderator's muster.

The basics of etiquette in this group aren't very different from general online etiquette (netiquette) discussed in chapter 1. The participants in this forum want the topics of discussion to relate to genealogy or family history, however, and it's held that anything a subscriber thinks is appropriate is, if it relates to genealogy.

Assume an attitude of courtesy among subscribers and readers. Remember that your postings and comments might be seen by as many as 20,000 readers on different networks in many different countries throughout the world. Remember the rules outlined in chapter 1:

Read carefully what you receive to be certain that you understand the message before you reply.

Read carefully what you send to ensure your message won't be misunderstood. As a matter of fact, routinely let a reply sit overnight, then read it again before sending. It prevents that sinking feeling of regret when you realize what you posted is not what you meant.

Avoid sarcasm if at all possible. If humor seems appropriate, clearly label it as such. Humor should be indicated by a smiley face. It's easy to misunderstand what's being said when there's no tone of voice, facial expressions, or body language to go by.

Know your audience and double-check addresses. Make sure that the person or list of people to whom you're sending your message are the appropriate one(s) with whom to communicate.

Be tolerant of newcomers, as you expect others to be tolerant of you. None of us were born knowing all about the Internet nor Usenet. Don't abuse new users of computer networks for their lack of knowledge. As you become more expert, be patient as others first learn to paddle, then swim, then surf the Internet. And be an active participant in teaching them.

Avoid cluttering your messages with excessive emphasis (**, !!, caps, and so on). It can make the message hard to follow.

When you respond to a message, either include the relevant part of the original message or explicitly refer to the original's contents. People will commonly read your reply to the message before they read the original. (Remember the convention to precede each quoted line of the original message you include with the > character.) Don't quote more than necessary to make your point clear, and please don't quote the entire message. Learn what happens on your particular system when you reply to messages. Is the message sent to the originator of the message or to the list, and when is it sent? When responding to another message, your subject line should be the same, with RE: at the beginning.

Always include a precise subject line in your message. A recent discussion on Roots-L was about the effective use of the subject line. It should get attention and the only way to do that is to make sure it describes the main point of your message.

If you're seeking information about a family, include the surname in uppercase in the message subject. Many readers don't have time to read the contents of all messages. The following is a bad example of a subject line:

```
Wondering if anyone on soc.roots is looking for JONES
```

And here are some good examples:

```
Researching surname JONES
Researching surname JONES in Arkansas
Delaware BLIZZARDs pre-1845
```

Remember that passages in all uppercase are considered shouting. The exception to this rule in the case of genealogy echos is that surnames should be in uppercase, just as in any query.

Try to keep messages to only one subject. This allows readers to quickly decide whether they need to read the message in full. Second subjects within a single message are often missed. Questions are often the exception to this rule. When you ask a question, end it with a ? and press the Return key. That should be the end of that line. Cliff Manis, who helps run Roots-L, explains, "If you do, your question will be so much easier to answer and see. Yes, only one question per line. There is no limit to lines with questions. We are all here to help each other!"

Be specific, especially when asking questions. If you ask about a person, identify when and where the person might have lived. In questions concerning specific genealogical software, make it clear what sort of computer (PC/MS-DOS, Windows, Apple Macintosh, etc.) is involved. People in the genealogy newsgroups are very helpful but very busy, and are more likely to answer if they don't have to ask what you mean.

Always, always put your name in the text of your message, and also your best e-mail address for a reply. The end of the message is a good place for your name and e-mail address. Furthermore, the genealogy newsgroups are read by many people who have read-only privileges. They can't reply by e-mail, so it's a good idea to also put your postal address in your messages for replies.

Some other rules about questions that apply only to the genealogy messages:

All questions concerning the possibility of access to the LDS database from Usenet or any other technique will be answered "no," so please

don't ask. No one has electronic access to the LDS (Latter-Day Saints) database. Period. And telnet or FTP access to the data isn't possible.

As of this writing, the newest PAF and IGI files weren't available by CD-ROM. They might be licensed for electronic read-only access by libraries, but that hasn't yet come to fruition.

Some tips

Whenever any newsgroup posts an FAQ, read it. If you can't find an FAQ message or file, make one of your first questions on the group, "Where and when can I get the frequently asked questions for this group?"

You might see a mention of alt.genealogy on some lists. This is a spurious newsgroup. Because of the difficulty of removing a dormant newsgroup, it refuses to go away. Most telegenealogists are in the soc.genealogy groups, which get about a hundred posts a day. The best thing to do is to ignore the group.

Sometimes (as when, in early 1994, rotten weather, an earthquake, and a national holiday all converged on a certain Monday) you'll find the Usenet news feed absolutely clogged with messages because so many people found themselves unable or not required to go to work. In that case you must choose what to read based on subject line or sender, because it's impossible to read everything posted to the group that day. This is when a news reader that lets you search the subject headings is invaluable!

There are several places where you can search Usenet newsgroups, one or several or all at a time. Two of them use the Web:

InfoSeek Guide has the last two weeks of all Usenet newsgroups in a searchable database. Use a Web browser (see chapter 5) and go to http://www.infoseek.com. Click the little circle next to Newsgroups, and type in the surnames you want. InfoSeek Guide will return a list of the messages. Each message title is a link; click on it to read it. However, this guide won't let you choose which groups to search!

That's why DejaNews is my favorite way to search the Web. DejaNews has more like a month's worth of messages. Go to http://www.deja .news.com with a Web browser, click on Search, then click on Create a Query Filter. Type in soc.genealogy.* for all the groups, or just the full name of the one you want (see Fig. 4-5). Click on Submit Filter and you're back to the search page. Now type in the surnames you're looking for and within seconds DejaNews will return a list of messages that match the search!

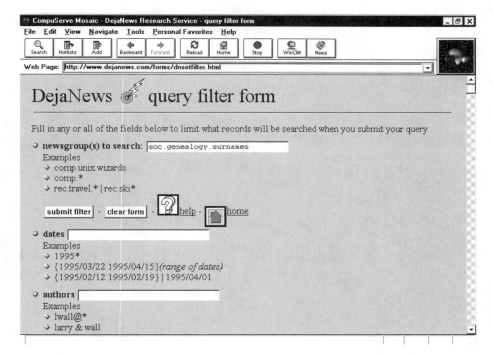

Figure 4-5

You can search all or just one of the genealogy newsgroups for a specific surname with DejaNews; handy for when you've been away from the computer for a while!

Beyond Usenet

There's more to communicating with others on the Internet than just Usenet, of course. And some people find delivery to their own mailbox more convenient than Usenet. For that, there are mail lists, the subject of the next chapter.

5

Roots-L and
other mail lists

CHAPTER 5

FOR many people, just reading several dozen messages a day on Usenet is great. But there's so much more on the Internet that has to do with genealogy, and Usenet is really just a tiny part of it. Another way to exchange information and queries with other genealogists is to use mail lists. Mail lists, like Usenet, are discussion groups: you post a message that's seen by everyone else on the mail list. The other members respond to the mail list with comments and answers. The differences are in how you send and receive the messages of the discussion list. While Usenet is sent and received mainly with news readers, you read messages from and post messages to a mail list with your mail program, whether that's Eudora, MicroSoft Mail, or the mail function of your favorite online commercial service such as CompuServe or America Online.

If you want to jump ahead to the next chapter, on the World Wide Web, you can use your browser to get to the Roots-L home page at:

```
http://www.smartlink.net/~leverich/roots-l.html
```

But for now let's deal with just the mail lists. There are dozens of mail lists that can help genealogists, and many of them are listed at the end of this chapter. But let's look at a very popular one, Roots-L, for an example of how mail lists can be useful.

Roots-L is a discussion list where those with an interest in genealogy can communicate via e-mail messages in order to find family history information. Subscribers to Roots-L form what is in effect a single electronic community. The membership of this community spans many different countries.

Roots-L has undergone many changes since the first edition of this book; It's no longer echoed in a Usenet newsgroup, and it no longer resides at North Dakota University. But the number-one rule still holds: Everyone is welcome, and any message pertinent to genealogy is gladly received. This list was created for the following purposes:

➤ To allow subscribers to communicate and request information about genealogy (family history), not to refight old wars or discuss religion or politics.

➤ To provide a forum for communication, since we have no campus on which we can regularly congregate and exchange ideas. This means the list is open to people from all over the world, not just the U.S.

➤ To provide a means of keeping informed of activities taking place in the genealogical community. However, be aware that rumors spread as fast as news!

➤ To be a meeting place for those who want to learn about finding information concerning their own family history, as well as share what they've learned.

➤ To help people learn to spell the word *genealogy*. Spell it correctly in your messages!

Advertising or selling a product isn't generally regarded as acceptable on this list. Posting the announcement of a product is acceptable. Roots-L, the mail list, used to correspond to soc.roots; each echoed the other and the only difference was how you retrieved the message. That connection was severed in June 1994, and new newsgroups and mail lists resulted. People you should know about on Roots-L are:

Roots-L owner alf.christophersen@nutri.uio.no (Alf Christophersen)

FAMILY file maintainer karen@RAND.ORG (Karen E. Isaacson)

GENEALOG file maintainer cmanis@csoftec.csf.com (Cliff Manis)

VITALS file maintainer green@plains.nodak.edu (Bill Green)

FAQ (frequently asked questions) file maintainer
dennett@Kodak.COM (Charles Dennett)

You subscribe to Roots-L using the program called listserv. The first step in doing this is to learn how to send messages from your system to the Internet. Then, to subscribe to the list, send an e-mail message to listserv@mail.eworld.com. In the body of the message, have this line:

```
SUBSCRIBE ROOTS-L your_full_name
```

For example:

```
SUBSCRIBE ROOTS-L Libbi Crowe
```

The process is easy to reverse: To unsubscribe or sign off, just send the following line:

```
SIGNOFF ROOTS-L
```

Your name isn't needed in this command; indeed, it won't work if you add it. There's something at this point you must master in using Roots-L. Stop a moment, now, and memorize the following two rules:

➤ Messages to people go to roots-l@mail.eworld.com.

➤ Commands to programs go to listserv@mail.eworld.com.

This is true of any listserver. The messages go to the address of the list, and the commands to use the list in various ways must go to the listserver, even though everything after the @ is identical.

If you send the command SIGNOFF ROOTS-L to the roots-l@mail .eworld.com address, you won't be signed off and everyone on the list will get the sign-off message. If you send a genealogy-related message to the listserv@mail.eworld.com address, no one will get to read it, and the message will be bounced back to you as an "unrecognized command."

It's possible that for some reason you might stop receiving Roots-L, even if you didn't send a sign-off command. In this case, it might be that your subscription to Roots-L was deleted. This can happen if your site isn't receiving the mail sent to you, and if so you probably won't even receive the message saying that your subscription was deleted. If you don't receive any mail for two days, then simply subscribe again when your system is working. Your subscription could also be deleted if your e-mail address has changed. In that case, you must resubscribe from your new e-mail address.

Listserv commands

When your subscription command is received, you'll get some helpful text files on how the system works. Then each and every message addressed to listserv@mail.eworld.com will come to your mailbox. With most commercial online and BBS systems, you can download the contents of your mailbox to be read offline. Most mail programs allow you to read the subject line of e-mail messages to see whether you want to read them.

Fortunately, listserv supports more commands than SUBSCRIBE and SIGNON/SIGNOFF. You can control your subscription from your e-mail program, but you must send your command from the same e-mail address from which you subscribed to make adjustments to your subscription. These commands are handled automatically by the list processor. Just remember to use the listserv address when you send one of these commands.

 # SET

This is an important command to set your options on a certain list. The syntax is SET *list_name options*, and the options include:

Ack/NoAck/MsgAck This sets whether you receive a computer-generated acknowledgments for your postings to the list.

Conceal/NoConceal This sets whether your name and e-mail address appear when a REVIEW command is sent (by anyone).

Files/NoFiles Sometimes files that are pictures or programs are sent as attachments; this command toggles whether those are sent to you.

Mail/NoMail When you go on vacation, rather than let your mailbox get clogged with hundreds of unread messages, you can use this command to stop delivery to you until you send the MAIL command.

Digests/NoDigests This asks for digests or message indexes rather than getting messages as they're posted. If it's turned on, the messages are collected into large messages and are sent once or twice a day.

Repro/NoRepro This controls whether you receive a copy of your own postings.

 # TOPICS: ALL

Some lists are divided into specific topics, and all messages to those lists must have the topic in the subject line. For such a list you can select topics to receive. You can use the subcommand TOPICS: *topic_name*, with a plus or a minus sign in front of it for specific topics, or leave it at the default of ALL.

 # Index *list_name*

This command sends a directory of available archive files for the list, if postings are archived. Roots-L are.

 # Lists *option*

This command sends you a list of mail lists. The options are as follows:

(no option) Lists are handled by that listserver only, one line per list.

Detailed Lists are handled by that listserver, and full information is returned in a file.

Global All known lists, one line per list, are sent as a large file.

Global /xyz This specifies all known lists whose name or title contains the letters xyz.

Summary *host* This produces a membership summary for all lists on the specified host.

Summary ALL This specifies all hosts and all lists. Don't use this one unless you *really* need to know!

Summary Total This will give you just the total for all hosts.

Query *list_name*

This command will send you a list of your subscription options for a particular list (use the SET command to change them). Follow it with an asterisk instead of a list name, and it will send you your option settings for all lists you're subscribed to on that server.

Review *listname options*

This command will get information about a list and its subscribers. If your options are set to Conceal, you won't appear on the results. The options for this command are:

❋ **By** *sort_field*

This will sort the list in a certain order, with the options for *sort_field* as follows:

Country By country of origin

Name By name (last, then first)

NodeID By host name or node ID

UserID By user ID

You can also specify more than one sort field if they're both enclosed by parentheses, for example BY (node name). If you're specifying more than one country, the sort field is Countries rather than Country.

✳ **Local**

This specifies not to forward the request to your peers.

✳ **NoHeader**

This specifies not to send the list header.

✳ **Short**

This doesn't list the subscribers.

SCAN *listname text*

This command will scan a list's membership for a name or address. It's useful if you're looking for people with the same surname.

STATS *listname options*

This command will get statistics about a list.

Some commands are simply to give you information. Sending the word *help* in a message to a listserver will tell you about the commands that listserver can use. Sending the word *info* by itself will get you a listserv manual; sending the line INFO ROOTS-L will get you information on Roots-L (you can substitute the name of any other list on that server), and INFO SET would give you the ins and outs of the command SET (you can substitute the name of any other command).

Other commands can help you with files. If you want to know the last time a file on a listserver was updated, send the command QUERY FILE fn ft *file_list* and you'll get date and time of the last update of a file, as well as the get/put file access code (who can get it and who's allowed to put it on the server).

Other mail lists

Not all mail lists run on a list server. Some are done "by hand" by someone who receives messages and then forwards them to all the subscribers. You can subscribe to such lists by sending a politely worded message its address (such as afrigeneas-request@drum .ncsc.org). It will go to the list owner, who will read it when he or she can and add you as soon as possible. When the subscription information in a list shows an address including the word *request*, assume your message is going to a real, live person, not a machine, so word your request accordingly (use complete sentences). If the subscription message is to a listserv, assume you're talking to a machine and use the commands described in the previous section.

Once you've mastered how Roots-L works, you're ready to sample other mailing lists. The rest of this chapter lists just a few; where noted, the messages are gatewayed to the specified newsgroup on Usenet. If a list is available on eWorld, you can get it only in the Mail + Digest mode. Index mode won't be available and archives won't be searchable until sometime in 1996.

Generally, you'll get a welcome message when you subscribe, telling you about the group, the server, and the associated files. Sometimes a list is aimed at particular countries and areas of the world. While these lists aren't devoted to genealogy, the list owners have indicated that genealogy is an acceptable, though in some cases unusual, subject for the list.

Lists come in many subjects, some only tangentially touching genealogy. Some of the ones I've listed in the following sections touch on heritage, culture, and genealogy of particular ethnic groups, some of specific family names, some on specific historical periods, some on research in specific regions, regardless of ethnic background, some on software and other computer-related topics, and some strictly on general genealogy topics. Here are some to get you started; you'll find one list often has messages referring to another, and it just snowballs!

Ethnic groups

These lists often aren't specifically genealogy, but are rather about culture, history, and current events in a particular ethnic group. Still, most of them will accept an occasional genealogy query, and most also are good to "lurk" in, just to glean information you perhaps didn't know.

AfriGeneas A private mailing list created as a place to discuss and promote family history research. This is a place for African descendants in particular to communicate their genealogical interests, needs, concerns, history, culture, and resources. Discussion areas include but are not limited to queries on surnames, records/events, "how do I start," census, locations, people and places, and resources. The mailing address for postings is afrigeneas@drum.ncsc.org. To subscribe, send e-mail to afrigeneas-request@drum.ncsc.org with the subject "Add Me."

AfroAm-L A discussion group focusing on the pivotal issues that confront the everyday life of African-Americans—an extremely busy list, with up to 25 messages an hour! Postings of specific genealogical queries are not considered appropriate, but postings regarding the broader areas of interest to genealogists are acceptable. The mailing address for postings is afroam-l@harvarda.harvard.edu. To subscribe, send e-mail to listserv@harvarda.harvard.edu with the message "Subscribe AfroAm-L *first_name last_name*."

Albanian A mailing list dedicated to the exchange of news and discussion of issues on Albania and Albanian people not only in Albania, but also other areas in the Balkans (Kosova, Macedonia, Montenegro) and around the world. The languages used are both Albanian and English. The mailing address for postings is albanian@ubvm.cc.buffalo.edu. To subscribe, send the message "Subscribe Albanian *first_name last_name*" to listserv@ubvm.cc.buffalo.edu.

APSA-L A list devoted to the subject of literature and cultures of the Portuguese-speaking world, especially Brazil and Portugal. Although associated with the American Portuguese Studies Association (APSA),

the list is not restricted to members of the association. The mailing address for postings is majordomo@beacon.bryant.edu; send the message "Subscribe APSA-L."

Arab-American A moderated list with the goal of fostering and building community among North Americans of Arabic descent. Arab-Canadians, Arab-Mexicans, and Arabs in the United States might find this list of interest. Any topic directly relating to the experience of Arab-Americans is welcome. The mailing address for postings is arab-american@carleton.edu. To subscribe, send the message "Subscribe Arab-American *first_name last_name*" to mailserv@carleton.edu.

Argentina General discussion and information on Argentine and Latin-American social/political issues (the list contents are almost exclusively in Spanish). The mailing address for postings is argentina@journal.math.indiana.edu. This is the main list; there are several sublists concerning more specialized aspects of Argentina. To subscribe, send your name, e-mail address, phone number, address, and topics of interest to argentina-requests@journal.math.indiana.edu.

Balt-L Online forum devoted to communicating to and about the Baltic Republics of Lithuania, Latvia, and Estonia. Anyone with skills or interests relevant to the Baltic region, or who just wants to know what's going on, is welcome to join this list. Short requests to help locate families or villages are carried in general-interest digest messages. The mailing address for postings is balt-l@ubvm.cc.buffalo.edu. To subscribe, send the message "Subscribe Balt-L *first_name last_name*" to listserv@ubvm.cc.buffalo.edu.

Banat A mailing list for those doing research in the Banat region of what was formerly Hungary. The mailing address for postings is banat@sierra.net. To subscribe, send the message "Subscribe Banat" to majordomo@sierra.net.

Basque-L A forum for the dissemination and exchange of information on Basque culture. Genealogy-related issues are often discussed on the list, though the main topics of discussion are socio-political current affairs, gastronomy, Basque music, poetry, anthropology (the origin of Basques), etc. Basque, Spanish, French, and English are used, and any other languages are welcome. The

mailing address for postings is basque-l@cunyvm.cuny.edu. To subscribe, send the message "Subscribe Basque-L *first_name last_name*" to listserv@cunyvm.cuny.edu.

Bras-Net A mail list for Brazilians, conducted in Portuguese, with no specific subject orientation. The mailing address for postings is bras-net@cs.columbia.edu. To subscribe, send the message "Subscribe Bras-Net *first_name last_name*" to bras-net-request@cs.columbia.edu.

Canada-L A discussion forum for political, social, cultural, and economic issues in Canada. The mailing address for postings is canada-l@vm1.mcgill.ca. To subscribe, send the message "Subscribe Canada-L *first_name last_name*" to listserv@vm1.mcgill.ca.

Catrachos A list that unites Hondurans and people interested in topics related to Honduras throughout the world. The languages of preference are English and Spanish. The topics of discussion range from local interests to politics. The mailing address for postings is catrachos@andrew.cmu.edu. To subscribe, send a politely worded request to stanmarder@aol.com (Stanley Marrder).

CentAm-L This list is intended to provide students from Central America and those interested in discussing issues concerning these countries (Guatemala, Belize, Honduras, El Salvador, Nicaragua, Costa Rica, and Panama) with a discussion list conducive to the exchange of ideas. The mailing address for postings is centam-l@ubvm.cc .buffalo.edu. To subscribe, send the message "Subscribe CentAm-L *first_name last_name*" to listserv@ubvm.cc.buffalo.edu.

E-List A moderated news and discussion list for Estonia-related matters. The primary readership is Estonians abroad and home, and both the Estonian and English languages are used. The typical content is Estonian- and English-language news and news reviews from some of the news agencies and foreign ministry of Estonia. The list also contains material from Estonian universities and other Estonian lists. Sometimes discussions on important subjects are held, and questions and requests from subscribers to the public are passed. All subjects can be covered, provided they might be interesting to current readership. The mailing address for postings is jaak.vilo@cs.helsinki.fi. To subscribe, send a politely worded request to jaak.vilo@cs.helsinki.fi.

Ec-Charla This list is a forum for discussion of Ecuadorian society, politics, culture, etc. List activities are conducted mostly in Spanish, but any language is welcome. The mailing address for postings is ec-charla@lac.net. To subscribe, send the message "Subscribe Ec-Charla *first_name last_name*" to listproc@lac.net.

Espana-L A mailing list to facilitate general discussion and exchange of information regarding Spain. All interested in Spain and Spanish culture are invited to join. The mailing address for postings is espana-l@uacsc2 .albany.edu. To subscribe, send the message "Subscribe Espana-L *first_name last_name*" to listserv@vm.stlawu.edu.

Gen-DE-L Gatewayed with the soc.genealogy.german newsgroup for the discussion of German genealogy. The mailing address for postings is gen-de-l@rz.uni-karlsruhe.de. To subscribe, send the message "Sub Gen-De-L *first_name last_name*" to listserv@rz.uni-karlsruhe.de.

Gen-FF-L Gatewayed with the fr.rec.genealogie newsgroup for the discussion of Francophone genealogy (the genealogy of French-speaking people). The traffic is mainly in French. The mailing address for postings is gen-ff-l@mail.eworld.com. To subscribe, send the message "Sub Gen-FF-L *first_name last_name*" to listserv@mail .eworld.com.

Gen-Fr-L Gatewayed with the soc.genealogy.french newsgroup for the discussion of Francophone genealogy (the genealogy of French-speaking people). The mailing address for postings is gen-fr-l@ mail.eworld.com. To subscribe, send the message "Subscribe Gen-Fr-L *first_name last_name*" to listserv@mail.eworld.com.

GenPol A mailing list for discussions of Polish genealogy. Postings are made in both English and Polish, but there's no guarantee that postings in English will receive replies in English. The mailing address for postings is genpol@chem.uw.edu.pl. To subscribe, send the message "Subscribe GenPol *first_name last_name*" to listproc@ chem.uw.edu.pl.

GenUKI-L Gatewayed with the soc.genealogy.uk+ireland newsgroup for the discussion of genealogy and family history among people researching ancestors and family members, as well as others who have

a genealogical connection to people in any part of the British Isles (England, Wales, Ireland, Scotland, the Channel Isles, and the Isle of Man). The mailing address for postings is genuki-l@postman .essex.ac.uk. To subscribe, send either "Subscribe GenUKI-Index" or "Subscribe GenUKI-Digest" to listproc@herald.co.uk.

Ger-Rus Germans from Russia. The mailing address for postings is ger-rus@vm1.nodak.edu. To subscribe, send the message "Subscribe Ger-Rus *first_name last_name*" to listserv@vm1.nodak.edu.

Hungary Discussion of Hungarian issues. The list is open to scholars and students from all disciplines. Although the working language of the group is English, contributions in other languages will be accepted and posted; however, they might not be understood by a significant proportion of the membership. Mailing list for postings is hungary@gwuvm.gwu.edu. To subscribe, send the message "Subscribe Hungary *first_name last_name*" to listserv@gwuvm.gwu.edu.

Indian-Roots Discussions of Native American genealogical and historical research. The mailing address for postings is indian-roots@rmgate.pop.indiana.edu. To subscribe, send the message "Sub Indian-Roots" to maiser@rmgate.pop.indiana.edu.

InRoots Discussions of Indiana genealogical and historical research. The mailing address for postings is inroots@rmgate.pop.indiana.edu. To subscribe, send the message "Sub InRoots" to maiser@rmgate .pop.indiana.edu.

JewishGen Discussions of Jewish genealogy. Gatewayed with the soc.genealogy.jewish newsgroup (JewGen is a synonym for JewishGen and postings to both will just give subscribers two copies of the same message). The mailing address for postings is jewishgen@mail .eworld.com. To subscribe, send the message "Subscribe JewishGen *first_name last_name*" to listserv@mail.eworld.com.

Llajta Discussion of any and all topics relating to Bolivia. The principle language for discussions is Spanish, although English, Quechua, and Portuguese messages have appeared. The mailing address for postings is llajta@io.dsd.litton.com. To subscribe, send the

message "Subscribe Llajta *first_name last_name*" to listserv@io .dsd.litton.com.

Makedon A moderated mailing list for discussions of the Macedonian Republic. Every posting made to this group is also automatically posted to the Informa BBS in Macedonia, and might also reach the Macedonian BBS in Canada. Acceptable languages for the group are Macedonian and English, with emphasis on Macedonian. The mailing address for postings is makedon@ubvm.cc.buffalo.edu. To subscribe, send the message "Subscribe Makedon *first_name last_name*" to listserv@ubvm.cc.buffalo.edu.

NamNet Anything related to Namibia (as of February 1995, mainly technical stuff). Small postings are preferred. The mailing address for postings is namnet@lisse.na. To subscribe, send the message "Subscribe" to namnet-request@lisse.na.

Nat-Lang A discussion list about Native American languages. To subscribe, send the message "Sub Nat-Lang" to listserv@tamvm1 .tamu.edu.

NyasaNet This list is for Malawians or people interested in discussing things Malawian. The mailing address for postings is nyasanet@unh.edu. To subscribe, send the message "Subscribe NyasaNet *first_name last_name*" to nyasanet-request@unh.edu.

Peru Discussion of Peruvian culture and other issues. This list is simply an echo site, so all posts get bounced from that address to all the people subscribed. The mailing address for postings is peru@cs.sfsu.edu (you have to be subscribed to post to this list). To subscribe, send the message "Subscribe Peru *first_name last_name*" with no subject to listproc@cs.sfsu.edu.

Pie A mailing list for people interested in topics related to Italian genealogy (over 160 people from around the world as of February 1995). The mailing address for postings is pie@jsoft.com. To subscribe, send the message "Subscribe Pie *first_name last_name*" to pie-request@jsoft.com, or "Subscribe Pie-Digest *first_name last_name*" to pie-digest@jsoft.com.

Poland-L Discussions of Polish culture and events, including all subjects related to Poland, Polish Americans, and Eastern Europe (related to Poland). The mailing address for postings is poland-l@vm1.nodak.edu. To subscribe, send the message "Subscribe Poland-L *first_name last_name*" to listserv@ubvm.cc.buffalo.edu.

Russian-Jews Dedicated to sharing information, discussions of history, announcements of upcoming events, etc. The mailing address for postings is russian-jews@shamash.nysernet.org. To subscribe, send the message "Sub Russian-Jews *first_name last_name*" to listproc@shamash.nysernet.org.

Sephard SIG A special-interest group of JewishGen, the Jewish Genealogy discussion group, established to develop resource lists for researchers of Sephardic genealogy. The definition of Sephardim is Jews who, after the expulsion from Spain in 1492, settled in northern Africa, Italy, Egypt, Palestine, Syria, the Balkans, and the Turkish Empire. Subsequently, these communities were reinforced by refugees from Portugal, who later established congregations in Amsterdam, London, Hamburg, Bordeaux, Bayonne, western Europe, and North America. The mailing address for postings is sephard@cgsg.com. To subscribe, send the message "Subscribe Sephard *first_name last_name*" to listserv@cgsg.com.

Slovak-L A mailing list for anyone interested in Slovak history, culture, politics, social life, economy, and anything else concerning the Republic of Slovakia and its people, or their descendants in other countries. The list is unmoderated and unlimited in scope. The mailing address for postings is slovak-l@ubvm.cc.buffalo.edu or slovak-l@ubvm.bitnet. To subscribe, send the message "Subscribe slovak-l *first_name last_name*" to listserv@ubvm.cc.buffalo.edu or listserv@ubvm.bitnet.

Slovak-World An unmoderated mailing list that can be used to contact Slovaks around the world to help find lost contacts, join relatives, meet new friends, etc. It is not limited to territory or to language and is open for all who have something in common with Slovaks and Slovakia. The mailing address for postings is slovak-world@fris.sk. To subscribe, send the message "Subscribe Slovak-World *first_name last_name*" to listproc@fris.sk.

Sudan-L A forum for sharing experience, ideas, thoughts, comments, and sources of information on issues concerning Sudan. The mailing address for postings is sudan-l@emuvm1.cc.emory.edu (you have to be subscribed to post to this list). To subscribe, send the message "Subscribe Sudan-L *first_name last_name*" to listserv@emuvm1.cc.emory.edu.

Suguselts An Estonian-language genealogy list (English and other languages such as German, French, and Finnish are acceptable). The mailing address for postings is suguselts@lists.ut.ee. To subscribe, send the message "Subscribe Suguselts *first_name last_name*" to lisproc@lists.ut.ee.

Welsh-L Aims to foster the amicable discussion of questions of the Welsh language, culture, history, and politics, and to offer a forum for speakers and learners of the Welsh language. Genealogical queries may be posted as long as the queries are in Welsh. (English may be used on Welsh-L to discuss questions of grammar). The mailing address for postings is welsh-l@irlearn.ucd.ie. To subscribe, send the message "Subscribe Welsh-L *first_name last_name*" to listserv@irlearn.ucd.ie.

 # Family name lists

These are lists for specific surnames or families. You usually have to ask to join.

Campbell-L A mailing list for Campbell descendants to discuss their possible kinship and for the various Campbell societies to discuss membership. The mailing address for postings is campbell-l@genealogy.emcee.com. To subscribe, send e-mail to campbell-l-request@genealogy.emcee.com with the subject "subscribe". No message is necessary. Queries are welcome; you should include your postal address so the clan can contact you.

Claflin Researchers of the surname Claflin (also Mackclothlan, MacLachlan, MacLachlan, Makclachlane, Maklauchlane, M'cLachlene, Makclauchlane, McLauchlane, M'lauchlane, M'cLauchlane, M'lauchan, McClauchlan, McLauchlane, M'cLachlane, M'cLaichlane, MacLaughlin,

and any other variation of the name you might be researching. Also, unless there's a mail list covering another surname, you're free to use this service to discuss those as well, as long as they're related to a Claflin (please try to limit it to Claflins). The mailing address for postings is claflin-l@genealogy.emcee.com. To subscribe, send a message to claflin-l-request@genealogy.emcee.com with "subscribe" in the subject line.

Clan-Henderson Researchers of the surname Henderson and variant spellings. To subscribe, send e-mail to ancanach@uabdpo .dpo.uab.edu with no message.

Clan-McCallum A list for the discussion of the MacCallum/Malcolm clan, chief, its gatherings, and genealogical research of the surnames Malcolm, McCallum, McCollum, Collum, and other variants. The mailing address for postings is clan-mccallum@csn.net. To subscribe, send the message "Subscribe Clan-McCallum *your_e-mail_address*" to majordomo@csn.org.

Cooley-L Researchers of the surname Cooley. The mailing address for postings is cooley-l@genealogy.emcee.com. To subscribe, send a request to be added to the list to cooley-l-request@genealogy .emcee.com.

Culp/Kolb Researchers of the Culp or Kolb families. To subscribe, send e-mail to John Culp at aa101932@midnet.csd.scarolina.edu.

Marjoribanks Researchers of the surname Marjoribanks family (a Border Scots family) and variants (Marchbanks, Marshbanks, Banks, etc.). Regardless of how it's spelled, all who claim Marjoribanks/ Marchbanks descent or who have an interest in the family are eligible for membership. If you want further information, you can contact the honorary secretary by e-mail at an770@freenet.carleton.ca, or the vice president at translaw@dgs.dgsys.com.

Mobley A small e-mail group (about 30 to 35) for discussions of the genealogy and history of the Mobley family. To subscribe or to post, send e-mail to moberley@freenet.fsu.edu.

Moore-L A mailing list for researchers of the surname Moore, anywhere, anytime. The mailing address for postings is moore-l@xx.zko.dec.com. To subscribe, send the message "Subscribe Moore-L" to majordomo@xx.zko.dec.com. (This listserver is case-sensitive; make sure to use lowercase.)

Pettit-L Researchers of the surname Pettit. The mailing address for postings is pettit-l@genealogy.emcee.com. To subscribe, send a request to be added to the list to pettit-l-request@genealogy.emcee.com.

Scol An informal group used to establish contact with people who have the name Sutfin/Sutphen/Sutphin/Zutphen (or people doing research on those families) in order to share information on their heritage. To subscribe, send e-mail to msutphin@fred.net with no message.

White-L Researchers of the surname White. The mailing address for postings is white-l@genealogy.emcee.com. To subscribe, send a message to white-l-request@genealogy.emcee.com with "subscribe" as the subject and no message.

General genealogy lists

These are lists with general genealogy in mind, apart from region and specific names. These are the ones a beginner should check out first.

Adoptees A discussion among people who have been adopted or have a family member who is adopted. The mailing address for postings is adoptees@ucsd.edu. If you have access to a WWW browser such as Mosaic, the preferred method to subscribe is to use the form linked to the Adoptees mailing list home page, located at http://psy.ucsd.edu/jhartung/adoptees.html. Otherwise, send the message "Subscribe *your_e-mail_address* adoptees" to listserv@ucsd.edu.

Adoption Discussion of anything and everything connected with adoption. The mailing address for postings is adoption@listserv.law .cornell.edu. To subscribe, send the message "Subscribe Adoption *first_name last_name*" to adoption-request@listserv.law.cornell.edu.

BrthPrnt A mailing list open to anyone wanting to discuss birth family issues. The mailing address for postings is bras-net-request@cs.columbia.edu. To subscribe, send the message "Sub BrthPrnt *first_name last_name*" to listserv@indycms.iupui.edu.

Elijah-L A list for members of the Church of Jesus Christ of Latter-Day Saints to discuss their ideas and experiences relating with genealogy in the LDS church (individuals not of the LDS faith are welcome to join, as long as they respect the beliefs of the LDS faith and do not deliberately offend these beliefs). To subscribe, send a message to Elijah-L-Request@genealogy.emcee.com with "archive" as the subject and "get charter" as the message. After reading and approving the charter, follow the instructions in the charter to subscribe. This list is to be used specifically for sharing LDS-related genealogy ideas, tools, and approaches, sharing LDS-related genealogy experiences and testimonies, and discussing answers to LDS-related genealogy questions and scriptures relating to genealogy. Members also share LDS-related genealogy news from throughout the world, as well as other LDS-related genealogical topics.

GenMsc-L A general discussion of genealogy for questions that don't fit the previous categories. Note: This list usually subscribes you in digest mode. If you want mail mode, you must use the command SET GENMSC-L MAIL. The mailing address for postings is genmsc-l@mail.eworld.com. To subscribe, send the message "Subscribe GenMsc-L *first_name last_name*" to listserv@mail.eworld.com.

GenMtd-L A general discussion of genealogy and methods of genealogical research. This list also usually subscribes you in digest mode. If you want mail mode, you must specify SET genmtd-l mail. This list is gatewayed with the soc.genealogy.methods newsgroup for the discussion of genealogy methods and resources. The mailing address for postings is genmtd-l@mail.eworld.com. To subscribe, send the message "Subscribe GenMtd-L *first_name last_name*" to listserv@mail.eworld.com.

GenNam-L Gatewayed with the soc.genealogy.surnames newsgroup for surname queries and tafels. The mailing address for postings is gennam-l@mail.eworld.com. To subscribe, send the message

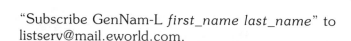

"Subscribe GenNam-L *first_name last_name*" to listserv@mail.eworld.com.

GenWeb Discussions of the implementation of a genealogical information exchange system using the World Wide Web. The mailing address for postings is genweb@uscd.edu. To subscribe, send the message "Add GenWeb" to listserv@ucsd.edu.

Roots-L The best known genealogy mailing list, with over 4,000 subscribers from around the world. The mailing address for postings is roots-l@vm1.nodak.edu. To subscribe, send the message "Subscribe Roots-L *first_name last_name*" to listserv@vm1.nodak.edu.

 # Historical groups

MennoLink A mailing list for and about Mennonites, including a fair bit of genealogy. The mailing address for postings is menno@uci.com. To subscribe to the complete list, which includes a great deal of discussion, send the message "Sub menno.d *first_name last_name*" to listserv@uci.com. (To receive mail once a day in digest mode, include a second line with the command SET memmo.d mail digest). To subscribe to an abbreviated form of the list that includes informational messages but not the discussion, send the message "Sub menno *first_name last_name*" to listserv@uci.com.

Quaker-L Moderated, online discussion of all aspects of Quakerism and the Religious Society of Friends. Such discussion might include (but is not limited to) Quaker worship, decision-making, and publications. Social and activist Quaker issues such as peace, justice, and ecology are discussed on Quaker-P. The mailing address for postings is quaker-l@vmd.cso.uiuc.edu. You must subscribe in order to post to Quaker-L. To subscribe, send the message "Subscribe Quaker-L *first_name last_name*" to listserv@vmd.cso.uiuc.edu.

Historical Gen-Medieval Gatewayed with the soc.genealogy .medieval newsgroup for genealogy and family history discussion among people researching individuals living during medieval times (loosely defined as the period from the fall of Rome until the time public records relating to the general population began to be kept,

extending roughly from AD 500 to AD 1600). The mailing address for postings is gen-medieval@mail.eworld.com. To subscribe, send the message "Subscribe Gen-Medieval *first_name last_name*" to listserv@mail.eworld.com.

RusHist A forum for the reasonable discussion of any aspect of the history of Russia from the reign of Ivan III (1462–1505) to the end of the Romanov dynasty in the person of Nicholas II (1894–1917). Any element of this period is discussable. The mailing address for postings is rushist@vm.usc.edu. To subscribe, send the message "Subscribe RusHist *first_name last_name*" to listserv@vm.usc.edu.

Overland-Trails Devoted to discussions concerning the history, preservation, and promotion of the Oregon, California, Sante Fe, and other historic trails in the western U.S. One project particularly interesting to genealogists is that all of the names inscribed as graffiti on the various rocks along the trails have been put into a database. Therefore, if someone's ancestor was suspected to have traveled the trail, there's a possibility that the route and dates can be pinpointed. The mailing address for postings (you have to be subscribed) is overland-trails@hipp.etsu.edu. To subscribe, send the message "Subscribe Overland-Trails *first_name last_name*" to listserv@hipp.etsu.edu.

➡ Regional groups

4Corners-Roots A genealogy discussion list for the Colorado-Utah-Arizona-New Mexico area. Send the message "Sub 4Corners-Roots" to maiser@rmgate.pop.indiana.edu.

Canadian-Roots A discussion list for Canadian genealogy. To subscribe, send a message that says "Sub Canadian-Roots" to maiser@rmgate.pop.indiana.edu.

Capitol-Roots A discussion of genealogy for the New Jersey-Maryland-Delaware-District of Columbia region. To subscribe, send the message "Sub Capitol-Roots" to maiser@rmgate.pop.indiana.edu.

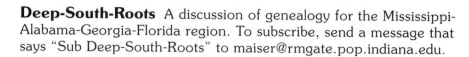
Deep-South-Roots A discussion of genealogy for the Mississippi-Alabama-Georgia-Florida region. To subscribe, send a message that says "Sub Deep-South-Roots" to maiser@rmgate.pop.indiana.edu.

Erie-Roots A discussion of genealogy for the New York-Pennsylvania-Ohio region. To subscribe, send the message "Sub Erie-Roots" to maiser@rmgate.pop.indiana.edu.

Far-West-Roots A discussion list for the California-Nevada-Hawaii region. To subscribe, send the message "Sub Far-West-Roots" to maiser@rmgate.pop.indiana.edu.

Kansas-L Announcements and activities of the Kansas State Historical Society, a clearing house for announcements by other organizations and a public forum for the discussion of Kansas heritage, both past and present. The mailing address for postings is kansas-l@ukanaix.cc.ukans.edu. To subscribe, send the message "Subscribe Kansas-L *first_name last_name*" to listserv@ukanaix.cc.ukans.edu.

KYRoots Discussions of Kentucky genealogical and historical research. The mailing address for postings is kyroots@ukcc.uky.edu. To subscribe, send the message "Subscribe KYRoots *first_name last_name*" to listserv@ukcc.uky.edu.

LA-Cajun-Roots A discussion of genealogy in Louisiana and for those of Cajun heritage. To subscribe, send the message "Sub LA-Cajun-Roots" to maiser@rmgate.pop.indiana.edu.

MI/WI-Roots A discussion of genealogy for the Michigan-Wisconsin area. To subscribe, send the message "Sub MI/WI-Roots" to maiser@rmgate.pop.indiana.edu.

Mid-Plains-Roots A discussion of genealogy for the Arkansas-Missouri-Iowa-Illinois-Nebraska area. To subscribe, send the message "Sub Mid-Plains-Roots" to maiser@rmgate.pop.indiana.edu.

NC/SC-Roots A discussion of genealogy for the North Carolina-South Carolina area. (Note: NCRoots and SCRoots are synonyms for NC/SC-Roots.) To subscribe, send the message "Sub NC/SC-Roots"

to maiser@rmgate.pop.indiana.edu. The mailing address for postings is nc/sc-roots@rmgate.pop.indiana.edu.

NDSDMN-L Discussions of genealogical and historical research for the North Dakota-South Dakota-Minnesota region. To subscribe, send a message with "Subscribe" as the subject to ndsdmn-l-request@ genealogy.emcee.com. The mailing address for postings is ndsdmn-l@ genealogy.emcee.com.

No.Slekt Norwegian genealogy conference called Slekt (family) on NordicNet (a PCBoard BBS network connected to Internet NetNews via Thunderball Cave and distributed on NetNews as no.slekt). To subscribe, send the message "Subscribe No.Slekt" to majordomo@ news.uninett.no.

Northeast-Roots A genealogy discussion list for Maine, Vermont, New Hampshire, Rhode Island, Massachusetts, and Connecticut. To subscribe, send the message "Sub Northeast-Roots" to maiser@ rmgate.pop.indiana.edu.

Northwest-Roots A genealogy discussion list for Washington, Oregon, Alaska, Idaho, Montana, and Wyoming. To subscribe, send the message "Sub Northwest-Roots" to maiser@rmgate.pop .indiana.edu.

Soc.Genealogy.Benelux, Soc.Genealogy.Dutch, or GenBnl-L Research in the Benelux region (Belgium, the Netherlands, and Luxembourg). For details on usage, send e-mail to maiser@omega .ufsia.ac.be with the word "help" in the message. The mailing address for postings is genbnl-l@omega.ufsia.ac.be. To subscribe, send the message "Sub Soc.Genealogy.Benelux" to maiser@omega.ufsia.ac.be.

Texahoma-Roots A discussion list of genealogy for the Texas-Oklahoma area. Send the message "Sub Texahoma-Roots" to maiser@rmgate.pop.indiana.edu.

TNRoots Discussions of Tennessee genealogical and historical research. The mailing address for postings is tnroots@rmgate .pop.indiana.edu. To subscribe, send the message "Sub TNRoots" to maiser@rmgate.pop.indiana.edu.

VA-Roots A discussion of Virginia genealogy. (This is *not* the same as VARoots.) This group allows researchers in the field of Virginia family history to share information about current work, pose queries to list members, share information about resources, debate issues, and discuss the techniques of genealogical research. The mailing address for postings is va-roots@leo.vsla.edu. To subscribe, send the message "Subscribe VA-Roots *first_name last_name*" to listserver@leo.vsla.edu.

VA/WVA-Roots A discussion of genealogy for the Virginia and West Virginia areas. (Note: VARoots and WVRoots are synonyms for VA/WVA-Roots.) Send "Sub VA/WVA-Roots" to maiser@rmgate .pop.indiana.edu. The mailing address for postings is va/wvaroots@ rmgate.pop.indiana.edu.

WVA-L West Virginia discussion list. The mailing address for postings is wva-l@world.std.com. To subscribe, send the message "Subscribe WVA-L" to majordomo@world.std.com.

WVA-LA Discussion of anything and everything related to West Virginia. Not genealogical, per se, but another good list to lurk on. This is *not* the same as WVRoots. To subscribe, send the message "Sub WVA-L" to majordomo@world.std.com.

 # Software lists

GenCmp-L A general discussion of genealogy and its relation to computing and computers. Note: This list usually subscribes you in digest mode. If you want mail mode, you must send the following command and message to the listserver (listserv@mail.eworld.com): "SET GenCmp-L mail" and "Sub GenCmp-L."

No.Slekt.Programmer Norwegian genealogy conference called SlektsProgram (family) on NordicNet (a BBS network connected to Internet NetNews via Thunderball Cave and distributed on Netnews as no.slekt.programmer). To subscribe, send the message "Subscribe No.Slekt.Programmer" to majordomo@news.uninett.no.

Software.FTMTech-L A mailing list maintained by Banner Blue Software for the discussion and technical support of the Family Tree

Maker genealogy program and the Family Archive CDs. Paul Burchfield, one of Banner Blue's technical support representatives, will answer technical questions posted to this list. The mailing address for postings is ftmtech-l@best.com. To subscribe, send the message "Subscribe FTMTech-L" to majordomo@best.com.

Software BBAnnounce-L A mailing list maintained by Banner Blue Software for product announcements (10 to 15 postings a year). To subscribe, send the message "Subscribe BBAnnounce-L" to majordomo@best.com.

Software BK An experience exchange platform for the Brother's Keeper genealogical program. The mailing address for postings is bk@omega.ufsia.ac.be. To subscribe, send the message "Sub BK" to maiser@omega.ufsia.ac.be.

Software BK5-L A mailing list for the discussion of the Brother's Keeper genealogy program. The mailing address for postings is bk5-l @genealogy.emcee.com. To subscribe, send e-mail to bk5-l-request@ genealogy.emcee.com with "Subscribe" as the subject and no message.

Software Lines-L Serves as a vehicle for topics related to the enhancement of LifeLines Genealogical Database and Report Generator (an experimental, second-generation genealogical system). Don't subscribe unless your computer runs on UNIX, you know who Tom Wetmore is, and you run LifeLines. The mailing address for postings is lines-l@vm1.nodak.edu. To subscribe, send the message "Subscribe Lines-L *first_name last_name*" to listserv@vm1.nodak.edu.

Software Progen An experience exchange group for the Progen genealogical program. The mailing address for postings is progen@omega.ufsia.ac.be. To subscribe, send the message "Sub Progen" to maiser@omega.ufsia.ac.be.

Software TMG-L A mailing list for those interested in The Master Genealogist program. The mailing address for postings is tmg-l@netcom.com. To subscribe, send the message "Subscribe "TMG-L" to listserv@netcom.com.

Software.GEDCOM-L A technical mailing list to discuss GEDCOM specifications. If you aren't a computer programmer, a serious genealogical computer user, or haven't read the GEDCOM specification, then this list is definitely not for you. The mailing address for postings is gedcom-l@vm1.nodak.edu. To subscribe, send the message "Sub GEDCOM-L *first_name last_name*" to listserv@vm1.nodak.edu.

Software.GenCmp-L Gatewayed with the soc.genealogy.computing newsgroup for the discussion of genealogical computing and net resources. The mailing address for postings is gencmp-l@mail.eworld.com. To subscribe, send the message "Subscribe GenCmp-L *first_name last_name*" to listserv@mail.eworld.com.

Software.PAF-L Mailing list for the discussion of issues relating to the Personal Ancestral File genealogy program. The mailing address for postings is paf-l@genesplicer.org. To subscribe, send the message "Subscribe PAF-L *first_name last_name*" to listserv@genesplicer.org.

GenWeb A discussion list for RootsBook, a project to link genealogy trees on a mass basis. Send "Sub GenWeb" to listserv@ucsd.edu.

FTP, gopher, and the World Wide Web

A T the beginning of the previous chapter on mail lists, when I listed the people you should know about, you might have noticed that each one was in charge of a certain set of files. These files are stored in places called *anonymous FTP sites*, where the general public is invited to log in and download various files. How you get them is to use an FTP program. The acronym FTP, by the way, stands for *file transfer protocol*.

File transfer protocol is one Internet service, just as e-mail is an Internet service, and you can use various programs, called *clients*, to use FTP. Some will be on the machine your Internet service provider (ISP) allows you to connect to, or you can have various file transfer programs on your own machine. WS-FTP32 for PCs and Fetch for Macintosh are good choices, and they're relatively cheap. They both have features that I enjoy: the ability to read text files, saving the addresses of FTP sites you visit, and to batch send and receive. Every FTP program is different, so when you get one, poke around its help file or manual to discover its particular tricks. Some let you store the settings for getting to several different FTP sites, or let you set a default FTP site. Many that store sites also let you set the initial directory to search, such as /PUB.

You might also consider FSP. FSP is a protocol, a bit like FTP, for moving files around. The name is the subject of some jocular debate: some people say it stands for *file service protocol*, some call it *FTP's sexier partner*, and others refer to it as *file slurping protocol*, or *flaky stream protocol*.

FSP has some nice features that FTP doesn't have, like the ability to transfer only the part of a file that was interrupted instead of starting all over from the beginning. To use FSP, you must get a client program and find FSP sites. A good place to look for clients is on ftp.germany.eu.net, and you can ask for sites in alt.comp.fsp (read the FAQ at http://mclachlan.rdg.ac.uk/misc/fsp/faq/faq.htm first).

WinFSP (which is freeware) certainly connected nicely and quickly got a file for me, but there's no function for saving the address of a site you want to visit again. Each time you connect, you have to type in the site address and the port number by hand. And the port number is essential in FSP, where in my experience it hasn't been all that

important in FTP. In all, WinFSP is very bare bones compared to WINFTP32, but if short, simple and sweet is what you want, definitely give it a try. The "official" place for FSP software is ftp.germany.eu.net.

To use FTP, you simply give the program an address (like the one at the end of the last paragraph). You log in as "anonymous" and give your e-mail address as a password. If anonymous doesn't work as a login name, try ftp. Use the CD command to change directories, LIST to look at filenames, and GET to retrieve them. That's FTP in a nutshell, but in practice it's a little more complicated.

In FTP, case, spelling, and punctuation count. If you try to get to FOOBAR.some.edu with foobar.some.edu, it probably won't work. If you try to get a file called FAMILY.LOCLIST.README.html, you must follow that punctuation and capitalization exactly or you'll get a "file not found" error message.

Many of the remote computers you're FTPing to are big machines running UNIX and DOS, and they've more or less adopted UNIX's subdirectory structure. So if you know DOS, you can wend your way through a remote computer's labyrinthine subdirectories.

If the server you want to access is always busy, one way to get in is to repeatedly try until you hit the exact moment when someone has just logged off. Another trick is to figure out which time zone the remote site is in and access it during local mealtimes or rush hours. A server in the UK, for instance, will be easier to access at 4 p.m. UK time when everyone is at tea. Granted, the Internet is international in nature, but a computer tied to a given university or organization will have peak usage at fairly predictable times—so use that to your advantage.

If you lack a Web browser or all you have is a Web address, you might be able to get something from the site. Ignore the http://www and FTP to the rest of the address. You can often log on to the system, dig through subdirectories, and find what you want. However, be warned that directories vary widely from site to site in name and organization. But there's almost always a README file, and most FTP programs can display it on the spot. The README file usually describes what you'll find at the site, and whether another site "mirrors" this one's

contents. If a mirror site is closer to you geographically, you're better off logging in there. Another important file is called INDEX or 00_INDEX. The index contains filenames, sizes, and descriptions of everything in that directory, or a list of what's in other subdirectories.

Another convention of FTP sites is that the /PUB directory almost always holds files and subdirectories that can be publicly accessed. Directories called /BIN, /ETC, and /INCOMING usually aren't open to anonymous logins.

If you're using a shell account (you've dialed up your Internet provider with a communications program and you're using the provider's UNIX FTP program), when you download (GET) a file, it will be stored on your provider's machine. Remember to use your communications program to download the files to your PC.

Many Web browsers, including America Online's, have a built-in FTP program. If you want to jump to an FTP site, just enter the address by prefacing it with FTP://. And remember that FTP site addresses are always changing. The Internet is dynamic, so expect a few detours along the way.

Anytime you're using FTP, you need to know some conventions. Files that end in .zip, .lzh, .exe, .arj, .arc, and .com are binary and should be transferred in binary mode. Files that end in anything else are probably text files and should be transferred in ASCII mode. If you're transferring files to a UNIX system, binary is generally the best mode to use for all transfers. The programs for uncompressing files are available at many BBSs, as well as at FTP.cac.psu.edu.

Binaries will usually be compressed, with a file extension of .zip. A self-extracting copy of PKware's shareware programs PKZip and PKUnzip is in the DOS file pkz204g.exe. Zip files can also be read with the DOS program unz50p1.exe.

Some files are also compressed with lharc, and end in .lzh. The software to unpack those files can be found in the self-extracting DOS archive lha213.exe. Files that end with .arj can be uncompressed with unarj.exe, which is in the zip file unarj230.zip. Compressed .arc files can be decompressed with a program in pk361.exe. There are also

several files that end with .exe. These are generally either self-extracting DOS archives or DOS programs.

Files ending in .Z have been compressed with UNIX Compress. Files ending in .gz have been compressed with GZip.

 # An example

You'll probably eventually own an FTP client that can type the commands for you as you point and click with your mouse. But let's do an example on Delphi, because its interface is typical for a text-based program. With a Delphi account, you're using a "shell" program that lets you type commands from your computer to Delphi's UNIX system. So to sign on, type the following from the main Delphi menu:

```
go internet FTP
```

From there you'll be asked what "address" you want to go to. Type the following:

```
ftp.cac.psu.edu
```

When connected, the computer will ask for a user name. Type:

```
anonymous
```

and for your password enter your e-mail address. For example:

```
etravel@delphi.com
```

The computer will generally give you a greeting message and the prompt "FTP." From there, type:

```
CD pub
```

and wait for a message that the directory has changed. Then type:

```
CD genealogy/
```

to access the genealogy directory. You can use DIR to list files and other directories. When you find a file you want, type:

```
GET filename
```

and remember that the filename must be typed *exactly* as it appears in the directory, including capitalization and punctuation. When the file is transferred, it will be sent to your Delphi workspace, and you can download it to your machine. If you've connected with an Internet service provider, the FTP might send it directly to your machine or your account at the ISP. You have to ask your system administrator exactly how your system works, but most ISPs are set up to send it straight to your machine. To go from a subdirectory back to the parent directory, type two periods (..). To get out of the site, type:

```
goodbye
```

And those are the basics of FTP!

 # A treasure chest of FTP files

So what kind of files should you, could you, would you get if you have FTP on your machine? I suggest you begin with some basic how-to files. The following directory:

```
ftp.cac.psu.edu
cd /pub/genealogy/text/guides
```

contains text files with information of interest to genealogists (see Fig. 6-1). Files that end with .zip or .lzh are in zip or lharc archive formats and must be transferred as binary files. Programs to extract the text files from these archives are available in the /genealogy/utils directory of the same site. The guides range from very general information to guides to specific libraries and collections:

hipp.etsu.edu
192.43.199.82
cd pub/genealogy
LDS research guides. This archive is maintained by Bob Wier
(weir@merlin.etsu.edu).

Figure 6-1

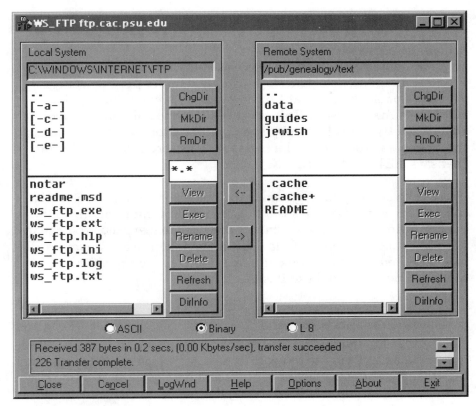

FTP with WS-FTP to ftp.cac.psu.edu in the directory
/pub/genealogy/text/guides, which will show you the three subdirectories:
data, guides, and jewish. To transfer a file in this program, simply highlight
the file with your mouse cursor, then click on the left arrow.

ftp.essex.ac.uk
155.245.10.133
cd pub/genealogy
Files from a 2% sample of the 1851 UK census.

hoth.stsci.edu
130.167.1.163
cd gedcom53 or cd lines
The latest GEDCOM specs and Lifelines genealogy program.

 # The Roots-L list of surnames

Several useful files for genealogical research are kept at the FTP sites emcee.com in the pub/genealogy/RSL and in the pub/genealogy /roots-1/family directory at ftp.cac.psu.edu. Among these is the Roots-L Surname List or RSL, a list of thousands of names being researched by Roots-L members, and information on how to contact the searchers. You can send a message to listserv@mail.eworld.com that says GET FAMILY.INDEX.

The listserver will return by e-mail the names of the files containing the full, current index. This is a huge amount of information, so the list has been broken up into smaller pieces alphabetically. You can get the files mailed to you with the GET command or use anonymous FTP, as I described. First let's look at how these files are organized. In the file, you find data listed like this:

surname date1 date2 migration/nametag . . .

New entries are marked by a +, modified entries by an *, and expiring entries by an x. *Date1* is the earliest date for which the submitter has information, and *date2* is the most recent date. The *migration* shows where people of this line lived during the period listed. To contact the submitter of the information, use *nametag* to find the address of the submitter in the address list (stored in FAMILY ADDR1 and FAMILY ADDR2). For example:

```
Spencer 1763 1933 SomersetCo,PAPerryCo,OHGrantCo,IN gailcoie
```

This person has information on Spencers from 1763 to the 20th century who moved through Pennsylvania, Ohio, and Indiana. In the FAMADDR lists, you'll find how to contact gailcoie next to her alphabetized nametag. You, too, can submit by sending your information in the proper format.

Other files maintained on Roots-L include Books We Own (members do research for each others with these); Family Organizations (GENEALOG FAMORGS); and the LOC (location) files, where people list the geographical areas for which they have information, regardless of surname.

Gophers

The Internet has a great function called telnet. Telnet is your magic mirror, allowing you to see what's on a computer thousands of miles away. One of its most interesting uses is a companion program called *gopher*. Created by the University of Minnesota (whose mascot is the gopher), this program uses telnet to tell you what's on another computer and help you retrieve it.

In brief, a gopher goes for titles of files on various computers that have to do with a subject of your choice. Sometimes it takes you to that computer. You'll be using them as you look at online library card catalogs in chapter 14, because it's usually through a gopher that you connect to the library of your choice. But for now, let's try the gophers on Delphi. (On Delphi's system, you can also find and connect to different anonymous FTP archives using gopher.) From Delphi's main menu, type:

```
GO Internet Gopher
```

and you'll be presented with this menu:

```
Internet SIG GopherPage 1 of 1
1 PERSONAL FAVORITES                            Menu
2 "ABOUT DELPHI'S GOPHER SERVICE"               Text
3 FAQ: FREQUENTLY ASKED QUESTIONS)              Menu
4 ALL THE GOPHER SERVERS IN THE WORLD           Menu
5 ARTS, LITERATURE, AND RELIGION                Menu
6 BUSINESS AND ECONOMICS                        Menu
7 COMPUTERS                                     Menu
8 FREE-NETS AND COMMUNITY ACCESS                Menu
9 FTP: DOWNLOADABLE PROGRAMS, IMAGES, SOUNDS    Menu
10 GAMES AND MUDS, MUSHES, MUSES, AND MOOS      Menu
11 GOVERNMENT AND POLITICS                      Menu
12 HEALTH AND MEDICINE                          Menu
13 INTERNET SEARCH UTILITIES AND INFORMATION    Menu
14 LAW                                          Menu
15 LIBRARIES, GUIDES, AND RESEARCH              Menu
16 MATHEMATICS, SCIENCE, AND TECHNOLOGY         Menu
17 SCHOOLHOUSE (K-12)                           Menu
18 SOCIAL SCIENCES, HISTORY, AND EDUCATION      Menu
19 THE GRAB BAG (WITH 'NEW THIS WEEK 1/17')     Menu
Enter Item Number, ?, or EXIT:
```

(The first time you use this menu, there will be nothing under PERSONAL FAVORITES. When you find a useful site, you save it; Delphi will then remember it for you for the next time.)

This is a very typical gopher menu. Sometimes the choices are more menus, to telnet to another computer, or to search a set of titles by a string you input. That last choice of this particular menu uses a companion program called Veronica, which searches sites with archives of files called Archie. All these programs reside on the Internet computers.

Let's look at choice 4, All the Gopher Servers in the World. This is the menu on Delphi:

```
ALL THE GOPHER SERVERS IN THE WORLD                Page 1 of 2
1 Connect to any gopher (Type a gopher address)    Search . . .
[entries deleted for space] . .
24   South America                                 Menu
25   All the Gopher Servers in the World (full list) Menu
26   Search titles in Gopherspace using veronica   Menu
Enter Item Number, PREV, ?, or BACK: 26
```

In the last choice, you see Veronica, the program that can search for certain text strings for you. Let's use that one.

```
Search titles in Gopherspace using veronica   Page 1 of 1
1 Search gopherspace at NYSERNet         Search
2 Search gopherspace at UNR              Search
3 Search gopherspace at PSINet           Search
4 Search gopherspace at U. of Manitoba   Search
5 Search gopherspace at SUNET            Search
[entries deleted for space]
Enter Item Number, SAVE, ?, or BACK: 1
```

All of these gopher sites have interesting possibilities, and I urge you to explore them on your own. But for now, let's just search the first one for the term *genealogy*. So enter 1 and you'd get:

```
"Search gopherspace at NYSERNet" is an indexed service. Please specify a
word or words to search.
Search for:
```

and you'd type:

```
genealogy
```

As this is a very general term, you'll get several hits. You could input a surname, a county and state, or any term you think will help you with your search. Sometimes you'll come up with nothing at that site, so try another. The computers take a while to search, so be patient and don't worry if nothing happens for a minute or two.

In this case, the computer will return with five screens of hits. (This looks like a good place to save as a personal favorite.) Some of them are text files, and some will lead to another menu of choices. Some are binary, which means they're either programs or compressed files. I won't show all the screens to you, but let's pretend item number 86 interests you:

```
Page 5 of 5

77  Genealogy software for a Mac                          Text
[entries deleted for space]
85   929  Genealogy, names, insignia                       Menu
86   E-MAIL Bulletin Boards for Genealogy ... L_CHRISTOPHE%USE.UI   Text


Enter Item Number, PREV, SAVE, ?, or BACK: 86

Date: Thu, 24 Sep 87 18:34:17 +0200
Reply-To: Info-Nets@Think.COM
Sender: General network forum <INFONETS@EB0UB011
Comments: To: info-nets@oz.ai.mit.edu
Comments: Warning_original Sender: tag was INFONETS@BITNIC
From: Alf Christophersen <L_CHRISTOPHE%USE.UIO.UNINETT@TOR.NTA.NO
Subject: E-MAIL Bulletin Boards for Genealogy reachable from Norway?


Does anybody out in the netland know about any Bulletin Boards for
genealogy interested computer fans? I am interested to hear from people
of Norwegian ancestry in hope that somebody could help me in tracing
people who emigrated from Norway (of my family, of course).


Addresses:
From ARPA:  L_CHRISTOPHE@INGER.ARPA
From EAN: L_CHRISTOPHE@USE.UIO.UNINETT
From BITNET: L_CHRISTOPHE%USE.UIO.UNINETT@CERNVAX.BITNET
From UUCP:  <mcvax!use.uio.uninett!l_christophe


We don't have any 300 baud modem connection with U.S., so please don't
tell me about such bulletin boards!

Alf Christophersen
Dep. of Nutrition Research
P.O. box 1046, Blindern
N-OSLO 3 Norway
```

Please remember that, with a gopher, you're in read-only mode. You cannot submit anything to a site using gopher. To answer this query, you must write down the e-mail address and send a message with your mail program later.

This is a short, simple example that only begins to show what a gopher can do. I hope this illustration gets you excited about cruising the Internet with gophers and Veronica. They're powerful search tools, and can really help your research.

A few cautions are in order, however. You never know which computer you'll wind up connected to with gophers, so you need to keep careful notes of how you got there. Always make sure your communications program emulates a VT100 terminal. Not all sites require it, but if gopher connects you to one that does and you aren't in VT100 mode, you'll suddenly be presented with a screen full of strange characters and be unable to submit new commands. That can be extremely frustrating, especially if you're paying for your Internet connection by the hour. In this case, you have to log off and try again.

Logging off, however, is a drastic measure and leaves the host computer hanging, so to speak. Whenever possible, try to close each connection before you leave, by typing exit or back until you're back at your original connection, in this case Delphi. Your Internet service provider might have similar services to Delphi's.

Also, remember that browsers, which I'll discuss in the following section, can use gophers. Simply type in the address in the "go" box or input line, like this:

```
gopher://gort.canisius.edu:70/1m/.otherlib/.discussion/.lists/roots-l
```

This is the address of the gopher that archives messages from the Roots-L mail list.

World Wide Web

An exciting new development in the Internet world is the World Wide Web. Started by scientists in Switzerland, it is an attempt to link information all over the world on the Internet. Of course, genealogists are involved in this, too!

You access the links through hypertext. Hypertext is a system of embedded pointers and associated "pages" on the Web. You click on a pointer (a highlighted word or phrase), and you're taken to another document, perhaps at another site, that has information related to the pointer—or a sound bite or a picture, if you have the proper hardware to handle them. (Warning: sound and pictures across the Internet are very slow as of this writing!)

To access the WWW, you must have a WWW *browser*, or be able to connect to one. What is wonderful about the Web is that most browsers combine the services I've talked about; they allow you to send e-mail (only a few browsers can receive e-mail), read and post to Usenet, transfer files with FTP, and search for files with gopher—all in one program.

The best way to access the Web is to run a browser yourself. Browsers are available for many platforms, both in source and executable forms. The browser business is booming, and it's beyond the scope of this book to try to list them all. But in general, browsers are either line-

Figure 6-2

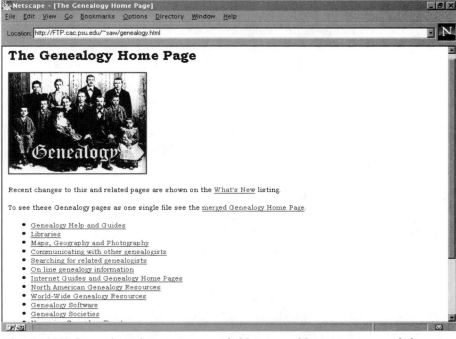

The WWW Genealogy home page with Netscape Navigator, one of the most popular graphical browsers, available for Macintoshes and PCs.

Figure 6-3

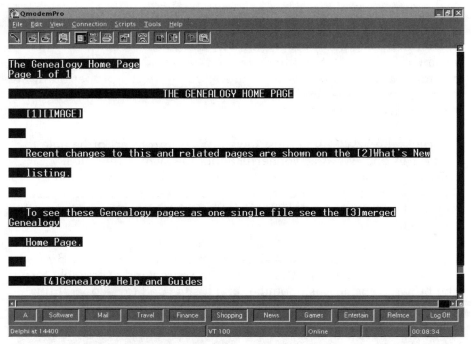

The WWW Genealogy home page with a line-oriented browser, called Lynx. The highlighted numbers are hypertext pointers to other resources.

oriented or graphical. The Genealogy home page is shown via the graphical browser Netscape (Fig. 6-2), the line-oriented browser Lynx (Fig. 6-3), and the graphical Windows 95 Internet Explorer (Fig. 6-4).

This is a new world, with new terminology. These terms can be confusing and are constantly changing, but here are a few you should know before you get going:

HTML The language that turns a text document into a WWW-browsable one. Many shareware and commercial products have popped up in the past year to help you create HTML documents, but if you get a good book on the subject, you can create HTML code in any word or text processor.

URL Stands for *uniform resource locator*. It's an address in the WWW. The format of a URL is *access_method://machine.name/*

Figure 6-4

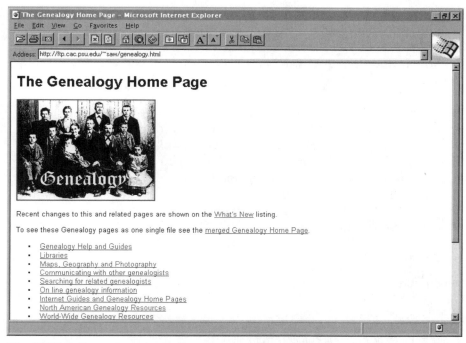

The WWW Genealogy home page with Microsoft's Internet Explorer for Windows.

directory/file. The access method can be FTP, http, gopher, or any other Internet service. When you see "check out this URL" in a message, you use your browser's method to get there. On some it's Go, on others Jump. For example, to get to the page shown in Figs. 6-2, 6-3, and 6-4, you'd type:

```
GO http://FTP.cac.psu.edu/~saw/genealogy.html
```

in the text browser. All you'd need to do in the graphical browsers is type the URL in the box. You can also use the menu options File, then Open in the graphical ones.

So let's try it, using Netscape as an example. Dialing up my Internet service provider, I click on the icon to start Netscape. Either using the menu commands File and Open or simply typing in http://FTP.cac .psu.edu/~saw/genealogy.html into the Location box will connect me.

If I don't want to type the address every time I visit the Genealogy home page, I can make a bookmark (called a *hot list* or *favorite place* in other browsers). In Netscape's case, I click on Bookmark in the menu bar and then click on Add Bookmark. You can sort and arrange your bookmarks to suit you.

Since the first publication of this book, the number of genealogy-related Web pages have gone from a handful to hundreds. After checking out a great many of them, I've compiled a list of the ones I think you should start with. They'll all lead you to other pages, eventually narrowing in scope, hopefully providing you with what you need. I've listed the pages with the name of the page on the first line, followed by the URL on the second line and a short description of what's there on the third:

Afrigeneas (African-American Roots)
http://drum.ncat.edu/~afrigen/
African-American genealogy, online and offline information pointers.

American Civil War Home Page
http://cobweb.utcc.utk.edu/~hoemann/warweb.html
Links to fantastic online documents from all sorts of sources.

Ancestors PBS Show
http://kbyuwww.byu.edu/ancestor.html
A family history and genealogy series coming to PBS stations in the fall of 1996: hosts, overview, pictures, and more!

Ancestry Inc.'s Discovering Your Heritage
http://www.ancestry.com/dyh/intro2.html
Basic beginner's how-to information on genealogy.

Bob Fieg's
http://www.getnet.com/~bfieg/
A typical home page, but with genealogy and pedigree chart software.

Canadian Genealogy Sources
gopher://Alpha.CC.UToledo.edu:70/11GOPHER_ROOT%3a%5b000000
.RESEARCH-RESOURCES.GENEALOGY.canadian-genealogy%5d
A list of sources to get you started in Canada.

Canadian Heritage Information Network
http://www.chin.gc.ca/
In French or English. It's a subscription service, but worth looking at.

Carrie's Adoptee & Genealogy Page
http://www.mtjeff.com/~bodenst/page3.html
Links to resources for adoptees, those of German heritage, and general genealogy.

Census Bureau Home Page
http://www.census.gov/ftp/pub/genealogy/www/
Frequently occurring names in the U.S. in 1990, among other things.

CLIO (The National Archives Information Server, Genealogy)
http://gopher.nara.gov:70/1/genealog
List holdings of the National Archives.

David Eppstein's Home Page http://www.ics.uci.edu/~eppstein/gene/
Information on Eppstein's shareware program Gene for Macintosh.

Dott's Genealogy Home Page
http://www.electriciti.com/~dotts/
Lots of great information on Iowa and Ohio resources.

Everton's Guide to Genealogy on the World Wide Web
http://www.everton.com/
Including an online version of the venerable Helper.

Excite Netsearch
http://www.excite.com/
Put "genealogy" in the search box.

Genealogy Resources on the Internet
http://www.umich.edu/~cgaunt/gen_int1.html
Tries to list it all; does a pretty good job.

Genealogy SF
http://roxy.sfo.com/~genealogysf/
Software, data, research tips, and a WWW hot list.

GenNam-L Archive, Folio Infobase
http://www.folio.com/folio.pgi/gennam-l_archive?
20,000+ messages from the GenNam-L mailing list, searchable.

GenServ (Genealogical Server Information)
http://soback.kornet.nm.kr/~cmanis/
GenServ's home page and information on how to register.

GenWeb Database Index
http://www.doit.com/tdoyle/genweb/ or http://sillyg.doit.com/genweb/
Links to all known genealogical databases searchable through the Web.

GenWeb Discussion List
http://demo.genweb.org/genweblist/genweblist.html
Discussions about the GenWeb database.

Helm's Genealogy Toolbox
http://aries.uihr.uiuc.edu/helm/genealogy.html
Categorized guide to genealogy on the WWW. Great starting place.

InfoSeek Net Guide
http://www.infoseek.com
Put "genealogy" in the search box.

Janyce's Root Diggin' Dept.
http://www.janyce.com/gene/rootdig.html
Good beginner's starting place.

List of Genealogy Bulletin Board Systems home page
http://genealogy.org:80/PAF/www/gbbs/
All the BBSs that carry Fidonet genealogy echos, searchable.

Lori Bushman's home page
http://www.holli.com/~lbushman/welcome.html
Has information about her family tree and Clinton County, Indiana.

Lycos Web Search
http://www.lycos.com/
Put "genealogy" in the search box.

National Genealogical Society
http://genealogy.org/NGS/
The granddaddy of all genealogical societies. Much of what's on the BBS is here, too.

Quick Guide to Genealogy in Ireland
http://www.bess.tcd.ie/roots/prototyp/qguide.htm
Great beginner's guide to Irish genealogical resources.

RAND Genealogy Club Home Page
http://www.rand.org:80/personal/Genea/
Search for surnames and locations, and get Soundex codes.

Registry of genealogists with home pages
http://www.wolfe.net/~janyce/genealogy/gene.cgi
A guide to individual genealogy pages. When your page is up, register!

RootsBook on the Web
http://mlane2.inhouse.compuserve.com:8000/Search.htm

A big database made up of a lot of little databases; a cooperative effort of lots of people.

Roots-L Resources Page
http://www.smartlink.net/~leverich/roots-l.html
Home page of the Roots-L mailing list.

Southern Genealogy
http://www.traveller.com/genealogy/
Southern families, Civil War pages, government Web servers, genealogy software companies, family societies and associations pages, books for sale, and genealogy newsgroups.

U.S. Gazetteer
http://wings.buffalo.edu/geogw
Type in a city and/or state, and a map will appear showing its location.

Webcrawler
http://www.webcrawler.com
Put "genealogy" in the search box.

Xerox Map Server
http://pubweb.parc.xerox.com/map
Interactive maps for finding any place in the world.

Yahoo
http://www.yahoo.com
Put "genealogy" in the search box.

Finding out more

This chapter has only touched on the basics of the Internet. As you become more confident and experienced, you'll want to learn more about traveling this way. The files I've mentioned so far will give you a good start, but there are quite a few detailed, technical books on Internet techniques when you're ready for more information.

Genealogy One: The National Genealogical Society BBS

BULLETIN board systems in general were covered in chapter 2. This chapter is devoted to Genealogy One, the source for many of the messages you'll find on other systems. Further, it's the place to dial to find the BBS nearest you that carries the NGS message systems. And, as BBSs go, it's one of the easiest to use once you set your preferences. Finally, this BBS is a source of information about the NGS itself. For all these reasons, I felt this BBS deserved a chapter all to itself.

The NGS BBS (see Fig. 7-1) is sponsored and provided as one of the services of the National Genealogical Society Computer Interest Group. Use of NGS is free, except for your toll charges if you have to dial long distance. Its sysops are Richard Pence, Frank Williams, and Don Wilson, and the BBS has two telephone numbers. The second line is on a rotary switch, so by calling 703-528-2612 you'll get either line 1 or, if it's busy, line 2. If you call 703-528-2612 you'll receive whichever modem isn't busy—therefore it's the best number for most

Figure 7-1

The opening screen of the NGS BBS.

people to call. Both modems should answer on the first ring. If you get more than one ring, then Pence is probably doing maintenance on the BBS and the system is down temporarily. If you get a busy signal calling 703-528-2612, then both lines are busy—not an uncommon occurrence! Here is the BBS's address, phone numbers, and additional information:

4527 17th St. North
Arlington, VA 22207-2399
703-525-0050 (voice)
703-528-2612 (BBS)
109/302 (Fidonet)

Both modems are capable of speeds up to and including 9,600 bps, and both support MNP 4 error-correcting protocol and MNP 5 file compression. The modem on 703-528-2612 is a Fastcom FDX model 9696, operating V.32 protocol to 9,600 bps. The modem on 703-528-8570 is a U.S. Robotics HST dual standard, and handles HST transfers up to 14,400 bps and V.32 transfers to 9,600 bps. Both modems are capable of MNP4/5 error-correcting and file-compression protocols at 2,400 or 9,600 bps.

During the sign-up process, choose and record your password carefully; this BBS software is case-sensitive when it comes to passwords. Once you've registered, you can do a fast sign-on by typing the following at the first name prompt:

```
first name;last name;;password
```

then hit the Enter key. Don't use any spaces and separate the fields with semicolons. Make sure to hit Enter only at the end of the line.

How it began

"It started in my basement," Richard Pence says. He had seen a BBS with some genealogy on it and thought it was a great idea. A friend said he had a computer to donate if someone would set it up. Pence did, and ran it out of his home for a while until it really took off.

"We had come from a conference in 1982, right before we had this meeting [that started the BBS]. Paul Anderek had had an early experience, and kids had messed up his system, so we learned from that quickly," says Pence. There's nothing on the board of interest to game-playing, security-cracking adolescents.

The board was one of the first to log onto the Fidonet genealogy echo; now it's sort of "home base" for that set of messages on Fidonet. In early 1994, the echo alone had 950 participants and 500 messages a day.

Pence is famous throughout the online genealogy world for his monthly updates on boards carrying Fidonet genealogy echos. The list of genealogy BBSs, now compiled by Richard Cleaveland, is in file area 2 in GBBS*yymm*.ZIP and GBBS*yymm*.TXT, where *yy* and *mm* are the year and month of the file. You can download the text file and read it in any text or word processor.

The system also has an online search function for genealogy bulletin boards, so you can capture just the ones in your area code instead of downloading Pence's comprehensive file, which often runs over 90K. To do this, choose Database Search from the main menu, then BBS from the next menu (see Fig. 7-2). You can enter a city name and a two-letter abbreviation for a state in the U.S., or simply input your area code and city, followed by a minus sign. The BBS within that area code will appear.

As a new user on NGS BBS, your first step should be to read the bulletins and the system information files available from the main menu (see Figs. 7-3 and 7-4). These will help you learn to use the system more effectively. Capture them to your buffer file to refer to later.

This information about the National Genealogical Society is also in file area 2. You can download the file NGS.ZIP to get all the information in the ten or so separate files. All the files on this BBS available for download are also in file area 2 in the file NGS-BBS.ZIP.

Figure 7-2

The Fidonet BBS database helps you find a local-call BBS that carries the NGS message base.

Figure 7-3

The bulletins are all worth reading. Download them in your first message download.

Figure 7-4

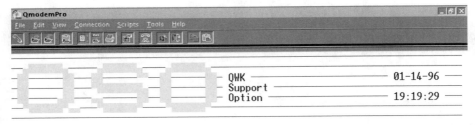

The QSO helps you make each visit to Genealogy One as fast (and cheap!) as possible. Set up your preferences, then each call simply downloads the latest messages, bulletins, and files so you can peruse them offline.

⇨ Messages

An abundance of messages on any genealogical topic you can imagine is the primary feature of this BBS. You can leave public or private messages on NGS to seek assistance with your research or respond to others looking for help. The only places you can leave private messages on this system are in the Local Message and NetMail areas. Even then, you're reminded that the sysops can read all private messages. All messages entered into the Fidonet national and international conferences are public messages and can be read by all callers. The NGS BBS has national/international message areas for the following subjects:

General Genealogy All are public messages.

NGC (National Genealogical Conference), mostly U.S. This is the most widely read genealogy echo and your messages will receive the greatest distribution here.

Genealogy Software Information about all genealogy software programs.

European Genealogy (International Genealogical Conference) This echo area is for messages pertaining to international genealogy only; please do not use this area for U.S.-only genealogy messages.

Jewish Genealogy For special Jewish-related problems.

South-East U.S. Genealogy Use this area only for messages concerning the "Dixie" states.

Genealogy Data Use this area only to circulate a Tiny Tafel; the replies to messages you see here should be sent by U.S. mail or net mail, or placed in the NGC message area.

The local message areas are:

Messages to the Sysop Private questions about using the BBS.

Local Messages Public or private messages to callers of this BBS. These messages aren't transmitted to any other BBS. Private messages can be read by the sysops and the addressee only.

TechNet 109 This area is echoed to over 100 BBSs in the local area and is intended for technical computer hardware or operating system questions. Place genealogy or genealogy software issues in the NGC or Genealogy Software areas.

The BBS is set to delete messages over 30 days old. It will keep about 15,000 messages available in the message areas. Messages are renumbered each Tuesday morning, once a week.

The messages are available through the QSO mail reader (see Fig. 7-4). QSO allows you to use any offline reader that supports the QWK packet

format to interact with TBBS, the bulletin board software. When used in conjunction with a QWK-compatible offline reader, QSO allows you to:

➤ Download mail from selected conferences (either all mail or only mail that's addressed to you) for reading offline.

➤ Reply offline using any reader that supports the QWK format, and use QSO to bulk-upload your replies and have them integrated into the message base as though you had made those replies online. All reply linkages, private/public flags, etc. are maintained as if you had entered the messages online.

➤ Customize its operation so that only desired actions take place.

➤ Reduce connect time. Instead of staying online to read and reply to messages, you can do this offline. If you're calling long distance, this can result in a drastically reduced phone bill.

➤ Read and reply to messages at your leisure. Once you download a bundle of mail, you can read messages in that bundle any time you want. Upload the replies back to the system whenever you want.

You need to obtain a QWK-compatible offline mail reader before you can use QSO. Since most are released as shareware, they're usually available from BBSs supporting QWK offline readers. On NGS BBS, they can be found in file area 1 with other general utilities. Remember, if your reader is shareware, you should register your copy with its author.

When you first select the TBBS menu item that enters QSO, you'll see an opening screen with the following options:

➤ Configure User Parameters

➤ Download Messages

➤ Upload Messages

➤ Keyword File Upload

➤ Goodbye (Hangup)

➤ Go Back to the Main Menu (Quit)

Configure User Parameters

If you've never used QSO before, you must first press C to select the Configure User Parameters menu. There you'll select the message conferences you want QSO to get for you, and configure several options. You must at least select some message areas before QSO will do anything else useful. Many QWK interfaces also allow you to select which archive format is used. QSO uses only the PKZip 1.x implode archiving format, so this can't be selected. You must set your offline reader to use PKZip with QSO. (PKZ110.EXE is available for download in file area 1.) The options you can choose to set are as follows:

✳ **Option Change**

Selecting this command allows you to enter the number of one of the options listed on the status portion of the screen in order to toggle it from No to Yes, and vice versa. These options configure the operation of QSO for you in several detailed ways. Let's examine what each one does:

Include Enclosed Files If this option is set to Yes, QSO will include any files enclosed in messages you retrieve in your QWK packet automatically. Note that if there's more than one enclosed file with the same name, you might have trouble retrieving the files from the QWK packet. If this option is set to No, then only the message text will be in your QWK packet.

Download Your Replies If you set this option to Yes, your QWK packet will include any messages you've previously posted (either online or by uploading them as replies using QSO). If this option is set to No, the messages you originate won't be enclosed in your QWK packet.

Send Welcome Screen If this option is set to Yes, then QSO will include the initial welcome file you see when you log onto this BBS in your QWK packet.

Send News Screen If this option is set to Yes, then QSO will include the system news file for NGS BBS in your QWK packet. Note that this

option has been set to include the news file only when the file has changed.

Send Logoff Screen If this option is set to Yes, QSO will include the goodbye file you see when you log off this BBS in your QWK packet.

BBS Time Stamp on Replies If this option is set to No, QSO will post your replies with the time and date your offline reader puts in them. If you set this option to Yes, then QSO will post your replies with the time and date it enters them into the BBS message base.

Logoff after U/L Replies Normally QSO returns to its main menu after you upload your reply packet and QSO processes it. If this option is set to Yes, then QSO will automatically log you off after your uploaded packet is processed. Note that, if set to Yes, you should do your upload as the last part of your QSO session or you'll have to dial back into the system to carry on with your session.

Logoff after D/L Msgs Normally QSO returns to its main menu after you download your QWK packet. If this option is set to Yes, then QSO will automatically log you off after your QWK packet is successfully downloaded. Note that this means you should do your download last.

Suppress NDX File Creation This option should probably be set to No. For some offline reader programs, however, the NDX files aren't necessary. If you have such a program, then you can set this option to Yes and no NDX files will be included in your QWK packets, saving disk space.

Scan for New Bulletins If this option is set to Yes, then QSO will send you any of the bulletin files from this BBS that have been updated since your last call. If this option is set to No, then no bulletin files will be included in your QWK packet.

D/L Packet w/o Messages Sometimes when you scan for new messages, you'll find that none have been found since your last QSO session. If this option is set to No, then no packet will be downloaded until messages are available. If you set the option to Yes, however, QSO will still package any new bulletins, service files, and other

nonmessage data and transmit it to you in a QWK packet that has no messages.

D/L New Files Listing If this option is set to Yes, QSO will include a listing of any new files that have been posted since your last call. This option is very time-consuming. Don't select it on a regular basis unless you're willing to wait the time (and pay the toll) it takes to scan all file areas for new files.

Only Selected Confs in DAT If this option is set to No, then QSO will include the names and numbers of all conferences this BBS provides to you in your QWK packet's CONTROL.DAT file. This allows you to use the remote configuration Add and Drop options. When a system provides many conferences, however, it can be annoying to see all the conferences listed on your offline reader screen. You can set this option to Yes to limit the list to only those conferences you've selected to download.

Send Session Log If this option is set to Yes, QSO will include the file SESSION.TXT in your QWK packet. This file is a transcript of your online session, and it includes all QSO screens and your input as it occurred. If this option is set to No, then SESSION.TXT isn't included in your QWK packet.

Omit Download Verify Prompt If this option is set to No, QSO will prompt you after the message scan to begin the download. If you set the option to Yes, then QSO will immediately begin the download process when the message scan completes. I keep this set to No so I can abort more easily.

✳ Conference Selection

This command will display all the message conferences available to you through QSO. Some conference numbers might be missing, either because the BBS doesn't use them or because you haven't been given access to a particular message conference. You'll see one or more screens of conference names that look much like this (a leading asterisk indicates the conference is selected):

```
Available Conferences
3 LOCAL
```

```
4  GENEALOGY
5  JEWISHGEN
9  GENE_EUR
11 GENDATA
15 TECHNET109
16 SE_GENEALOGY
17 GENSOFT
Select Conference, (HELP or QUIT)?
```

At this prompt you can use the commands Select, Deselect, or Reset to select conferences and/or reset the high message pointers. You can also simply enter conference numbers to toggle the selected status. Conference numbers can be listed individually or as a range (specified by lowest number and highest number), like this: 4–17. You can also select all conferences with the keyword *all*.

The high message pointer indicates which messages will be scanned and placed in your QWK packet. You can set the high message pointer explicitly using the Reset command, or include a pointer reset command as part of a Select command. The syntax of the Select command is:

```
SELECT conference(s) [pointer_setting]
```

where *conference(s)* specifies one or more conferences (a single number, range of numbers, or the keyword *all*). The variable *pointer_setting* specifies the new value of the high message; you can specify either an explicit message number, LOW+n (n above the lowest message in the conference), or HIGH-n (n below the highest message in the conference). For example, the following:

```
SELECT ALL HIGH-50
```

would select all listed conferences and reset all high pointers to 50 below the highest message in the conference. This one:

```
SELECT 1
```

would select conference 1, which doesn't affect the high message pointer. High message pointers default to the high message pointer you had on the conference before entering QSO. The following:

```
SELECT 10-15 HIGH-10
```

would select conferences 10, 11, 12, 13, 14, and 15 and set the high message pointer to 10 below the last message in each conference. The Deselect command has the same syntax as the Select command, except it doesn't allow you to reset the high message pointer. For example:

```
DESELECT 5-11
```

would deselect any selected conferences in the range 5 through 11. The Reset command has the same syntax as the Select command, but it won't select any deselected message conferences. It allows you to reset high message pointers without affecting the select status. For example:

```
RESET 10-15 HIGH-10
```

would set the high message pointers of any selected conferences between 10 and 15 to 10 less than the highest message in the conference.

✳ Protocol Selection

This command allows you to select your preferred file transfer protocol for use when uploading and downloading QWK packets to and from QSO. You can either be prompted for your protocol selection each time, or pick a default that will be used automatically.

✳ Limits Configuration

This command allows you to set your own limits for QWK packet creation. When selected, you'll be prompted for the maximum number of messages QSO is allowed to place in one packet, as well as the maximum number of messages allowed per conference. Some offline mail readers have internal limits on the number of messages they can handle per packet and per conference. If your reader has such limits, you should configure QSO not to exceed them.

⇨ Download Messages

This is one of the two QSO commands you'll use most often. Press D and you'll cause QSO to scan all the conferences you've selected for

new messages and package them into a QWK packet for transmission to your offline reader. QSO will also add any other files you've selected to this packet. After the packet has been assembled, it's then downloaded to you. You download a QWK packet just as you would any other file.

If you have many messages to scan, this process can take a good while. If you want to abort the scan, press either S to stop or Ctrl–C or Esc to abort. The scanning will abort immediately and you'll return to the main QSO menu. All pointers will be reset to their status prior to the scan (there will be no effects from the partial scan you aborted).

Begin the download process by answering Y to the prompt at the end of the message scan. QSO will then prepare the message portion of the QWK packet and add any nonmessage files (bulletins, services, etc.) that your configuration demands. All these files are combined into a file named *id*.QWK (where *id* is the identifier the sysop has established for this system) as a PKZip format archive.

Note that if you've already downloaded a packet earlier in the day, QSO will change the last letter of the packet name to prevent overwriting your previous packet. The change creates files named .QW1, .QW2, etc., then .QWA through .QWJ, for a total of 21 unique packet names in a 24-hour period. Not all mail packagers do this!

 # Upload Messages

This is the other most frequently used QSO main menu command. When you select this command, QSO will prompt you to upload the NGS-BBS.REP file that your offline reader produced when you entered replies to messages previously obtained with the Download Messages command. After you've uploaded this file to QSO, it will unzip it and enter your replies into the message base.

As you read messages offline (using your QWK-compatible offline reader), you can reply to messages. When doing so, your reader program will generate a file named NGS-BBS.REP, which contains those replies. To post those messages on the BBS, you need to select the Upload Messages command from the main QSO menu.

You'll be prompted to select a protocol (if you haven't set a default), and then you can upload the .REP file. Once the file is uploaded, QSO will decompress it and post your reply messages into the TBBS message base. Once this process is complete, you'll return to the main QSO menu (unless you've set your configuration to log off after uploading replies).

A final word about messages: Be sure to leave a message to the sysop as you sign off if you have questions or encounter problems. That person will do his or her best to answer as quickly as possible, usually within a week.

 Keyword File Upload

This command will prompt you to upload an ASCII file that contains keywords to qualify the Download Messages command's actions for this session with QSO. You can use up to 25 keywords in this file. The format of a keyword file is discussed later in this chapter.

You can condition a message scan to select only certain messages by uploading a keyword file prior to specifying the Download Messages command. To upload a keyword file, you must select the Keyword File Upload command from the main QSO menu. You'll be prompted to upload the file, and QSO will receive it. This file is stored in your temporary directory for use during the next Download Messages command.

A keyword file is an ASCII file that allows you to select which messages you want to receive. Each line of the file is a one-key selection filter, and you can have a maximum of 20 keys in a single key file. The keys are not case sensitive, so they'll match either upper- or lowercase strings in the message. The format of a key line is as follows:

```
[/] [+ or -] [(conference)] key_text
```

If the line begins with the / character, then this key applies only to the From: and To: name fields in the message. If there's no leading / character, then the key applies to the message's Subject: field and the

body of the message text. The + or − characters indicate whether you want only messages that contain this key (+) or only messages that don't contain this key (−). If neither + or − is specified, then + is assumed. This is how you can filter out messages from a certain person, often called a "twit filter."

If a conference number in parentheses precedes the key, then this key applies to only the specified conference. If no conference number is given, then the key applies to all conferences. The remainder of the line (beginning with the first nonblank character) is the key text to use for the selection. Keyword files are deleted after the scan is done, so you can do multiple scans with different keyword files by uploading a new keyword file between each scan.

⇨ Goodbye (hangup)

This command causes an immediate log off from the system.

⇨ Quit to TBBS

This command exits QSO and returns to the TBBS menu from which you entered QSO (the main menu).

Everton
Publisher's BBS

THIS chapter will show you a typical for-fee genealogy BBS. The respected genealogical publishing house, Everton's, has for 47 years been in the vanguard of American genealogists, so it's no surprise that they have a helpful, usable, and valuable BBS. It's not as cozy as some of the homegrown ones, and of course there are fees, but it's very good. Figure 8-1 shows the welcome screen to On-Line Search, Everton Publisher's genealogical bulletin board. The following is Everton's address and access numbers:

P.O. Box 368
Logan, UT 84323-0368
Attn: Online Search
800-443-6325 (voice)
801-752-6095 (data)
801-752-0425 (fax)
ale@cc.us.edu (e-mail)

Everton's BBS rates for subscribers to the publication *Genealogical Helper* are $59.50 for 6 months and $89.50 for 12 months. For

Figure 8-1

The welcome screen to On-Line Search, Everton Publisher's for-fee bulletin board.

nonsubscribers to *Genealogical Helper*, you can use the BBS for $79.50 for 6 months and $119.50 for 12 months. You can register online by credit card, or send a check.

Besides several Fidonet echoes, the outstanding feature of this board is a set of searchable databases, which I'll show you later. On-Line Search began in September 1992, with two computers and two phone lines. Today it has four computers, four lines, and a unique searchable database of about 2 million names. It's not information you'll find anywhere else, and it's cross-referenced with the names and addresses of over 150,000 submitters.

The BBS software here is PCBoard, version 15.0, which has a built-in QWK mail function and a door to an offline mail reader. There's also a chat option, but it isn't used much. The first time you log on and thereafter as a nonsubscriber, you get about 15 minutes a day.

The first time you log on, you'll be presented with the screen in Fig. 8-2, warning you about some of the rules of the place. Then you'll be

Figure 8-2

```
? (C)
           Welcome, Elizabeth!  Please read the following carefully:
                        ++  DISCLAIMER ++
           Any information entered on this system that is intended to be PRIVATE
will be treated in strict confidence.  HOWEVER, pursuant to the Electronic and
Communications Privacy Act of 1986. 18 USC 2510 et. seq., notice is hereby
given that THERE ARE NO ABSOLUTELY SECURE FACILITIES PROVIDED BY THIS SYSTEM
for SENDING or RECEIVING PRIVATE OR CONFIDENTIAL ELECTRONIC COMMUNICATIONS.
ALL messages should be deemed to be readily accessible to the general public.
Do not use this system for any communication which you intend to be strictly
confidential.  Notice is hereby given that ALL messages entered into this
system can and may be read by the operators of this system, WHETHER OR NOT
they are the intended recipient(s).
           Everton Publishers, Inc. and it's employees can not be held liable for
damages arising from the use of this system or any information obtained from
it.  Please note that this is mainly a subscription service. Non-subscribing
users have limited access, and we reserve the right to remove non-subscribing
accounts at any time without notice.  To become a subscriber, type "REGISTER"
at (almost) any menu, or call our toll-free order line at 1-800-443-6325.

           By answering "Yes" to the following question or accessing this system
beyond this point, you submit that you have read and agreed to the above
conditions.  Answer "No" to decline to the above agreement and disconnect.
Would you like to try out the system, Elizabeth? (Enter)=yes? (Y)
```

The new user disclaimer.

Figure 8-3

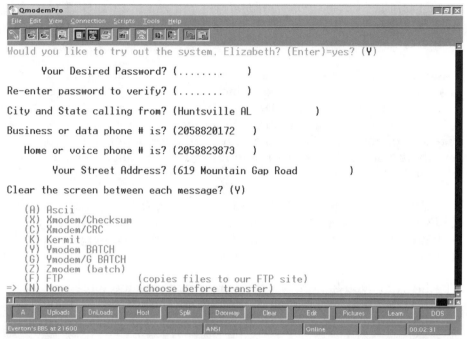

The system will collect some data from you, even if you don't register as a subscriber.

led through a preregistration sequence (see Fig. 8-3). Be sure to select the protocol for downloads you want to use; it will save time later. At the main menu, type register to subscribe to On-Line Search. As a subscriber, you'll be able to:

➢ Access the BBS for 30 minutes each day

➢ Access all the databases

➢ Leave messages for other users

➢ Reply to messages

➢ Access future databases or conferences when available

Each time you log on, you'll be told whether there are new items in News and Bulletins. A sample News screen is shown in Fig. 8-4.

Figure 8-4

```
o                                                                o
o    ▪| GEDSRCH Growing! |▪              ▪| Dated 12-08-1995 |▪   o
o                                                                o
o       Thanks to one and all who have contributed to           o
o    our GEDSRCH database.  We have been overwhelmed by          o
o    the responce to our free month of OLS for                  o
o    submitting a Gedcom.  Thanks Everyone.                      o
o       We are currently adding around 50,000 names to          o
o    this database each week.  The current total size           o
o    around 700,000 names.  Thanks again everyone.              o
o                                                                o
```

(26 min left), (H)elp, Enter for More, (N)o More?

Current news for the system is presented at logon. By typing N, you can avoid the automatic display and read it from the News menu instead.

⇨ Meet the sysop

Lee Everton, the sysop at On-Line Search, says the databases are the main focus of the board. "With On-Line Search, we don't have a large list of files to download. We have been concentrating on the databases. Information from the databases is searched and then the chosen information can be downloaded in a zipped file to the user's computer," Everton explains. An example will be given later in this chapter.

Everton also says that, "As for actual files to download, we have two areas. The first contains utility files and genealogy files. The genealogy area consists of about six files that looked interesting. The utility file area has about a dozen files . . . anything from PKUnzip to some text files about searching. When we start working on greater amounts of files, we will create a listing." To get to this file area, choose conference 5 (JOIN 5 from the main menu, as shown in Fig. 8-5).

Figure 8-5

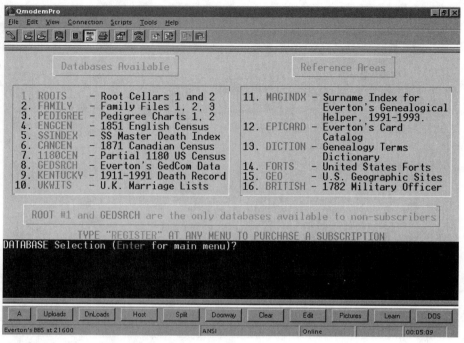

On-Line Search's main menu.

"One other area that we have is the GEDCOM file area. This is conference 3 from the main menu (available only to paid subscribers). This area does contain quite a few files, but (the inevitable 'but') these areas can be scanned to see if there are any possible matches. For example: a person would choose conference 3 from the main menu, then TS and enter the text to search for. For me, I might enter EVERTON and press Enter. If there were any matches in the filename or the file description, it would be highlighted and I would know which file contained information on EVERTON as well as who submitted the information," he says. Then you could choose a transfer protocol (T from the main menu) and download (D) to retrieve the file.

 # Messages

PCBoard always asks if you want to see your mail first, before you even get to the main menu. If you answer yes, you'll read and reply to those messages first, online. If you want to download them later, say

no. But if you just want to see what conferences have mail for you, scan the message base (PCBoard gives you this option right after offering to let you read the mail first). A typical scan looks like this:

```
Scan Message Base Since 'Last Read' (Enter)=yes?
(Ctrl-K) or (Ctrl-X) Aborts, (Ctrl-S) Suspends.
Num     Conference    To You    Found
----    -----------   -------   -------
   0    Main Board        2         6
   5    Utility Files     0         0
   9    A.R.T. Demo       0         0
  10    GENEALOGY    +    0      1868
  11    JEWISHGEN    +    0       324
  12    JOURNAL      +    0        16
  13    GENDATA      +    0       148
  14    WGW          +    0       115
  15    WGA_GEN      +    0         0
  16    WGA_WGW      +    0         0
  17    EUROPE GEN   +    0       583
  18    AUSTRALIAN   +    0        84
  19    FRENCH GEN   +    0         8
  20    B-N-L GEN         0         1
  21    CANADA GEN   +    0        23
  22    GERMAN       +    0        41
  23    GENSOFT      +    0        78
  24    IRE & U.K.   +    0       141
  25    ITALIAN GEN  +    0        10
  26    MIDWEST      +    0        80
  27    NEW ZEALAND  +    0        12
  28    POLAND GEN   +    0         3
  29    REUNIONS     +    0         0
  30    SOUTHEAST    +    0       146
  31    SPANISH      +    0         3
```

To read your messages, type R and then Y; R and S will show you your messages since you were last on. Reply allows you to answer the messages, and Enter will retrieve the next message.

You can read one conference at a time. Suppose you typed join 12 at the Main Board menu in Fig. 8-5. Your next menu would be the screen shown in Fig. 8-6. You can instruct PCBoard to search these messages for a certain string, mark them for later download, answer them, and so on.

Offline messages

The offline mail reader (OLM) is carefully explained in a file you should download called OFFLINE.TXT. An excerpt of that file, written

Figure 8-6

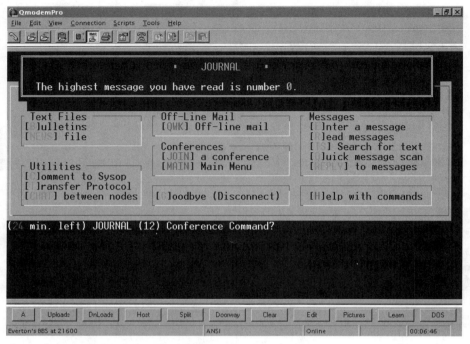

A conference menu, from which you can read messages in a single message conference. From this menu you can use TS to search for a specific string within those messages.

by Lee Everton, is as follows: "There are all sorts of readers available, from the extremely simple to the sophisticated packages, complete with spell checkers and other features. If you are using Qmodem Pro from Mustang Software as your terminal program, you already have a built-in QWK reader called On-Line Xpress (OLX). My favorite reader is a simple one called Jabber. Jabber is easy to learn and includes a built-in message editor without all the complex features that I don't need. You can download a shareware copy of Jabber from . . . Everton's On-Line Search . . . under the name JABR12.ZIP."

JABR12.ZIP is compressed with PKZip version 2.04g. If you're not too familiar with how to decompress files, download the file QWKPACK.EXE instead. QWKPACK.EXE is a self-extracting compressed file (it will uncompress itself). QWKPACK also contains the PKZip and PKUnzip files you'll need to uncompress messages and

compress your replies. QWKPACK is larger than JABR12, so it will take longer to download.

Using OLM on PCBoard is really just as easy as reading a message. Instead of the Read command, just give the BBS the QWK command. It will scan all the conferences for new mail, and then pack them into a compressed file named ONLINE.QWK. The .QWK extension tells you that it's a QWK mail file. When you enter replies, they're packed into the file ONLINE.REP. The extension .REP tells you it's a reply file. If you enter any replies or post any new messages of your own, they're put into the ONLINE.REP file, not the ONLINE.QWK file. After reading the mail and entering any messages you want, you need to upload the ONLINE.REP file to the BBS from your computer.

 # Searching the databases

As mentioned before, an outstanding feature of this board is the databases. The following example will perform a search in Roots Cellar, Volume 1 (ROOT1). This one is available to you the first time you call; the other databases are open only to subscribers. All the databases have a similar design and use the same commands for the searches. This example will take you through the search process, narrowing the search and adding the information to a download list.

First, enter the ROOT1 database. To do this, type open and then press Enter at the Main Board command line. You'll then be shown the screen in Fig. 8-7. Choose 1.

To search for the surname Spencer, press A. This will take you to the surname field. Type spencer in the surname field and then press Enter. To start the search, type S. Searching the entire ROOT1 database will take approximately 35 seconds, and will yield several records. (If you want to stop the search, press any key.)

You should now have the results of the search for Spencer. With the results on the screen, you can move to the next page (type N), the previous page (type P), or a certain page (type O and then enter the number of the page).

Figure 8-7

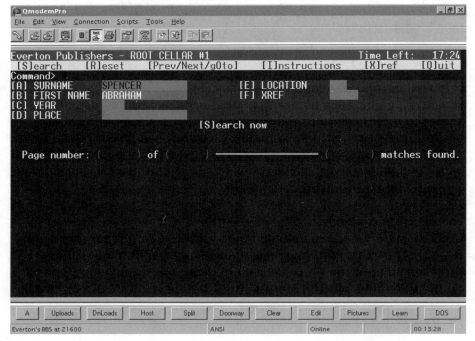

*The search menu for an On-Line Search database. This one, Root Cellar
#1, is open to everyone, even first-time callers. The commands are the
same for all databases.*

If you want to narrow the search by adding a first name, type B. The
cursor will move to the first name field. Type abraham for the first
name and press Enter. (When the cursor returns to the top of the
screen after you enter a search criterion, you can either press S to
search again or add more criteria for the search.) The screen in Fig. 8-8
will appear.

If you want to add a date and event for the example, type C and the
cursor will move to the event field. The available events are: B (birth),
D (death), M (marriage), and R (resided). Type the letter for the event
you want to search and press Enter. Then type D. The cursor will
move to the date field. You can enter dates in two ways. First, you can
type the entire year if you know it, for example 1878. Second, If you
want to have the entire decade searched you can type 187. The
second option would give you any of the Spencers in the 1870s.

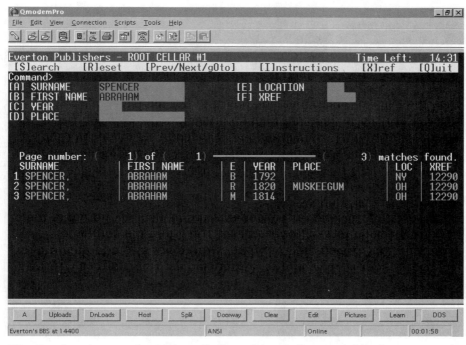

Figure 8-8

The results of a search on Root Cellar #1, with Spencer, Abraham.

A useful command is Cross-Reference to the Submitter. Once you have some results, type X. You'll be asked:

```
Cross-reference which number? [ ]
```

For this example the submitter number (in the far right-hand column) was 12290, so type this number and press Enter. You'll be shown the person who submitted the information (see Fig. 8-9). When you get the submitter's address, you'll be asked:

```
Do you want to add this information to the download list? [ ]
```

If you choose Y, the name will be added to a list in preparation for downloading. If you'd like to add the ancestor names to a list to download, press L. You'll be asked:

```
From which page? [
```

Figure 8-9

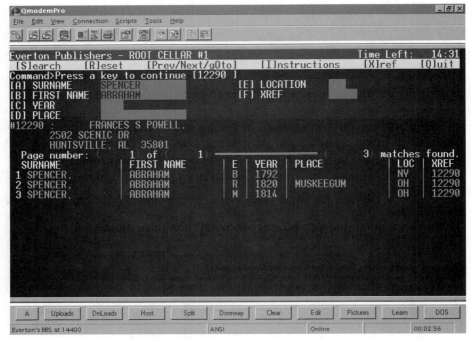

The Cross Reference command (X) will give you the name and address of the information's original submitter, which can be added to your download list.

Type in the starting page number. Then at the following prompt:

```
To which page? [
```

type the ending page number. The download limit for each database is 90 individuals per database per day—about eight pages. The computer will then ask:

```
Are you sure?
```

At this point, you're ready to download the information that you've searched to your computer with the D command. As this board is accessible up to 14.4K, you can get a lot of information in a short visit!

America Online's
Genealogy Forum

ONLINE genealogy has been on America Online almost from the beginning, according to George Ferguson, host of the America Online Genealogy Forum (GENGeorge is his screen name). George is just one of the helpful people there, and we'll hear more from him later. America Online's address and other information is as follows:

8619 Westwood Center Dr.
Vienna, VA 22182-2285
cs@aol.com (e-mail)
1-800-227-6364 (phone)

America Online is "open" 24 hours a day, seven days a week. Their basic rate is free startup, $9.95 for the first five hours, and $2.95 per hour after that. It's more for overseas accounts. Your Internet address as an AOL user is *screen_name*@aol.com. The keyword to use is Genealogy or Roots.

Getting started

First, let's set up for a session. When you call the 800 number, you'll receive free front-end software to sign up on AOL. Generally, you'll dial a local number to connect (if available), just as you do for CompuServe, Delphi, and other online commercial services. You'll register, choosing a screen name and a password. Your screen name can be close to your real name (as mine is, see Fig. 9-1) or it can be totally whimsical and fictitious. AOL will know who you really are from the sign-up routine. If more than one person in your family uses AOL, your account can have a total of five screen names at no extra charge. You cannot, however, change or delete your original screen name. This is where AOL stores all your account information. To add or delete a screen name, use the keyword Names.

But before you click on Sign On, you can set yourself up to get to the Genealogy area quickly. Throughout the system, AOL has keywords that are shortcuts to where you want to go. By clicking on Go To in the top menu bar and choosing Go To Menu Editor, you'll get the dialog box in Fig. 9-2.

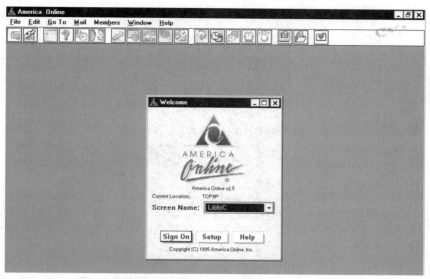

Figure 9-1

Your screen name is shown in the Welcome box when you load the AOL software. You can have several names assigned to one account, for family members to use.

Figure 9-2

Make life easy on yourself: Click on the Go To | Edit Go To menu and add the Genealogy area to the list. Then two keystrokes will get you to the AOL genealogy resources.

Conveniently, the keyword you need is either Roots or Genealogy. Simply enter that in the dialog box. Menu Entry can be anything you care to call it. Keyword must be the exact spelling of the AOL keyword, although capitalization doesn't matter. Once you click OK, the entry is saved. Then you can use Ctrl–1 (number one) to get to the Genealogy Club from anywhere in AOL when you're online.

Now double-click on Sign On. When the program connects, type in the password you chose (later, you can input your password in Members, then Personal Choices, which will automate your connection for flash sessions). A few moments later you'll be online. The very first screen will tell you whether you have private mail. If not, choose the Go To Main Menu, shown in Fig. 9-3. From here, you can click on Clubs & Interests to find the Genealogy area, or use the Go To list keystrokes.

Figure 9-3

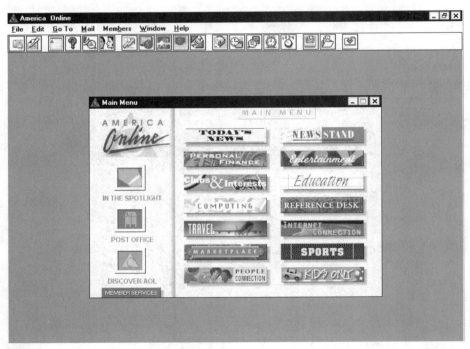

The main menu of AOL can take you to Clubs and Interests, where the Genealogy Club is. Or you can use the Go To menu from the menu bar at the top of the screen.

The resources

When you arrive at Genealogy Club, your choices are shown in Fig. 9-4. The icons that look like pieces of paper represent text files. You can read them online, save them to your disk, and so on. The file folders are links to another menu; the red intertwined lines are an interactive area. The pin and card icon is for the messages, the tiny diskettes for files, and the two faces for live, online chat.

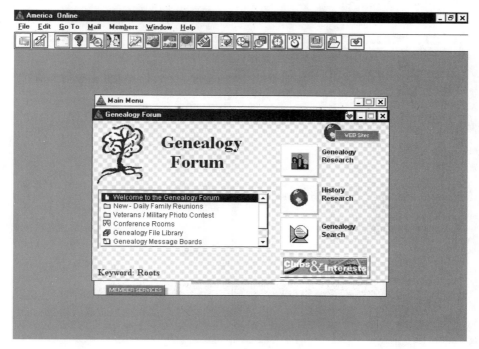

Figure 9-4

The Genealogy area on AOL has lots of choices.

You also have easy access to 6 to 12 sites on the World Wide Web that AOL's genealogy sysops find useful; this list is updated often. If you choose this one, the AOL Web browser will open in the AOL window and you'll be connected to that site. I'll discuss the browser later.

To choose any of them, double-click on one with the mouse. If you choose the message area, you'll get the screen in Fig. 9-5. This screen explains the categories and their uses. Clicking on any one topic area will call up the screen in Fig. 9-6. The first time you visit, all messages (sometimes more than 10,000 in an area, in different topics!) will be new to you. As it's impractical to read even the subject lines of that many, and as AOL won't let you search them, choose Find Since . . . to see just the new messages in the last day. After that, you can look at just the new topics and messages since your last visit, and things will be more manageable.

Figure 9-5

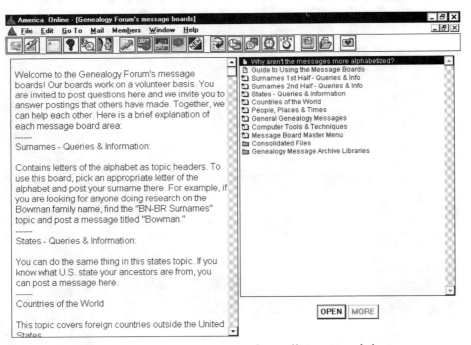

The Genealogy Forum's message area is logically arranged, but not searchable, one of AOL's major flaws.

AOL's greatest weakness is that all forum message reading must be done online (except the archives of messages, described later), while the meter is ticking. You can't download forum messages to disk as you can with any other commercial online service, and there's no

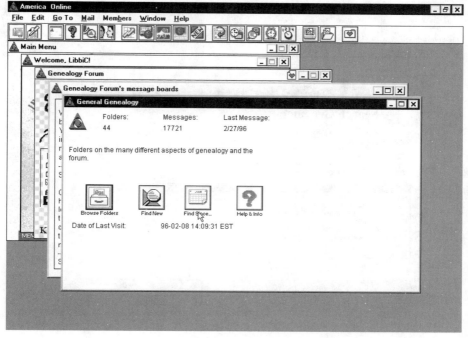

Figure 9-6

The first time you visit the forum, click on New Since and read the last day's messages.

provision in the program for replying to forum messages except while connected.

If you're new to genealogy, check out the Genealogy Research area (see Figure 9-7). This provides conference areas, message boards, software and text files, tips and tricks for the beginner, and a question-and-answer area called Dear Myrtle. You'll also find a calendar of genealogy events across the U.S., lists of genealogical societies, and more to help you get started.

History Research is similar, only it's for finding background on a particular historical topic that might help you decide the best place to search for that ancestor.

Search Genealogy (see Fig. 9-8) will find text articles in all the genealogy areas that match your input keywords. Searching for

Figure 9-7

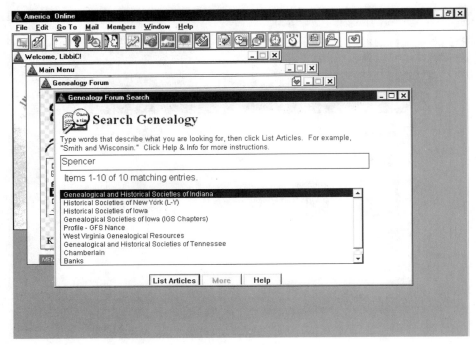

The Research area has files on how to do genealogy and data uploaded by members on their family lines.

Spencer will not only get some GEDCOMs, but also information about historical societies in Spencer counties in several states. Unfortunately, this doesn't search any message bases, which is AOL's second major deficiency.

The Consolidated Files area is where surnames and e-mail screen names from all the postings (archived on AOL from 1989 to the present) are stored. You can download it to your disk; it's a text file, so you can use a word processor or text editor to search through the several hundred thousand names offline, to find out who else is researching your lines. Their AOL user names are included, so you can e-mail them. You'll also find old messages sorted alphabetically by surname search here; use them similarly.

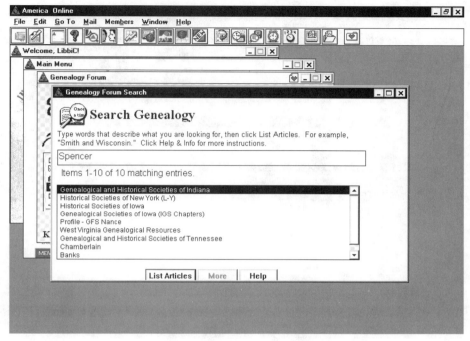

Figure 9-8

Search Genealogy finds your keywords in text files, but not forum messages.

⇨ Flash mail

If you have AOL for Windows 2.0 or AOL for Macintosh 2.5.1 or later, you can have AOL fetch you mail (and Usenet newsgroups) for you automatically or at the click of a button. This is fast and easy, and really saves on the connect time. The new messages are put under Mail, Read Incoming Mail, and you can save your replies on disk for the next flash session.

To set it up, choose Mail and then Flash Sessions from the AOL program menu bar (see Figure 9-9). If you choose Walk Me Through, the program will ask you a series of questions about how you want your automatic mail retrievals to go, and then you're all set. Each screen name that you use flash sessions with has its own incoming mailbox, outgoing mailbox, and download manager for files. Flash

Figure 9-9

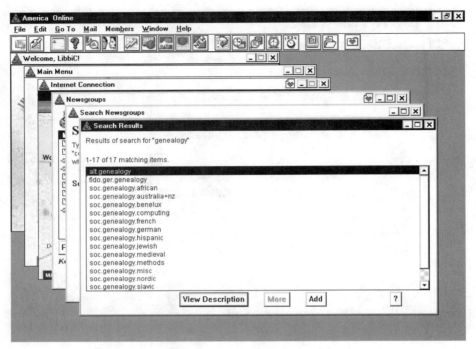

Descriptions of Usenet newsgroups on AOL.

session settings (schedules, actions to be performed, etc.) and preferences apply to all screen names. You can set it up to be performed at several different intervals, and you can choose what days of the week the flash sessions will be run.

Note that your scheduled flash sessions can occur only if the America Online application is open at the scheduled time. You'll be reminded of this if you try to close the application while there are flash sessions scheduled. The number of items that can be stored in a flash sessions mailbox is limited only by the amount of available disk space on your computer, but the largest message that can be stored and displayed is 64K.

To use your AOL account to subscribe to a mail list such as Roots-L, simply send an e-mail message to the proper listserver, and the messages will begin to pour in!

Usenet on AOL

AOL has a Usenet reader, and it's quite easy to use. Click on Internet from the main menu and then click on Usenet (or use the keyword Usenet). Click on Search Newsgroups, type genealogy, and read the descriptions, as shown in Fig. 9-9. When you find one you think you'd like, click on Add to choose the ones you want to subscribe to.

Now you're ready to read; close the subscribing window and choose Read My Newsgroups. The message headers (subject lines) will appear, and you can read and/or reply to one by double-clicking on it. But of course, all of this is while the meter is ticking.

If you want to read and reply to these offline, use the keyword Usenet and click on Read Off-line. From the list on the left, put the ones you want included in your flash sessions in the box on the right (see Fig. 9-10). Then go to Mail, Flash Sessions and put check marks in the

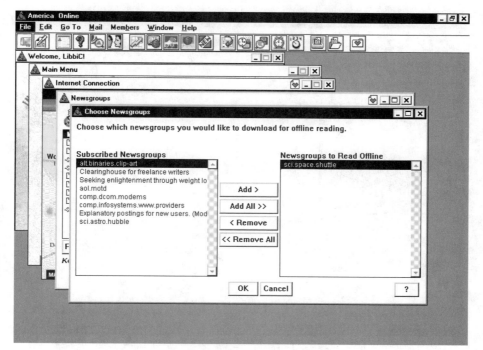

Figure 9-10

To read Usenet offline and therefore more cheaply, set the preferences in both the Usenet area and your Flash Sessions setting.

Retrieve and Send Newsgroup Messages boxes. Your flash sessions will now be longer, but all the reading and replying will be offline. To read Usenet messages retrieved by flash sessions, click on Mail and then Personal Filing Cabinet. At the bottom will be your Usenet articles.

Web browsing with AOL

America Online's software now offers a Web browser. It's part of the program, and you don't have to do anything special to call it up. It's just one more window in the AOL desktop.

When you click on the little world icon, you open up a list of Web sites, and clicking on one of these will launch the AOL Web browser (see Fig. 9-11). As a browser, AOL's is a little clunky. It loads pictures, sounds, and other files very slowly. To configure it, you can click on Members, Personal Choices, Preferences, and WWW; that's what to do if you don't want it to load pictures automatically on a page.

Figure 9-11

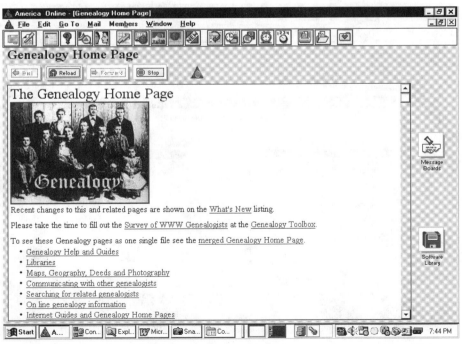

You can launch the Web browser from the Genealogy area, and you'll have links back to the files and messages there.

If you launch the browser from the Genealogy area, you'll still see icons to take you back to the genealogy messages and files. If you want to call up the browser without going to the Genealogy area first, simply choose Go To and type www in the keyword box. If you launch it yourself, you'll see a slightly different window with the favorite places, preferences, and URL input boxes (see Fig. 9-12).

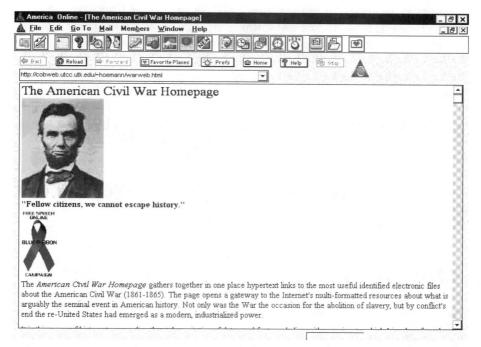

Figure 9-12

When you launch the Web browser yourself, you have more controls over the tool bar.

Also, AOL's browser doesn't recognize the HTML commands for centering, tables, and many other things people do to make their pages look nice. So don't be surprised if pages on AOL look a lot different from what you've seen in books and magazines.

Still, for a first shot at World Wide Web browsing, AOL's software is at least easy to understand. If you don't want to see a page that's loading after all, click on the Stop button. If you like a page and want to come again sometime, click on the little folder with a heart, located

on the toolbar, and put in the URL. This will save it in your favorite places folder. If you've read about a genealogy page you'd like to visit, type it in the URL box at the top and press Enter.

AOL's Internet offerings

Many people are putting genealogical data into their home pages on the web. AOL now allows personal home pages at no extra charge. Great programs are available to inexpensively and easily convert GEDCOM data directly into home pages (one is GED2HTML, a $20 shareware program by Eugene W. Stark, found at www.cs.sunysb .edu/~stark).

AOL lets you compose your own home page and gives you up to two megabytes of space to store it. Use the keywords Web Diner, choose Free! How to Put Up Your Website, and you'll get all the details.

AOL also has a gopher and an FTP server. They work pretty much as I described in chapter 6. You can either click on Internet Connection from the main menu or use the keywords FTP and Gopher.

The people

The club leader is GFAGeorge. Other club assistants are GFATerry, GFABeth, GFARoben, and GFADrew; there are also coordinators for various special-interest groups (SIGs). You'll find the complete, updated list by clicking on Welcome to the Genealogy Forum at the keywords Roots Window.

When you post a message introducing yourself, you'll receive an e-mail message explaining the major points of the Genealogy Club. Either GFARobin or GFATerry will send your mailbox a Genealogy Club newsletter occasionally, but they go a few months between issues, so read the Club Business message board to get the latest news.

In addition to message boards and software libraries, the sysops hold regular "live" Genealogy Club meetings. The regularly scheduled

general conferences, or meetings, are on Sunday nights at 9:00 and Thursday nights at 10:00, Eastern Standard Time.

Formal meetings, which are on a planned topic with observed protocol, are held the first Sunday of each month and the second Thursday of each month. There are also several special-interest groups. One is an African-American SIG, which meets on Tuesday nights at 9:00 EST. Others are a Scottish/Irish SIG, which meets on Friday nights at 9 p.m. EST; a Southern Genealogy SIG, which meets on Saturday nights at 10:00 EST; and a Reunion SIG with meetings on Thursday nights at 9:00 EST.

Some meetings are hosted by club assistants and members. You can drop by the "ancestral digs" any time to see what's going on. Most of the meetings are informal; others have a special speaker who will present a lecture for about 15 to 20 minutes, after which you can type in questions. Also, you might want to catch the Beginners' Class, which is held every second and fourth Tuesday at 10:00 p.m. EST in the Ancestral Digs conference room. Other special-interest groups form and hold meetings. Check the message boards for announcements about various other group meetings.

When you want to conference with people, double-click (or Tab to highlight and hit Return) on Online Chat in the main menu of the Genealogy Club. You can type your messages in the white bar below the main messages area. When you click on Send, your message will appear to the others in the room.

Clicking on the People button will tell you about the other people in that room. You can color-code each person so you can tell messages apart more easily. And you can select individual people in the room and send them private, real-time messages.

You can also "squelch" conversations; say you're talking with three people in the room about Civil War records, while three other people are talking about the War of 1812. You can click the People button and temporarily make the other conversation invisible until your discussion is done. Or you can all agree to go to another room by clicking on Rooms and creating your own space. The Help & Info

button, as you would expect, will tell you more about how this function works.

Messages are encouraged

The message boards operate on a volunteer basis; you're invited to post any questions you might have and are encouraged to post a reply in answer to anybody else's question for which you have information. Also, don't forget to post the family names you're looking for in the message board under the Surname category.

If you need help downloading or learning how to use the front-end software, you can go to the Members Helping Members area and post questions. I recommend this because it's free (it won't cost you any online charges) and is geared for beginners as they learn their way around America Online.

If you choose to upload a file to the Genealogy Forum, put it in plain ASCII text format. That way more people can read it. Most people can read an ASCII text file, but only a few might have the same word processor that you use.

GFATerry would be glad to help you if you have any questions; she's also the director of a family history center (FHC) and would be glad to answer questions about the use of an FHC.

"I have been working in the Genealogy Club for years," GFATerry says. "It started in about 1986 when I joined Q-Link (the first network from the owners of AOL for Commodore computers). I worked in the genealogy area of Q-Link as a staff member. When AOL came about and when my husband and I upgraded to an IBM, we joined this network. I was already a staff member on Q-Link (owned by the same company), so it was possible to become one here, too.

"My duties cover many things. I greet the new members, answer some of the questions on the message boards, do some librarian duties as I help make files go live, archive message boards, host meetings—well, there's a lot to do, but I enjoy it very much."

The network has helped her with her genealogy as well, and she says: "I have made contact with several folks by posting the surnames I was looking for. I even found a distant cousin! This all works on a volunteer principle—folks helping other folks. One of them lived in Connecticut, where I have ancestors, and looked up some information for me. In turn I looked up some information for her from Georgia. There are helpful text files in the genealogy libraries, too."

⇨ Questions and answers

Over the Internet, I interviewed the head sysop (host in AOL parlance), GFAGeorge, and found him a most helpful gentleman:

Q. How long have you been teleresearching genealogy?

A. I started teleresearching genealogy the day after I got my first modem, though it might have been the same day. That was in 1987.

Q. How long have you been associated with AOL's genealogy BBS?

A. I was one of the original beta testers of the America Online software back when it was strictly an Apple II service known as AppleLink Personal Edition. There must have been about 30 of us from the Boston Computer Society who started in February of 1988. I had grown up with genealogy, since it was a passion of my father's also, so it was only natural that I wanted to start the genealogy forum on this new service.

Q. What are the best features about AOL's BBS?

A. The best feature of the America Online Genealogy Forum would have to be the ability to get 48 people from all over the country together in one online room and talk about genealogy. It's great because you don't have to leave the comfort of your own home, but you can get all kinds of questions answered. We also have an outstanding collection of downloadable files. We have programs and utilities for IBM-compatible systems, Macintosh systems, even Apple II systems. We have hundreds of lineage files, GEDCOM database files, genealogical records files, tiny tafel files, alphabetic surname files, and logs of past meetings. We have a surnames area where anyone can

post a message about someone they are looking for. We also have message boards that are designed to exchange information about computer- and noncomputer-related genealogical subjects.

Q. What do you hope to improve in the future?

A. We have started several special-interest groups (SIGs), which are becoming quite popular. On different nights we have beginners' classes, an African-American genealogy SIG, a Southern SIG, and a Scot-Irish SIG. In the near future we hope to expand these offerings with expanded beginner services, a New England research SIG, and a reunion software users' group.

Q. How helpful are the online real-time conversations?

A. The online real-time conversations are great. We have many meetings where somebody finds a cousin or a possible link. It is also an opportunity to chat with people who have a similar interest, and you don't have to go out at night or drive into a big city to do it. Also, unlike the big genealogy groups that get together only once every month or so, we can get out and talk almost any night of the week.

Q. What are the things that are expected of the members?

A. We expect people to come and share their passion for genealogy. We expect nothing, but hope that everyone will share what they have with the rest of us and have fun doing it. What we find is that people freely give of themselves and that we can have a good time while learning different ways of investigating the past.

 # Classes

Another AOL feature are the online genealogy courses. One is for experienced users who want to learn more about the available resources and LDS family history centers. You don't have to be an "advanced" genealogist to take this class; beginners will find useful information. Online interaction with the instructor can help you solve specific research problems and acquaint you in detail with resources available from the Salt Lake Family History Library. To join the class, sign on at the appointed time and go to the assigned "chat room."

The instructor presents material and the students ask questions. Each session lasts about two hours.

 # Tips and tricks

Like all services, some things are obvious about the best way to get around AOL and some aren't.

Unlike many genealogy forums and indeed some other forums on AOL itself, the Genealogy Club has no search function for either the messages or the data files. You simply have to click through menu after menu to see whether your topics of interest have been covered. Messages and files are grouped in broad categories, however, and that helps some. When you find a file title you think is interesting, double-click on it or use the Tab key to highlight it and press Return. A screen describing the file, who uploaded it, how long it will take to download, and other details will appear. You can flag several files for batch downloading, or for retrieval by flash sessions.

On a related note, AOL's latest software will support 28.8 Kbps. Most connections to AOL, however, are still at 9,600 bps. Some 28.8-Kbps sites are up and running, but the majority are at the slower pace. So some large files might cost a dollar or two of connect charges to download. Remember that connect charges are suspended when you upload a file to the system, so don't hesitate to contribute your research!

One way to get faster access: If you have a TCP/IP dial-up account, the new AOL software will connect via PPP. So you could dial your local ISP as fast as your modem can go, and connect via TCP/IP. Choose Setup, Edit Location, and, in the Network drop-down box, TCP/IP. After that, dial the ISP first, then launch AOL, then connect.

The AOL message system won't tell you that a message you left previously on the genealogy message board has been answered, nor that you have a message in the Genealogy Club. All messages are to everyone (all). You have to remember which category and topic you employed to leave the message, search for new messages under that

topic, and read them all to see whether one of them answers your previous post. If you want a particular person's attention, send private e-mail to that person's AOL mailbox.

AOL has no way for you to download forum messages and read them offline. All messages must be read and answered online in the clubs.

The F3 key will log you off AOL from anywhere in the system, although it always asks first.

Typing Ctrl–F4 will close the topmost window, which is usually faster than clicking on the upper left corner. You can also switch from one window to another with a mouse click on the new window.

AOL's e-mail is connected to the Internet, and you can use it to get anonymous FTP files by mail.

Once you read a mail message, it goes into your "old mail" file. While online, click on the Mail menu and choose Mail You've Read to refer to it again. If you want to save it to your computer, use the File function to write it to a text file.

10

Delphi's custom forums

D ELPHI is a service of General Videotex Corporation, a developer of interactive and online services based in Cambridge, Massachusetts. It has two membership plans. The 10/4 plan is $10 per month and includes the first four hours of use; additional use is $4 per hour. The 20/20 advantage plan is $20 per month, includes 20 hours of use, and is only $1.80 per hour for additional time. The Internet service option is an extra $3 per month, including the transfer of 10 megabytes (the equivalent of about 3,000 typewritten pages). Access during business hours via SprintNet or Tymnet carries a surcharge; you can telnet from your ISP by typing telnet delphi.com and from there log in just as if you had dialed. The service is available 24 hours a day, but evenings and weekends are cheaper. Delphi's address and additional information are:

1030 Massachusetts Ave.
Cambridge, MA 02138
800-695-4005 (voice)
800-365-4636 (modem)
username@delphi.com (e-mail)

As of this writing, Rupert Murdoch was desperately trying to turn Delphi into an AOL/CIS/Prodigy clone, but the software was still in the testing phase. Because its text interface makes it one of the most reliable online services, I'm going to show you Delphi in that form. If it goes the GUI route, you can expect the format to be much like that of other commercial online services. Still, I hope the sense of community will survive the transition, when and if it comes.

Delphi has been around longer than many online systems, but it's not very well known. It was the first online encyclopedia, started in 1982, but they've been growing and adding services steadily ever since. It was named for the site of the famous Greek oracle. For the Greeks, Delphi was the center in which opposing creative forces—the rational creativity of Apollo and the irrational creativity of Dionysus—merged and from which all creative forms emerged. There's a little more of Dionysus than Apollo here, but both are amply represented.

Delphi uses an informal software setup. It has large file libraries containing both documents and software, and fun is an important component. Delphi is one of the few online services that doesn't require a special interface to make the service usable, but if you want you can download a shareware program called D-Lite. Registration for this program is $45, and I'll describe it later in this chapter. Try the newly introduced Rainbow by typing GO GROUPS 250. Another option is called Internav. It's free, but it doesn't do offline reading as D-Lite does. Use the command GO USING INTERNAV to download it and try it out.

Logging on

Delphi is on SprintNet, Tymnet, and DataPack in Canada, not to mention its regional services in Boston, Kansas City, Miami, and Argentina.

Set your parameters to 8-N-1 and your terminal emulation to VT100 or VT52. My computer in an ANSI terminal setting just didn't like Delphi's way of talking. The best way to join is to call 800-695-4005 and talk to a representative, who can give you a password, user name, and the nearest phone number to dial. User names on Delphi are all lowercase with no spaces. Your user name need not reflect your real name, but once you have it you're stuck with it unless you close that account and start another. When you order something online, though, and at certain SIGs, you'll be asked your real-life name before you can participate. Your user name also becomes your Internet address, in the following form: *user_name*@delphi.com.

Delphi's vocabulary

Delphi uses terminology that's a bit different from other places you've seen so far in this book:

Conference Typing online, real-time messages to others on Delphi is called a conference here. You can conference from any menu, setting up several conversations at once. You can block out people, leave to check something out (a buffer will tell you what was said while you were gone), and even upload a file in conference mode.

Forum The place to exchange messages and files is a forum, which is usually found in a menu for a SIG (special-interest group) or club.

Mail Mail from the main menu is not just e-mail (the command MAIL MAIL from the main menu). In Delphi, mail comes in many forms: telex (an extra charge), translation between English and many languages, the workspace, and fax. The workspace is available from almost any menu. It has a different prompt (WS>), and it lets you transfer, store, edit, copy, delete, view, and back up files. You can use it with e-mail, conferences, forums, and databases.

Database Database is the name for a files area (analogous to the library on CompuServe). Most files are free. Transfer protocols include ASCII (tricky in VT100 mode), kermit, Xmodem, Ymodem, and Zmodem. Uploading is free of connect charges.

Bye This is the quickest way to log off from any prompt. Ctrl–Z will take you up one menu level from anywhere in the system.

 # Initiation to the mysteries

When your user name and password are accepted, you come into the main menu, which might have some announcements. It will look like this:

```
MAIN Menu:
Business and Finance          News, Weather, and Sports
Computing Groups              Reference and Education
Conference                    Shopping
Entertainment and Games       Travel and Leisure
Groups and Clubs              Using DELPHI
Internet Services             Workspace
Mail                          HELP
Member Directory              EXIT
MAIN>What do you want to do?
Please respond.
```

With the Using Delphi Settings, however, you can change the first menu you see from the main menu to Custom Forums.

You can chain commands to save time. For instance, you can type CUSTOM for the customized groups, 124 for Irish Ancestry or 68 for Roots, then FOR for the messages (forum) or DATA for the files database. But at the main menu you could type GO CUS 68 FORUM instead, and you'll go straight there. This is what D-Lite does for you (explained later in the chapter). The following is a quick rundown of your choices from the main menu before you go on to Custom Forum 68:

Business and Finance This is where you'll find UPI Business News fees, a SIG for business-minded people, stock and commodity quotes, an online brokerage, and Dow Jones averages, plus other economic news and advice.

Computing Groups These are the SIGs, forums, and databases for several brands and flavors of computers.

Conference This allows you to chat online with people who are in the same menu as you at the moment. First, type WHO to see who else is around. Their user names will be displayed, and whether they're conferring. If they are, the group will have a name. To join a group that's conferring, type JOIN *group_name*. To page someone to come and enter a new group with you, type PAGE *user_name*. You must preface most of the conference commands with a slash (/) to distinguish them from text when using them in a conversation. To see a list of all of the commands, enter /HELP. /SEND allows you to send a direct message to any users currently on the system, unless they've used the /GAG command to prevent interruptions. The best way to learn about conferences is to go in there and try them out. Don't be shy; ask questions. You'll find that other users are very helpful and genuinely enjoy sharing their knowledge with new people.

Delphi/Regional This will take you to gateways for the regional setups of Delphi. Each has some unique features, and some have tie-ins with local universities.

Entertainment and Games This includes forums, real-time games, e-mail games, and more.

Groups and Clubs From Games to Writers, from Flight Simulators to the Environment, the general-interest SIGs are here.

The Internet From here you can visit the Internet SIG, as well as telnet, FTP, and gopher.

Mail As explained previously, this contains a wide range of communications services, both hardcopy and e-mail.

Member Directory This allows you to look someone up on Delphi by either user name or real name. Also, you can read short biographies of users here, and leave one of your own to introduce yourself to the other members.

News, Weather, Sports Newswire feeds on these subjects, movies, and more.

Reference and Education Here's where you'll find New Parent's Network, encyclopedias, medical-topic SIGs, and, for a surcharge, the Dialog research service.

Shopping Delphi has quite a lineup of online merchants, many of them related to computer software and hardware. But you'll also find greeting cards, gifts, books, and so on.

Travel and Leisure This contains not only the *Official Airlines Guide* and *Easy Sabre*, but profiles of cities and countries you might want to visit, information on lodging and ground transportation, tours, cruises, and convention services. You can even apply for a travel Visa online, handy for overseas ancestor hunting!

Using Delphi This should be the new user's first stop. Set your capture on and download all 31 of the tips from this menu. If you have a specific problem, there's a new-user SIG where sysops and administrators will help you. You're not billed for Delphi time while in this menu, so make good use of it.

Help This provides short descriptions of the commands from any menu.

Exit From the main menu, Exit will log you off. From any other menu, it will take you back one menu. Ctrl–Z will do the same thing. Also, if things are scrolling by too fast for you, Ctrl–S will stop the output until you hit Ctrl–Q.

Chain of command

You can get along just fine with Delphi's menus, but don't forget you can chain commands and selections to move past several menus at once. The Go command is the easiest way to do this, and it works with all the menus except e-mail. Exit, as in Exit Internet Forum, can take you from one SIG to another. You can change from one database topic to another using Set.

By far, the most popular feature on Delphi is conferencing. It works much the same as other conference systems, and makes Delphi seem small and cozy, with newcomers warmly welcomed. Delphi, however, is a large and powerful service. Explore and confer, research, and recommend. It's not the navel of the universe yet, but you can definitely increase your wisdom here.

 # Custom Forum 68

Started in August 1993, Custom Forum 68 (nicknamed Searching Our Roots or Genealogy) has about 200 active members, and is growing quickly. To get there manually from the main menu (at the Main> prompt), type:

```
CUS 68 FORUM
```

And you'll get the screen in Fig. 10-1. Jeff Seawell, the host or sysop of this custom forum, is in his 30s and lives in Lynchburg, Virginia. He's a second-shift computer operator for B&W Nuclear Technologies (BWNT) in Lynchburg, a company that services power-generating facilities worldwide. He graduated with a two-year degree in Computer Information Systems from Central Virginia Community College. He also enjoys fishing, coin collecting, computer programming, and genealogy. In fact, he discovered this group and genealogy at about the same time.

"In June of 1993, my grandfather, in New Jersey, had died and I went to the funeral. Not having lived in New Jersey since a child, I met all these relatives I never knew of before. I listened intently to all the

Figure 10-1

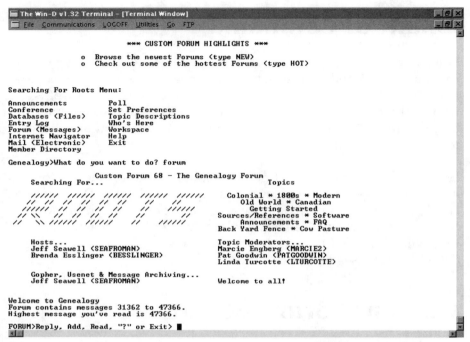

The opening screen of Delphi's Roots Forum shows the topic areas. Topics are covered both in the forum (messages) and in the database (Files area).

family stories they told and found them quite fascinating. It sparked an interest in learning a little about these folks. When I got back home, I read up on the subject of genealogy and learned about some of the means of obtaining information about past relatives, one of them being commercial online services. I had been a member of Delphi for a few months so I explored it to see what it might have had to offer. I came upon Custom Forum 68, which had just formed about a month prior. I mostly lurked a while because the folks who were posting messages were obviously more experienced at this than I was and I was afraid that they wouldn't want to be bothered with my beginner questions. Eventually, I posted a question and was surprised to get back several responses from these folks. I learned folks on this forum would help, but I would have to ask a question first."

Though Bob Cote and Bob Maddigan had gotten the ball rolling, momentum started slowing down in the new group. Then the original

hosts had to drop out, and Jeff found himself the new host. "I didn't feel the most qualified person for the position," he says, "but I didn't want to see the forum close up just because it didn't have a forum host."

Seawell says that what he enjoys about being the forum host is helping people, especially newcomers, with some of their research. Sometimes he's able to do specific research for folks and at other times all he can offer is advice and how-to information. "But it's extremely rewarding, when the bit of information I've passed on makes a difference in someone's research. It's kind of like being able to relive the moment I learned something new about my own ancestry. And it also inspires me to keep trying, even when things get a little slow in my own research."

Since taking over in early 1994, he has made a few changes, as requested by some of the active members, and he asked an experienced member, Brenda Esslinger (BEsslinger), to be cohost of the forum. Things seem to be working out well, so far, but there are still a few forum enhancements that he'd like to make, so it's bound to get better. The menu for the forum looks like this:

```
Custom Forum 68> menu
Genealogy Menu:
Conference                 Exit
Database                   Mail
Forum (Messages)           Poll
Usenet Discussion Groups   Workspace
Custom Forum 68>What do you want to do?
```

To read the messages, type FORUM at this menu. Delphi allows you to search the message base with the Directory command. It will begin this search at your last-read message; if you want to search the entire message base, you need to first reset your High message.

You can search the messages by sender, receiver, and subject line. The following shows how to search for messages with the word *spencer* in the subject line:

```
FORUM Menu:
ADD New Message (Thread)    FORWARD Message by Mail
REPLY To Current Message    DELETE Message
READ Message(s)             EDIT a Posted Message
```

```
FOLLOW Thread                   NEXT Message
BACK to Previous Message        TOPICS (Set/Show)
DIRECTORY of Messages           HIGH Message (Set/Show)
MAIL                            HELP
TAG Interesting Message         EXIT
FILE Message into Workspace
FORUM>Reply, Add, Read, "?" or Exit? Directory subject spencer
```

If you want to search for two words together (GENEALOGY PROGRAM, for example) use quotation marks around the search string. To read everything since you last signed on, type (at the Forum> prompt):

```
READ NEW
```

To read your messages, type:

```
READ WAITING
```

You can save messages to your workspace, reply to them, tag them for reference later, and so on.

 # Files

When you're ready to explore the files, type (at the Forum> prompt):

```
exit
```

and at the next Custom Forum 68> prompt, type:

```
DA DA 68 (Genealogy)
```

The database, you'll recall, is where the files are. This database is shared by several custom forums—each having just one topic. The topics are listed by forum number and name. If you simply type DATABASE at the menu prompt, without chaining commands, you'll see the following menu:

```
Databases Available Menu:
68  -  Searching for Roots        119 -  LinksVille USA
73  -  InfoTech Forum             52  -  The Comics Forum
90  -  United Methodists          40  -  Parrothead Madness
```

```
81  -  RPG Forum                    2   -  Desolate Weyr
123 -  Rotary Club Forum            92  -  Family Forum
88  -  Dittoheads Unlimited         25  -  DRAGONet
95  -  Telecommunications Forum     110 -  Educational Technology
102 -  Windows NT Forum
TOPIC>Which topic?
```

The database manager for all these files is Dick Evans (e-mail ellisco); he can help you with problems. Type 68 at the prompt following the lists of available databases, and you'll get the proper set of files, as follows:

```
TOPIC>Which topic? 68
DBASES:68 > menu
68  -  Searching for Roots Menu:
Directory of Groups      Set Topic
Read (and Download)      Submit (Upload)
Search (by Keyword)      Workspace
Narrow search            Help
Widen search             Exit
DBASES:68 > (Dir, Read, Set, Exit) search SPENCER
```

The Directory of Groups shows you all the groups sharing this database, and you can switch to another topic using the command Set Topic. Read and Download are for when you know exactly what you want. Searching by keyword is how you find out about specific files; the previous menu shows a search for Spencer. The search takes about 10 seconds, and then you can ask for a directory of the hits; narrow the search if it finds too many and widen the search if it finds too few. Workspace, Help, and Exit work just as they do on *every* Delphi menu. To list all the files:

```
DBASES:68 > DIR FULL NS
```

This is a small sample of the files you'll find in Forum 68's database:

Name: LHA compression program
Type: Program
Date: 24-Feb-1994 01:18 by PZAVON
Size: 44381
Count: 3

Name: Brothers Keeper, module 4 of 4
Type: Program
Date: 24-Feb-1994 00:10 by PZAVON
Size: 440104
Count: 0

Name: Roots surname list, 2/94 UPD
Type: Program
Date: 7-Feb-1994 19:09 by STANB
Size: 160952
Count: 12

FAM-LIST: February update for the Roots Surname List from VM1.NODAK.EDU.

Name: December '93 forum messages A9FB
Type: Program
Date: 31-Jan-1994 01:34 by SEAFROMAN
Size: 97294
Count: 6

A zipped text file of Custom Forum 68 (Genealogy Forum) forum messages for the month of December 1993. Part 3 of 3. Requires PKUNZIP204g.

Name: NQF Index
Type: Program
Date: 20-Jan-1994 01:32 by SEAFROMAN
Size: 146793
Count: 20

This is a surname index for the NQF (National Query Forum). It is a listing of the surnames submitted to the NQF, accompanied with the issue number in which these names can be found. It contains a utility viewer to view the list, and the viewer allows you to make searches of the list. There is also a utility to convert surnames to their Soundex representation. This viewer can be used to view other text files as well (an added bonus). Keywords are OTHER, NQF, INDEX, SURNAMES, and 01-20-94.

Name: Estidate Genealogical Date Estim
Type: Program
Date: 28-Oct-1993 00:57 by AJMORRIS
Size: 165084
Count: 4

A freeware program that calculates the target range of dates for vital events such as births, marriages, and deaths based on known facts and probable or logical human limits. Can be used to narrow the search for a particular person to the correct time range, or to see if "possible" relations are within realistic time limits. Keywords are OTHER, ESTIDATE DATES ESTIMATE, and VITAL RECORD RESEARCH.

Name: Spencer Genealogical & Historical
Type: Text
Date: 13-Sep-1993 14:49 by ETRAVEL
Size: 1920
Count: 6

A short description of SGHS, our journal and our biannual meeting. Keywords are OTHER, FAMILY, SOCIETIES, ASSOCIATIONS, and SPENCER.

Accessing soc.genealogy.misc through Custom Forum 68

Exit from the database back to the Custom Forum 68 menu, and you'll see a choice called Usenet. This menu choice is a shortcut to the genealogy newsgroups. This choice will bring you to the following menu:

```
Custom Forum 68>What do you want to do? usenet
```

As discussed before, alt.genealogy is a spurious newsgroup that won't go away; soc.genealogy.misc is the Usenet mirror of Roots-L. Personal Favorites is a menu you build by visiting Usenet and saving your preferred newsgroups.

If you choose 2 from this menu, you'll be taken directly to the newsreader and given a choice of the date from which you want to read. Then you can read, reply, and so on, as described in chapter 4. When you exit from there, you go back to Custom Forum 68.

 # The Internet is here

Delphi provides full access to the Internet, including real-time electronic mail, an excellent gopher, file transfers with FTP, and remote log-ins to other Internet hosts using telnet. Be warned, however, that the fastest available connection to Delphi right now is 9,600 baud, which can be a problem for really large files. Also, complaints often appear on the Internet forum that programs FTP'd from UNIX hosts to Delphi often come back corrupted. If you really get into Internet connections, this could be cumbersome for you.

A nice feature here on Delphi is a gopher dedicated to genealogy. Type GO CUSTOM 68 and choose the Internet from that menu to get to it (see Fig. 10-2). It's filled with genealogy-related sites and features to help you find files, and offers the only commercial-service direct link to Brigham Young University's genealogy gopher. It also ties into Delphi's gopher to allow you to wander through the Internet. With this

Figure 10-2

```
Genealogy>What do you want to do? internet

Type HELP for a list of commands

Searching For Roots Gopher
Page 1 of 1

1    PERSONAL FAVORITES                              Menu
2    A WARM WELCOME FROM JIMBO_SOUTH                 Text
3    ABOUT DELPHI'S GOPHER                           Menu
4    ABOUT THE CF68 GENEALOGY GOPHER (26-JAN-1995)   Text
5    US GENEALOGY GOPHERS                            Menu
6    USENET DISCUSSION NEWSGROUPS                    Menu
7    WWW - CONNECT TO ANY SITE                       Menu
8    DELPHI'S MAIN GOPHER (INTERNET SIG)             Menu

Enter Item Number, ?, or EXIT: █
```

The Delphi genealogy gopher leads you to a text-based Web browser, Usenet genealogy groups, and various gophers at other sites beyond Delphi. Read the About files (text) before you take off!

gopher, you can use Veronica to search for entries based on keywords. Or you can let Archie find a file for you, pick the site to FTP from, and download the file to your computer.

All this puts the Internet in your hands. If you want to add other genealogy-related locations to the CF68 gopher, drop a note to Jimbo_South (Jim Southworth), along with instructions on how you got there, and he'll add it to the Delphi gopher. If you're having trouble with the gopher or would like something particular in the CF68 genealogy gopher, drop a note to Jim and he'll do his best to help. Getting out of the gopher is a Ctrl–C or EX away.

 # Irish genealogy: Custom Forum 124

Soon after the Genealogy SIG started, a new one popped up for Irish genealogy—Custom Forum 124. This is the first message you'll get from this forum:

```
18OCT93-2003 General Discussion
Irish Genealogy
```

```
From: AJMORRIS    To: ALL
Is anyone out there doing Irish research? I'm the host of this new forum
so perhaps I should introduce myself. I have been doing genealogical
research professionally for over ten years now, specializing (yes, you
guessed it) in Irish ancestry. I also sell genealogy and history books on
microfiche, as well as MS-DOS software and databases. My own roots go
back to the Norman clan Morris, one of the Tribes of Galway, and a
Slattery line from the north of Tipperary. My direct Morris immigrant
ancestor was George Morris from county Mayo, who settled in Canada ca.
1833.
Andrew J. Morris, P.O. Box 535, Farmington, MI 48332
```

It didn't take long for people to discover this new forum, and the messages, files, and sections have grown. It now has seven topic areas into which your messages can be placed:

General Discussion For chit-chat, introductions, anything that doesn't fit better elsewhere.

Placename For sorting out those frustrating Irish locations, or expressing interest in a particular area in Ireland.

Surname For names you're searching, surname origins, family lines, etc.

Finding Records For information on particular source material, Griffith's Valuation, parish registers, and the what/where/when of them.

Research Methods To share techniques that have worked for you—distribution studies, correspondence techniques, etc.

Books & Video Where to offer others your personal comments/reviews of Irish interest publications (books, videos, magazines, tapes, etc.).

Software The place to share your experience using genealogy software and sources that improve Irish research by computer.

The discussions there are lively, from "Who was Strongbow?" (the most famous and powerful of the Normans to lead the Norman conquest of Ireland, and his real name was Richard FitzGilbert de Clare, The Earl of

Pembroke, came the answer from AJMorris) to ships' passenger lists. It's not as busy as the general genealogy SIG, but it's always interesting. All the functions work here just as they do in Custom Forum 68.

 # Reading and deleting your mail

As I've mentioned before, Delphi is a good choice if you want to subscribe to Roots-L and have either the index or all the messages that the Internet mail list delivers to you. (Let me again strongly recommend the index feature!) Your personal mailbox at Delphi can send and receive messages all over the Internet. Listservers, FTP, and people can all send you mail as often as you like.

The catch is that these messages are stored in your personal workspace, which is unnecessary if you also have them on your disk at home. So you must learn how to clear the old messages out. First I'll show you how to read the mail. From a menu, type:

```
GO mail mail
```

Then type (at the Mail> prompt):

```
DIRECTORY
```

and look at the messages you have. You can download them, read them while online, answer them, and so on from this menu. When you've finished, it's very important to delete the messages to avoid surcharges for storage. The Delete command deletes either the message you're currently reading or the message you just read, and moves it to the wastebasket folder. You can also delete several messages by using a range or list of messages. When you enter the Exit or Purge commands, your wastebasket folder empties automatically.

To recover a message accidentally deleted (while it's still in the wastebasket folder), select the wastebasket folder, read the desired message, and move it to another folder. The format for the Delete command is:

```
DELETE [message_list]
```

D-Lite, the front end for Delphi

D-Lite, a front-end program to make life easier and cheaper on Delphi, is shareware and downloadable from the D-Lite SIG. The developer is Perry and he's very active and helpful. Once you have D-Lite installed, you won't need any other software to connect to Delphi. (Keep your old software for connecting to places other than Delphi.) To get to the D-Lite area, just type GO COMP D-Lite at the prompt.

You can download a trial version from the databases and try it out for 30 days. At the end of that time, if you've found it has made Delphi simpler and cheaper to use (as I did), register with Perry. If you have any problems or suggestions for adding new features, send e-mail to Perry (perry@delphi.com), or better yet leave a message in the D-Lite SIG so everyone can see the answer!

The first thing you need to do with D-Lite is set up your password so the log on is completely automatic. Type Delphi to start the program, and choose Settings from the first screen (you have to use arrow keys; D-Lite doesn't support a mouse). Enter the information. (Notice that your password won't appear, and the file storing it encodes the password. Just keep in mind that, if you forget it, you won't be able to use D-Lite to look it up!)

Once that's done, go to Utilities and Add a SIG. Tell D-Lite to look under Custom, then 68. From then on, you can manipulate your messages and files from the SIG menu.

 ## Using D-Lite to read Usenet

The newest version of D-Lite allows you to treat any Usenet newsgroup just like a Delphi SIG; it downloads the latest messages, uploads your replies, and allows you to read the results offline, with a text-string searcher if you like. To use the Usenet feature, do the following with D-Lite:

❶ Under Utilities, choose Install a News SIG and call it Usenet.

❷ Choose Usenet as the menu location when prompted.

❸ Go to the SIG menu, and choose Usenet.

❹ Under the Usenet menu, choose Add Newsgroups, and type in the newsgroups you want (soc.genealogy.misc).

Be certain that the last three items of that menu have a >> in front of them. That means that D-Lite will get, post, and update messages for you on the next automatic pass. If it doesn't, use the arrow keys to highlight each, pressing the Enter key until the >> appears.

Say you want an automatic pass without visiting soc.genealogy.misc. To disable a specific newsgroup, go to Edit Newsgroups and, in the dialog box, insert any word in front of it, such as NO or SKIP or REM. There must be a space between the word and the name of the newsgroup. To reenable the newsgroup, delete the word in front of the group. For example, soc.genealogy.misc in the dialog box will get all new soc.genealogy.misc messages the next automatic pass. But entering SKIP soc.genealogy.misc will cause D-Lite to skip it until SKIP is removed.

When you first add a newsgroup, the default is to download messages beginning at midnight of the current date. Afterwards, it will download messages beginning at the date and time of the most recently downloaded message. You can override this in two ways—by using the Change Date option, which starts downloading messages posted since midnight on the date you specify, or by editing the date in the newsgroup list. Dates and times are stored in the format *yymmdd hhmmss*, so 8:30 P.M. on 9/26/93 would be 930926 203000.

Internav for Delphi

Another front end for Delphi is Internav, available either for download online or in kits at your local computer store for about $30. The kit includes some online time on Delphi and the official guide.

Internav will automate your sessions only with special scripts and it isn't an offline reader like D-Lite, but it does make real-time sessions with Delphi and the Internet much more comprehensible. Online on

Delphi, type GO USING INTERNAV and choose Database to find the latest version and scripts.

⇨ **Rainbow**

Rainbow, introduced for Delphi in late 1994, is another robot program. Tell Rainbow what forums, Usenet newsgroups, and mail you want to retrieve, and it will do it. Rainbow allows you to attach sounds and colors to your messages if you want. However, there's no keyword search for retrieving forum messages and Usenet articles, as with D-Lite.

11

CompuServe's Roots Forum and WWW page

CHAPTER 11

C OMPUSERVE'S basic rate is $9.95 per month, which includes five free hours of online time, $2.95 a minute thereafter. They almost always have a "try the first month free" offer going; call the toll-free number for information. Access can be over a usual data-switching packet network or their new PPP connection, allowing you full Internet access with your membership.

As a CIS member, your Internet address is *member_number* @compuserve.com; just remember to replace the comma in the member number with a period. As of 1996, you can also choose a name in addition to the number, such as epcrowe@compuserve.com. The service is accessible 24 hours a day, but is cheapest between 6 P.M. and 6 A.M. local time. Its address and phone number are:

5000 Arlington Centre Blvd.
P.O. Box 20212
Columbus, OH 43220
800-848-8199 (phone)

CompuServe, the granddaddy of online services, has over two million subscribers; of those, over 10,000 a week visit the Roots Forum, according to sysop Dick Eastman. However, true to form for most CIS forums, only about five percent of those who visit actually leave messages. That's a lot of lurkers! Yet the forum sees plenty of action, and the files and messages are valuable and worthwhile. CompuServe's online genealogy resources have much to offer:

➤ Online Social Security death records (CompuTrace).

➤ Online telephone directories, both residential and commercial (Phone*File and Biz*File).

➤ Nearly 2,000 genealogy book reviews available online in the Roots Forum.

➤ Tables of contents for hundreds of genealogy magazines, which allow you to quickly find the articles you want.

➤ More than 8,000 genealogy-related files, including shareware and free genealogy programs for Windows, MS-DOS, Macintosh, UNIX, Amiga, and even older computers.

The members of the forum are varied. There are online assistant sysops and some recognized professional genealogists who drop in; other members are rank beginners. Many are in between. The members are just as cooperative, outgoing, and friendly as anywhere online; in my opinion, this is one of the best online hangouts for the telegenealogist.

Before I delve into the forum, however, let's look at the system as a whole. Owned by H&R Block, CompuServe is a worldwide communications network that was designed for business use. It has a wealth of financial, business, and institutional information, as well as online reference works and highly technical information services such as IQuest. It also has an astounding variety of online stores, including several bookstores, which have good prices on reference books. This is the part that costs so much more during the day, but if you're willing to pay the online charges, it's all available to any CompuServe member.

As it's a business, CompuServe charges for connect time, but strives to be competitive in its pricing. Once you know how to use the system well and how to take advantage of some of the front ends, you can keep your online charges within a moderate range.

Access

Many modems come packed with a $15 to $25 credit on CompuServe, complete with a trial membership number and password. Another way to get on is to buy a CompuServe membership kit or a CompuServe Information Manager (CIM) software package for around $35, which will also have the number and password to get you started. Or you can call the 800 number and talk to customer service.

Many people find it beneficial to use CIM until they know what forums they like best, because it allows you to look through what's there with an easy-to-use interface and not worry about which command to use next. (Use GO CIS SOFTWARE to download a copy.) It's available for DOS (DOSCIM), Windows (WinCIM), and Macintosh (MacCIM). Yet

CIM is designed to work while you're connected to CompuServe (that is, while the meter is running). It's a great way to learn your way around, but when you're online, time is literally money.

So I strongly recommend getting some sort of front-end software for CompuServe, once you know exactly where you want to go and what's there for you. This sort of program can perform your habitual chores automatically, thus saving you time (and therefore money). Switching to another program such as The CompuServe Navigator (Windows or Macintosh, GO DVORAK, or OzCIS, GO OZCIS, or TapCIS, GO TAPCIS), where all the commands for uploading and downloading messages and files are typed offline, can save you money. All these programs are shareware: you download a trial version from the forums and try it for a month, then you pay anywhere from $35 to $99 to get the full-featured program. Any one of these programs will pay for itself in reduced online costs, especially at higher speeds. No front-end program, though, saves you much money during online conferences.

"We recommend that new users use the CompuServe Information Manager (CIM) because it's graphical and easy to use," says Debra Young of CompuServe. "The [front-end] products are batch-oriented and allow members to write their own scripts. Therefore, an online session takes minutes, thus saving time and money."

CIM comes free in CompuServe membership kits, and as I've mentioned it's available for DOS, Windows, and Macintosh platforms. Navigator is available as separate software and can be purchased online (downloaded and charged to your membership account).

The membership kits contain detailed instructions on how to set your modem, how to sign on, and the basic commands you need to know. Without any front-end software, you'll be in text-only mode, but that's not as hard as it sounds. The command prompt you'll encounter is an exclamation point. From the exclamation point, you can use several commands (such as Go, M for the previous menu, T for the top menu, and Off to logoff. Ctrl–S will stop text from scrolling on your screen, and Ctrl–Q will start it up again. I'll go over the text commands later, but you'll probably be using CIM or a front end.

The forums

As mentioned previously, research and business services abound on CompuServe, but many members belong to the forums and use little else. Forums on CompuServe are divided into three parts: messages, libraries, and conferences.

Messages have up to 17 different categories of topics. The libraries, which contain programs, text files, and graphics, are often designed to match the message structure. The Roots Forum has a searchable member database with information contributed by members on their surnames of interest. Conference areas are for live, online "chats," of which the Roots Forum has several, scheduled and unscheduled, each week.

All forums are arranged the same way; once you learn the forum software in one place on CompuServe, you can easily use it in another. The best way to do that is to try the Practice Forum (GO PRACTICE). This special forum is free of connect charges. It has message areas for you to discuss specific problems with sysops and has libraries of helpful files you can download and read later.

Find (the magnifying glass in CIM) is the command to discover what CompuServe areas cover your interests. WORKING, for instance, will uncover the Working from Home forum, where people talk about every possible way to run a business successfully from home (including professional genealogists). FIND GENEALOGY will show you the Roots Forum, as well as Information USA and Phone*File (an extra-charge service).

There are more than 200 forums on various topics, and the choices will seem overwhelming at first. But with Find and Go (the traffic signal button in CIM), you'll be able to navigate. Go, with a keyword, takes you to the forum you want. GO ROOTS, in this case, will take you to the Genealogy Forum.

 # A visit to Roots

Membership in the Genealogy Forum is free and open to everyone interested. When you first come to Roots, you're asked to join, which is simple to do. You're asked to use your full name, both first and last; "handles" are not permitted. Since this is a forum dealing with tracing surnames, it's assumed you're proud of yours! Then you can input any interests you have. Without a front end, your first menu at the Genealogy Forum is:

```
1 INSTRUCTIONS
2 MESSAGES
3 LIBRARIES (Files)
4 CONFERENCING (0 participating)
5 ANNOUNCEMENTS from sysops
6 MEMBER directory
7 OPTIONS for this forum
```

These options are represented in the forum tool bar (see Fig. 11-1). You can browse the messages, for example, by clicking the hand icon on pages, or you can search the messages for specific text in the subject line by clicking on the icon with pages and a magnifying glass. These are also available under the menu commands.

One of the first things to do is search the membership directory. There you should enter your name, how you prefer to be contacted, and the surnames you're searching. This database is searchable, but it's one of the largest member directories of any forum on CIS, so your search should be a little different here.

First, search for interests, not names, to find people looking for the same surnames you are. Second, if you're using CIM, you must change your interface.

To begin the session, use the Services menu to GO ASCII. You'll be put in terminal mode. You might also want to hit F5 to capture the session to a log. When online, type GO ROOTS. At the Forum menu, enter 6 (the members directory). From the next menu, choose 6, Interest, and enter the search string, for example, SPENCER. Be patient; there are more than 20,000 entries for the system to search.

Figure 11-1

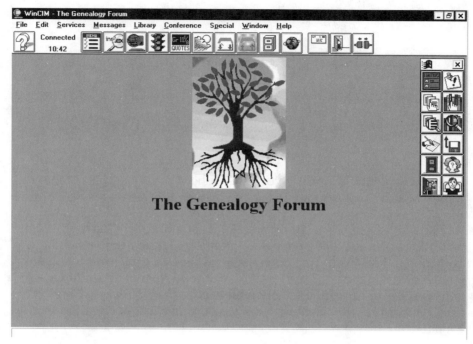

In WinCIM, click on the green light and type ROOTS to get to the Genealogy Forum. The toolbar to the right allows you to read and send messages and files, and participate in conferences.

The system will list Roots forum members, their member numbers, and the surnames they listed when they signed up.

Other front-end programs have different ways to access this feature. Check out ROOTS.MAP in Library 1 for details.

 # Messages: The heart of the forum

The message board gives you the following choices:

```
1 "I'm New and..."
2 U.S. Surnames A-G
3 U.S. Surnames H-M
4 U.S. Surnames N-S
5 U.S. Surnames T-Z
6 Canadian Genealogy
```

```
 7 UK & Irish Genealogy
 8 European Genealogy
 9 Latin America
10 All Other Countries
11 Jewish Genealogy
12 Societies/Libraries
13 How to Find Records
14 Software/Computers
15 History/Heraldry
16 Adoption Searches
17 Wandering Messages
18 Ask the Sysops
```

If you have any questions as to which subject area is applicable, leave a message to the sysop and ask. The Wandering Messages section is for all nongenealogy messages and chit-chat. Each section on the menu is followed by two numbers, which stand for the current number of topics and messages under that category. These numbers change constantly. The Hot Topic changes from time to time, and is usually whatever has genealogists stirred up at the moment: new software or a census release, for example. Keep an eye on the Software/Computers area concerning the latest genealogy programs just becoming available.

If you choose Read from the Message menu, you'll see the latest messages, which you can read and respond to if you want. To reply, click on the Reply button at the bottom of the window. The system will flag you when someone has posted a message to you—in WinCIM, the Waiting Messages button on the toolbar will be selectable; when you click it, the messages addressed to you will be listed in a window for you to read, reply to, and save as you choose. The system keeps track of what you read last and presents only new messages; you can change the highest number read under Options in the main forum menu. Another very nice thing about CompuServe's system is that it allows you to search both messages and files by keyword, submitter, and date.

You don't have to read all the messages and reply to them online, though, even with CIM. You can use the F5 key to mark those that catch your eye and then download those messages. You can read and answer them offline, when the meter isn't running. (All these actions can also be applied to files in the libraries, discussed later in this chapter.)

By double-clicking on a topic, you'll get a list of the messages in that topic. You can use your mouse to put a check mark next to each message you think you'd like to read. Then, by clicking on Messages and Retrieve Marked, all the messages you marked are downloaded. Uploading replies and files of your own is just as simple.

When CIM has logged you off, you can select Mail, open the Filing Cabinet, and read new messages in Genealogy+. Your replies will be stored on disk until you sign on again and tell CIM to deliver them. Manage the files as you ordinarily would— uncompressing, etc. if necessary.

With front ends such as OzCIS, the message and file process is even easier, as the Message and File menus are stored in OzCIS's software. Simply choose which forums to visit, and for each forum you'll have a catalog of the forum's message categories and all the libraries and files to select from. Before you sign on, simply tell OzCIS what you want and it takes care of the entire online session.

And those are just two examples of front-end programs and their potential to save you money when using CompuServe. Others are around, and I urge you to read AUTO.CIS and sample those that fit your platform.

Conferences

As mentioned previously, online conferences consist of members typing messages to each other in "conference rooms" while online.

Obviously, front-end programs such as OzCIS, NavCIS and TapCIS, won't help you here, as this is an interactive function that's different each time. Also, remember that the faster your modem speed at logon, the higher your charges for connect time to CompuServe. As you probably can't type or read at 14.4 Kbps, it's best to log on at lower speeds for conferences.

Often, special online conferences are announced in the forum's Announcements section. Recent topics have included:

> Tracing Your Roots in Eastern Europe, Elizabeth Rohaly, moderator.

> Southern U.S. Roots: Every 2nd Saturday, 7:00 P.M. Eastern, Karen Bosze moderator.

> Newcomers' Evening.

> Welcome to the Genealogy, History & Adoption Forum Conference Area

> Daily informal "anything (almost) goes" online conferences.

> Regular conferences are held each Tuesday evening at 10 P.M. EST in the Main Room.

> "Adoption Searches" Conference Room (Room 4) Sundays at 12:00 noon EST (9:00 A.M. PST, 17:00 GMT) and Wednesdays at 10:00 P.M. EST (7:00 P.M. PST, 03:00 A.M. GMT (Thursday mornings).

> Irregular conferences at the drop of a hat—anytime, anywhere.

The regular, "open topic" conferences are held every Tuesday evening. They start at 10:00 P.M. eastern standard time (7:00 P.M. pacific), and are open to all for anything you want to discuss. Often, the more productive conferences are saved and edited, then uploaded into the libraries for future reference.

When a conference you want to attend is scheduled, you sign on with CIM with GO ROOTS. (This should be in your favorite places list by now. If it isn't, click on the green light and type in ROOTS. When you have the forum's opening screen, click on Favorite Places, then Add. When the Genealogy Forum's address appears, click OK.)

In the forum toolbar, click on the door icon. You'll get a small window that lists the current "rooms" where people are typing messages to each other (see Fig. 11-2). Entering the room, you'll see a small window split into two panes. The top pane shows you the conversation as people type lines of messages and press Enter. The bottom pane is where your own messages appear until you press Enter; you can back up and correct typos here before your message

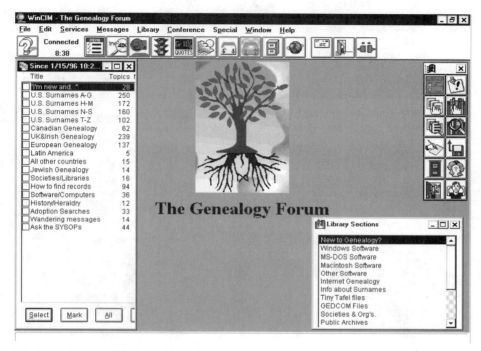

Figure 11-2

The messages and files are what most people use the Roots Forum to access.

appears to others. As shown in Fig. 11-3, the sender's name appears next to the message he or she typed.

Libraries

Libraries are where files are stored in CompuServe forums. These can be sample versions of the latest programs, text files on how to do genealogy; GEDCOMs of members' families, or anything else the Roots communities thought was worth sharing.

A notable feature of CompuServe's Genealogy Forum is the 1,400 genealogy book reviews written by professional reviewers, under Book Reviews. Hundreds of other files are available on this forum, covering basic techniques and historical background, GEDCOM files of famous people, PAF utilities, lists of genealogical societies and libraries, the

Figure 11-3

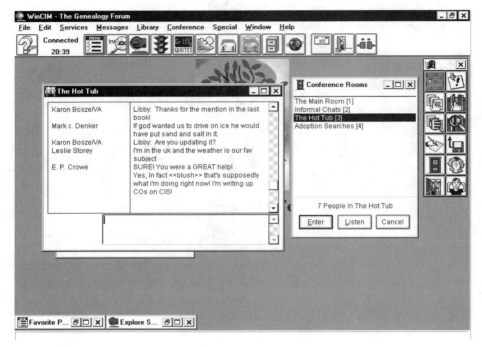

You can get into a conference with CIM via the door icon (Enter Room), which will give you a list of conference rooms. Click on Enter to get into the conversation.

Family History Library newsletter, and files from the Internet. Newcomers should find these files interesting:

SEARCH.TXT An excellent tutorial for the beginner and old-timer alike.

QUICK.TIP Sandy Clunies' excellent list of tips and advice.

ROOTS.MAP A frequently updated file about the forum, including how to search the membership directory.

HOW2.MSG A file on effective forum messages, effective answers, and so on.

GENBOOK.TXT A collection of messages discussing the best books for a beginning genealogist. (Such a discussion is called a *thread.*)

BOOKS.SIX Another thread resulting from Bill Ewing's posted question "If you could own a maximum of six books to generally aid your genealogical research, which six books would they be, and why would you pick them?" Enlightening.

WHATIS.TT A file defining tiny tafels and ahentafels.

COUSIN.TXT How to calculate relationships.

MASTER.ZIP A list of all the files in the forum. This is a compressed file, and must be unzipped to be read.

SUMMRY.ZIP Also a list of all the files in the forum, but the descriptions are abbreviated. Compressed, and much smaller than MASTER.ZIP.

AUTO.CIS A list of front-end programs for CompuServe on all platforms.

Browse is the button with a hand over books; it allows you to look at the list of categories and the list of files within each category. This is okay for a while, but you usually just want something on a particular subject. For that you use Search, the button with a magnifying glass over books.

Click the box next to the library or libraries, then type in the keyword(s) and the age (in days) to search. You'll get a list of which files match your criteria. You can read the descriptions and download the files with a click of the mouse.

Who's who

You'll find professional genealogists, software authors, and even genealogy publishers here. But, in keeping with CompuServe's policies, advertising is not allowed. Messages that contain advertising or solicitations for commercial services will be removed from public

view by the sysops. The Genealogy Forum sysops and staff are as follows:

Dick Eastman, Forum Manager (76701,263) Dick is the author of *Your Roots: Total Genealogy Planning on Your Computer* published by Ziff-Davis Press. He also lectures frequently on computer genealogy topics and will be featured in the upcoming "Ancestry" TV show on public television.

Gay Spencer, Associate Forum Manager (76702,1353) Gay is a doctoral candidate and an expert at genealogy research, photography, and electronic photo enhancements. She owns her own specialty photo processing business, and lives in Ohio.

Michael MacCannell, Associate Forum Manager (76702,445) Michael retired as a Captain in Naval Aviation and has been a long-time user of home computers. He resides in California.

Phil DeSilva, Associate Forum Manager (76702,1032) Phil is a long-time member of the National Genealogical Society and has been very active in promoting the use of home computers in genealogy work. He lives in Virginia.

Elizabeth Rohaly, Associate Forum Manager (76710,100) Elizabeth lives in North Yorkshire, England. She is an expert primarily in European research (particularly Ireland, Switzerland, Hungary, and Slovakia) and records pertaining to post-Civil War immigration to the United States.

Martha Reamy, Book Review Editor (71271,2042) Martha is past editor of the *Maryland Genealogical Quarterly* and has written a number of genealogy books. She lives in Hawaii and works as a volunteer at local Family History Centers.

Jacques Tucker (76710,105) Jacques has a good knowledge of New England genealogy as well as French, German, and Swedish sources. He's been involved in computing since tab card equipment, and lives in Kansas City, MO.

You can address messages to any of these people via their user IDs. You can also leave a message addressed to "sysop" (to make it a private message, precede the word *sysop* with an asterisk, like this: *sysop).

An interview with Dick Eastman

"It's lots of fun, but no money," Dick Eastman says of being a sysop. Along with several other Genealogy Forum members, he was at the 1994 GenTech conference in Texas to help promote the forum. That's just one of his many functions as sysop. He also manages the files, checks for viruses, keeps the messages where they should be, and offers advice to new genealogists. Eastman recruits assistant sysops as well. He's the buffer between the technical people at CompuServe headquarters and the CIS user. The goal is to keep problems to a minimum, both in using the service and in doing genealogy.

"We're very much a referral service," Eastman says. "Like a football coach, we won't play the game for you, but we'll help you learn the best game plans." He likes to do that on the forums, but, amazing as it is to him, he says that many people are too shy to post a public message; they send him private e-mail with their questions instead. He'd prefer to answer questions where all can benefit from the answers, though.

"We're a social group," he says, "and we have a lot of fun. We get together at conferences like this [GenTech] and meet face to face when we can. But I love the online environment. I'm a die-hard techie, and I think it's so much fun!"

Over and over, he says, people have found relatives either on the Roots Forum or because of it. One of the most affecting, he says, was when he was demonstrating Roots and the Phone*File system at a National Genealogical Society meeting. A woman found a name and number she thought might be her long-lost father, though she didn't dare hope. Still, she went to the pay phone, and sure enough, was talking to him in minutes, arranging a reunion after 30 years. "She

had tears running down her cheeks, because she was flying to Philadelphia to see her father that next week. I could hardly talk the rest of the day, I was so choked up," he says.

Gaye Spencer, one of the sysops, had a mysterious Amirilla Eastman in her lineage, whose parents she just couldn't place. That is, until one day a long message was posted on the Roots Forum about an Eastman family of the right period and all the siblings of that family—and there was Amirilla!

Dick Eastman himself found a relative he was able to help online. His French-Canadian Dubay line was hard to find, partly because of variant spellings. But he knew of a history professor of that name and, using Phone*File, discovered that the fellow lived within 25 miles of where Eastman knew his ancestors to be from.

Calling the gentleman, he found out that the professor had just self-published 1,200 copies of a genealogy of the family, and was having trouble selling them. Eastman sent the professor gummed labels with every Dubay (and variant spelling) he could find on Phone*File. The professor mailed each one a notice of the book, and the results were a wonderful Dubay reunion and a sold-out printing of the genealogy!

 # Eastman's Online Genealogy Newsletter

Dick Eastman has another service available: a weekly electronic newsletter on genealogy. Software, services, research resources, anything newsworthy is available in this free newsletter. To subscribe via e-mail, send a message to one of the following addresses:

76701,263 (CompuServe)
76701.263@compuserve.com (the Internet)
roots@cis.compuserve.com

Messages sent to any of those addresses will end up in the same mailbox. It won't do any good to post this message to the forum message areas; it has to be sent to one of the addresses. The message text should be the word *subscribe*. The rest of the message will be ignored. To unsubscribe, follow the same instructions, but use the message text of *unsubscribe*.

In addition, the latest copy of this newsletter and an archive of all previous editions are kept in the New to Genealogy library on the Genealogy Forum on CompuServe (GO ROOTS). Many people prefer to have their newsletter arrive by e-mail, but you can always obtain the latest ones online on the Genealogy Forum.

 # Genealogy Vendors' Forum

For help and information on books, magazines, software, and other genealogy products, visit the Genealogy Vendors' Forum (GO CIS:GENSUP). Here you'll find representatives from the New England Historic Genealogical Society; Wholly Genes Software, producers of The Master Genealogist; Leister Productions, producers of Reunion for Macintosh and Windows; Jim Steed, the author of Brothers Keeper; CommSoft, Inc., producers of Roots IV and Visual Roots; The Family Edge; Everton Publishers; the National Genealogical Society; and Schroeder & Fuelling (a genealogy research firm in Germany)—to name just a few. Messages, forums, conferences, and other functions are just as in the Genealogy Forum.

 # CompuTrace and Phone*FILE

CompuTrace (GO TRACE) is a surcharged area ($15 an hour), but many people use it because it's basically the Social Security death records in a searchable form (see Fig. 11-4). This database has information on over 100 million living and dead United States citizens. Available every day between 2 A.M. and midnight, CompuTrace verifies name, partial Social Security number, and year of birth; for living people, the data is much more limited.

To get there, click on the Go button in CIM and type TRACE. Select the menu option with the dollar sign and, when the Text menu comes up, type 2 for Begin Search. Then you have to select a database. For this exercise, let's choose 3, the Deceased File. Then select a state or

Figure 11-4

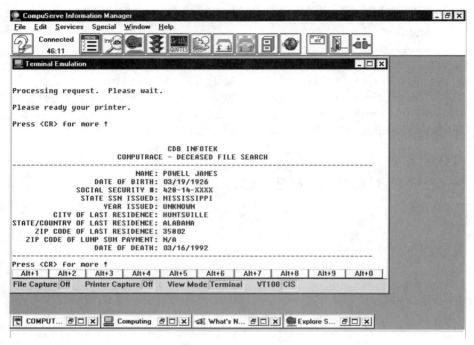

A CompuTrace search on death records.

states from the list, and input the first and last names. If you know the date of birth, enter it, as it will speed the search. Use File, Capture in CIM to save the results to disk; you don't want to waste time studying the list online at $15 per hour!

CompuTrace searches match individual information from either of two separate databases. The Deceased File includes over 40 million people who died after 1928; all individuals contained in this file were United States citizens residing anywhere in the United States or in one of 14 countries at the time the death was reported. The Living File includes over 90 million individuals whose names appear in public record filings throughout 27 states. But if you want to find living people who share surnames you're searching, try Phone*File (GO PHONEFILE), also for $15 per hour.

The setup is much the same as with CompuTrace: you type in a name, city, and any other information you know. You'll get back names, addresses, and phone numbers. The more you know, the faster the search. But if you enter the zip code, say, and the person no longer lives there, you won't get a match. The problem is usually the opposite, however: dozens of matches. Again, capture the results to a file and let them fly by as fast as possible at $15 an hour.

 # CompuServe and the Internet

CompuServe membership now includes full Internet access, including Usenet newsgroups, WWW access, and everything else covered in chapters 4, 5, and 6. The software for this all comes with CIM 2.0.1, and is quite simple to use.

 # Usenet on CompuServe

You can use the browser that comes with CIM, but it's really not the best way to read Usenet on CompuServe. Click on Go and type in USENET. (Once you're there, click on the Favorite Places icon and add it, so you don't have to type it every time.) Then click on the newsreader, CIM (see Fig. 11-5).

The first thing to do is select Subscribe to Newsgroups. From there, type in the keyword genealogy and click on Search. A list of genealogy newsgroups (19 at last count) will appear, and you can click on the ones you'd like to read regularly. You can preview a few messages before you subscribe, but it's not necessary.

Once you've subscribed to all the Usenet newsgroups you'd like, return to the first window by clicking Cancel until you get back there and choose Access Your Newsgroups. You can search newsgroups for specific text strings. This is a wonderful feature; you don't have to read soc.genealogy.surnames article by article, simply search for Spencer or Powell and the matching information will appear. You can mark them for retrieval to disk later. If any of them are encoded (pictures or programs changed to ASCII for transmission), CIS will decode them for you if you click on the Decoded button. The Clear

Figure 11-5

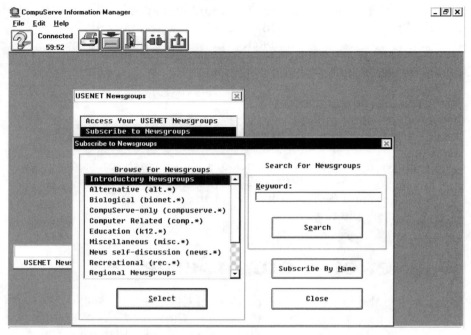

Usenet on CompuServe is really easy; it will search out the newsgroups you want and even let you download them for reading later.

option will mark them all as read, even if you didn't bother to read them.

Reading Usenet on CIS isn't really fast, but it's less hassle than on several other commercial online systems.

 # Roots Forum's home page

CompuServe's new set of programs means that you can dial up CIS's PPP network, fire up a Web browser, and get to CompuServe services via the Web. If you'd like to read more about the Roots Forum or check out what's new in the world of genealogy, go to (see Fig. 11-6):

```
http://ourworld.compuserve.com:80/hompages/roots/
```

Figure 11-6

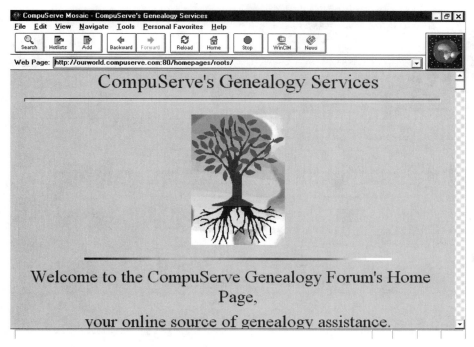

The Roots Forum's home page.

Here you'll find some tidbits and information, and a link that will call up CIM from the browser and take you to the Roots Forum. It also has information on links to other genealogy pages on the Web; it's updated frequently, so check it often for new sites.

 # Linkstar

Linkstar (see Fig. 11-7) is one of the nicest parts of CompuServe's genealogy Web site. Its address is as follows:

```
http://www.linkstar.com/home/partners/genealogy-forum-on-compuserve
```

A Web search engine, Linkstar can help you find Web pages. Type in genealogy as the keyword and any surname you're searching as the name to see if anyone out there has created a page with your lines on it!

Figure 11-7

CompuServe Mosaic - LinkStar - Genealogy Forum on CompuServe

File Edit View Navigate Tools Personal Favorites Help

Search Hotlists Add Backward Forward Reload Home Stop WinCIM News

Web Page: http://www.linkstar.com/home/partners/genealogy-forum-on-compuserve

INTERNET DIRECTORY   Add Free e-Card   Edit e-Card   Hot Web Sites   Return

Welcome to **Genealogy Forum on CompuServe's** Internet Search Page

KEYWORD SEARCH. Enter a keyword, name or phrase:

[   ] Search

Use any of the search fields below alone or together with the Keyword Search to perform the *most accurate* search on the Internet.

Company	
Person	
City	State/Province
Country	ANY	ZIP/Postal Code
Category	ANY	

Oops...Start Over   Display up to: 25

CATEGORY SEARCH

○ Business
○ Communications

Linkstar.

12

GEnie's Genealogy RoundTable

GENIE'S basic rate is $23.95 a month for nine hours, after which it's $2.75 an hour. There are GEnie premium services, whose prices vary per individual service (Charles Schwab, for example). The rates go up a dollar an hour during daytime hours; the basic rate is good for between 6 P.M. to 8 A.M. local time. You can reach GEnie at:

401 N. Washington St.
Rockville, MD 20849-6403
800-638-9636 (voice)
username@genie.geis.com (e-mail)

You can use GEnie with a common communications program such as Procomm Plus or Qmodem, typing in commands as you go. Or you can use the front-end program Aladdin, which allows you to type all the commands, messages, and such offline. It also logs on and performs your tasks, then logs off, cutting down the connect time. Or you can use the new GEnie front end for Windows and Macintosh, which is less time-consuming than typing all the commands yourself and has less of a learning curve than Aladdin. This chapter will assume you've gotten the GEnie front end, but I'll touch on how to use Aladdin.

Small but fun

The online community here is small but loyal. GEnie offers e-mail, Myra Vanderpool Gormley's weekly column, live conferences, and more, but their rates are nearly triple what they were four years ago, which has chased many users away. Although the smaller membership base means less people to share in the fun, those who come are very active.

One thing I recommend you do is buy Alfred Glossbrenner's *Master Guide to GEnie*, which includes a $12 credit to the service and the most comprehensive insider's tips anywhere. You can order it online (type ORDER at the main menu), or mail $41.95 to:

Glossbrenner's Choice
699 River Road
Yardley, PA 19067

New software

Late in 1995, GEnie finally came out with a graphical front end that makes getting around the service a little easier. Figure 12-1 shows the opening menu of GEnie through the new front-end program.

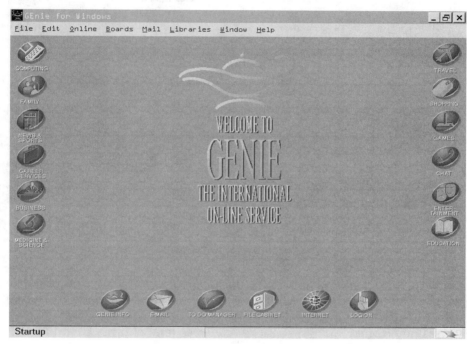

Figure 12-1

The new graphical interface makes your real-time online sessions with GEnie much more understandable.

You'll find all the genealogists at the Genealogy RoundTable (analogous to forums and bulletin boards in other services). Click on Log On and, when you're connected, you can go straight to the RoundTable by choosing Online and Move To from the menu bar and entering either M540 or GENEALOGY. You'll know you're there when you get the screen in Fig. 12-2. Then click on Online and then Customize Online Menu, and add the page. Now Genealogy is part of your Online menu. You can do this with any page on GEnie.

Figure 12-2

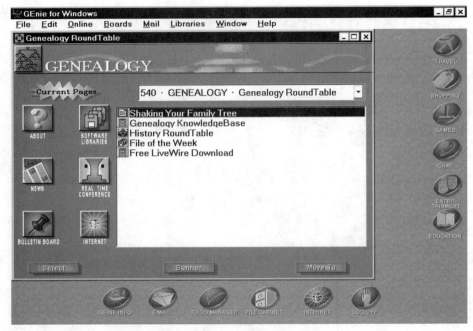

The welcome screen to page 540, the Genealogy page. You can add it to the Online drop-down menu by choosing Online and then Customize Online Menu.

On GEnie, a RoundTable (or RT) includes messages, files, and real-time conferences (chats). The libraries and the message base are set up with similar commands; learning one helps you learn the other. The Genealogy RoundTable (or GRT) also has several choices beyond the plain vanilla RT:

➢ Genealogy Bulletin Board (messages)

➢ Genealogy RT Conference (live chat)

➢ Genealogy RT Libraries (searchable files)

➢ About the RoundTable (rules)

➢ RoundTable News (bulletins and announcements; see Fig. 12-3)

➢ Shaking Your Family Tree (Myra's column)

➢ Genealogy KnowledgeBase (a searchable database of data from the members)

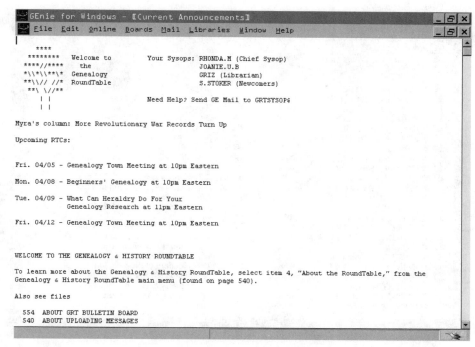

Figure 12-3

Check the button marked News about once a week for the latest announcements.

➤ History RoundTable

➤ Free Livewire Download (GEnie's online version of their membership magazine)

⇨ Files

The Software Libraries button will get you to the files. If you click the button List All Items, a screen like the one in Fig. 12-4 will appear. This is a lot of information, and you probably won't want to read each and every file description. Luckily, you don't have to.

On the menu bar, click on Libraries and then Search. Enter what interests you, such as a surname or a geographical name, as I've done in Fig. 12-5. You can narrow the search by date and category (looking

Figure 12-4

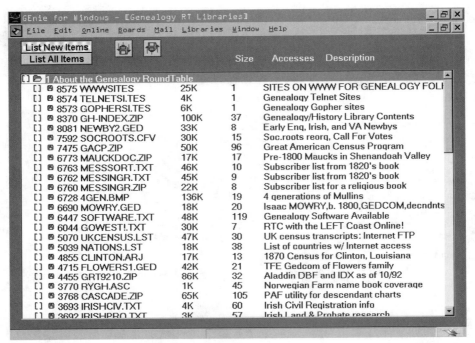

You'll find how-to files, tiny tafels, programs, and more in the library.

only at family histories and tiny tafels, for example). Click on Search, and the list of files and their appropriate categories will be narrowed to those that match your search. All this works with messages, too.

Members upload files with family histories, charts, tips on researching, software, scripts for Aladdin, and so on. Each file has a number and name assigned to it. A brief topic statement describing the contents and one or more keywords are also included to help you search through them.

If you find one you want, put a check mark in the box next to it. This is now on your To Do List. You can keep on finding messages, files, etc. to load to disk, but before you log off choose the To Do Manager from the GEnie desktop (look back at Fig. 12-1). The To Do Manager will download everything you've checked, and you can read it all offline when the meter isn't ticking. Simply log off and click on the file cabinet on the GEnie desktop.

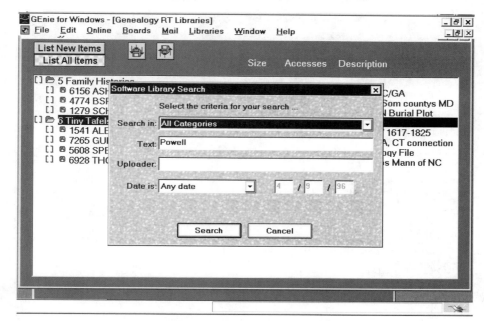

Figure 12-5

You can search the library file descriptions for surnames, place names, or any other string.

⇨ Messages

Click on Bulletin Board (messages) from the RT page, and you'll get the screen shown in Fig. 12-6.

The message organization is built on a hierarchy of categories, topics, and messages. Categories are determined by the sysops; users create the topics and messages. The shelf life of a message is two years in some categories. GEnie is generous with the amount of messages allowed to RoundTables, so the sysops decide how long topics and messages can hang around.

You can use the front end to download messages to the file cabinet just the way you do the files. One message you definitely want is the one listing the rules. To save you the connect time, I'll give it to you here:

```
Category: Welcome to the Genealogy BB
Topic: Sysop Notes - Read First!
Message: 1
```

Figure 12-6

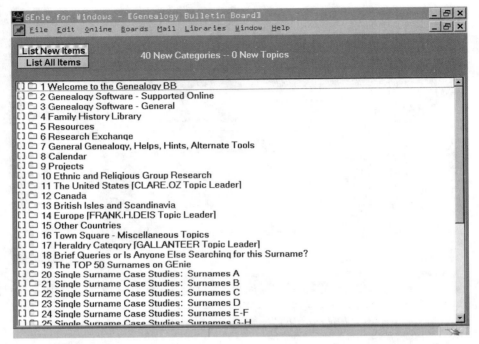

Message categories in the GRT bulletin board range from very general to very specific. Click on the file-folder icon to see the topics under each category.

All, below are the "guidelines" of the genealogy section of the Genealogy and History RoundTable. Please see Category 39, Topic 1 for the rules for the History Section.

1. Topics started in Categories 1, 8, 11, 18, or 19 will be moved to a more appropriate category.
2. Multiple surname discussions will be found in Categories 34-35. Topics for single surname discussions can be found in Categories 20-33. If a topic already exists for the surname you are discussing, your message will be moved to the existing topic and your topic deleted. Duplication of topics is not allowed per GEnie management.
3. A limit of 4 (four) topics in all the Surname Categories may be started by one person. If you have more than four, you will be asked to choose which you want to remain. This is to give all the chance to have a surname topic up and active.
4. Please read POLICY at any GEnie prompt for those guidelines that GEnie requires all over the GEnie system. These are adhered to in the G&HRT. We ask that you refrain from using any profane language.
5. All posts of longer than 62 lines will be sent back to the uploader, and he/she can either whittle it down to fit this requirement or upload

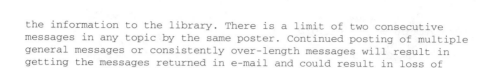

the information to the library. There is a limit of two consecutive
messages in any topic by the same poster. Continued posting of multiple
general messages or consistently over-length messages will result in
getting the messages returned in e-mail and could result in loss of
posting privileges.
6. Verbatim extracts from printed materials or computer databases must be
SMALL in nature. Limited verbatim messages from the NGC echos are allowed
(no more than 2 messages). There will be NO verbatim messages allowed
from Prodigy, CIS, or any other commercial board. These all have
compilation copyrights. All published material must have full citation
included. Verbatim messages in multiple topics are limited to 2 at any
one time. You are welcome to post in other topics over a period of days.
7. Signatures should be limited to 7 lines in length. Anything longer and
you will be asked to revise it to fit the limit.
8. Topics will be deleted for inactivity. Those that have been started
and then are never returned to will be deleted without any notification
to the sender at two-week intervals. Those that have been active will be
notified when their topic has reached 30 days of inactivity and will be
given a chance to save the topic from deletion.

The above guidelines will be consistently adhered to, though newcomers
will be given a "first offense" warning. If you have any questions, you
can discuss this in Category 1, Topic 2.

 # Genealogy KnowledgeBase

This is a surcharged service: $5.00 per hour above your GEnie
connect charges. You need to look before you leap and read the
guides and tips before you try to use it. There's a sample search,
which I recommend you capture and study offline, as well as some tips
on cost-effective searching that you should print out and keep by your
side. The most important tip: Don't do your thinking online, and plan
what to do before you sign on! You can use parentheses and Boolean
logic, so think it out.

In brief, the Genealogy KnowledgeBase is an ever-growing collection
of documents about sources for genealogical research, updated several
times a week. It's there to let you quickly find materials or
organizations that can help you in your genealogical research. Many
of the documents describe where to write for further information;
others include the following:

➢ Names and addresses of organizations or vendors

➢ Brief summaries about books or computer programs

> ➢ Brochures of organizations
> ➢ Publishers' catalogs
> ➢ Many other written materials

Some of the resources described in the Genealogy KnowledgeBase are:

> ➢ Genealogical and historical societies
> ➢ Computer-interest groups
> ➢ Books and magazines
> ➢ Publishers
> ➢ Family or surname associations
> ➢ Family or surname newsletters
> ➢ Software
> ➢ Research libraries
> ➢ Professional researchers
> ➢ Sources of vital records

The KnowledgeBase also contains summaries of the family research of members of the Genealogy and History RoundTable, in the form of tiny tafels, ahentafels, pedigree charts, and descendent charts.

You can search the KnowledgeBase by asking for any word or sequence of words, called *phrases*, in the text of the documents. For example, you could ask for all documents that mention the Tennessee Valley Genealogical Society. The Genealogy KnowledgeBase will then give you a list of these documents. You could ask for one or more of them to be displayed on your computer, saving to disk or printing them at the same time.

If you plan your search carefully, especially if you use a script such as you can create with Aladdin, this is a marvelous, affordable resource.

The Internet connection

You can use the GEnie front-end program to browse the Internet by clicking the Internet button on the GRT window. But GEnie's Internet interface is strictly text, and very small text at that. Look at Fig. 12-7 to see what I mean. It's good if you're interested primarily in fast access, bad if you want legible information.

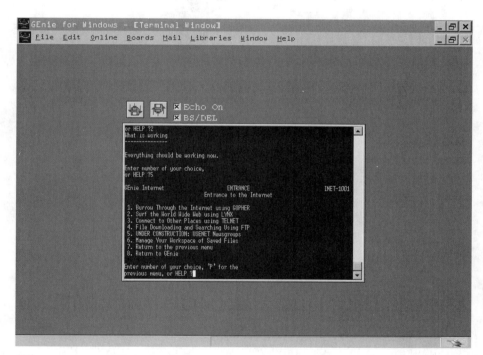

Figure 12-7

When you use GEnie for Internet access, you're in terminal mode, strictly text. Fast but not very pretty.

Clicking on the Internet button from GRT provides a list of several genealogically related sites, from magazines to personal genealogy databases. You can capture your session to a text file with a button click, and just let the text scroll by as small and as fast as it wants, reading it offline later. Reading Usenet from GEnie is pretty frustrating this way, and I wouldn't advise it.

 # Conferences

RTCs, or RoundTable conferences, are announced in the opening bulletin. They're commonly on topics such as "contributing to an ancestral file with a librarian from the Family History Library," "genealogy for beginners," or "Roots IV." A chat looks much like this:

```
<[Jim/Alad] GENIEUS.BB1> You will be prompted for a filename; Enter that,
hit Return, and it will start running for you.
<[Jim/Alad] GENIEUS.BB1> Then hit T to return to here.
<[Jim/Alad] GENIEUS.BB1> Sorry A, not S, to open it.
[Libbi] M.CROWE2> OH! So easy once you know how! Thank you!
<[Libbi] M.CROWE2> Thank you!
<[Jim/Alad] GENIEUS.BB1> Sure, Aladdin is MEANT to be easy! :)
Okay, I'm tacking into the wind no<[Jim/Alad] GENIEUS.BB1> Anything else
we can do for you?
!Thanks, but now I'm off to GENEALOGY! Appreciate it!
<[Libbi] M.CROWE2> Okay, I'm tacking into the wind now! Thanks, but now
I'm off to GENEALOGY! Appreciate it!
/exit
<[Jim/Alad] GENIEUS.BB1> There's a whole lot to do around this system, it
will take you awhile to find it all out.
** <[Libbi] M.CROWE2> has left.
```

The *handle*, or the nickname you use for the conference, is between the square brackets. The member name precedes the right-pointing angle brackets.

 # Aladdin

Aladdin is a great program that makes GEnie almost completely automatic, and once you know your way around the service and if you have an IBM compatible, Macintosh, or Atari ST, you really should get and learn to use Aladdin.

This free front-end program automates almost everything, but allows you to roam about the system when you want to. There are two Aladdin RoundTables, with live online help most evenings, and a 250K manual. To get it from GEnie, simply enter ALADDIN in the Online, Move To dialog box (or M110;1). From there, you can get information about Aladdin and the BBS, and download the version you need from the menu. Aladdin really helps make GEnie fun and easy to use. It's possible to find your way around without it, especially with Alfred Glossbrenner's book, but it's more fun to let Aladdin do it.

As the opening screen of the program explains, the fabled Aladdin obtained a magic lamp that, when rubbed, had the power to summon a genie to do his bidding. That's the function of this program.

The RoundTables section in your program comes set up for the Aladdin RT and your type of computer (it knows that from the version of Aladdin you downloaded). You can input the Genealogy RT very easily. Input your logon information into Aladdin, then press Escape and the F6 key. Choose Add an RT and fill in the blanks with M540 for Genealogy. Set the Auto Pass #1 to check for new messages and new files. If you want other options, put the cursor on that field and press F1. A window will pop up explaining all your choices for that field. This is true wherever you're in Aladdin.

Escape will save any changes you've made and quit the program. Now when you choose the Genealogy RT from the main menu, you'll have a two-page menu. The top is about messages; if you hit the Page Down key you'll get a second page of the menu to help you deal with files.

After an automatic pass, you'll have lists of categories, topics, and files to pick and choose from offline. Mark the topics that look interesting with N for new or A for all, and choose files from the list. Then have Aladdin do a second automatic pass to retrieve those files and messages. Earlier illustrations in this book have shown you what the messages will look like. From the second page of the menu, you can look at a short list of new files like the one shown in Fig. 12-8. Aladdin lets you search by text string, download the file's description, and so on.

Aladdin will also log you onto the GRT to take care of something manually, log you onto the GRTC for a chat, and other functions. If you get into the habit of this, the script function is worth learning. Here's an example. From the main menu, press F7 and then choose A

Figure 12-8

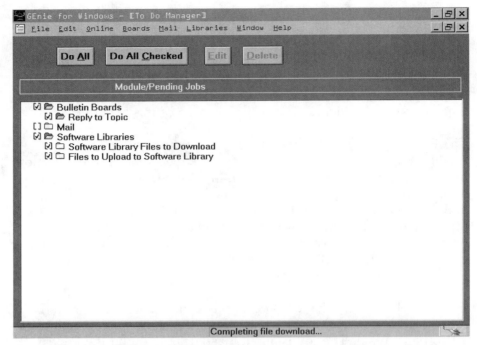

Check the files and message you're interested in as you browse, then have the To Do Manager download them to the filing cabinet. Do as much reading and replying offline as you can!

for Add a Script. Then you can type the following to have Aladdin retrieve Myra's column:

```
Script # Get Myra's Column for Thursday
ECHO OFF
CLEAR
NOTE ""
NOTE ""
NOTE ""
NOTE ""
NOTE ""
NOTE ""
NOTE "NOTE: Date is Year, Month, Day!"
NOTE "Enter Thursday's date of Myra's file (YY-MM-DD)"
GETSTRING 9
SETSTRING 8 "SHAK%9"
Log onTO "540"
If success
CAPTURE "%8"
```

```
SENDLINE "6"
WAITFORDATA STOP
WAITFORPROMPT
ENDCAPTURE
ENDIF
Log Off
EndScript
```

Here's an explanation of the different commands in that script:

Script # Get Myra's Column for Thursday Display the number and title on the main menu.

ECHO OFF Don't display the script as it executes.

CLEAR Clear the screen as the script begins.

NOTE " " Puts blank lines on the cleared screen. You can put in as many blank lines as you like.

NOTE "NOTE:Date is Year, Month, Day!" A helpful reminder.

NOTE "Enter Thursday's date of Myra's file (YY-MM-DD)" Asks which file you want.

GETSTRING 9 Accepts YY-MM-DD from the keyboard; it's now the variable 9.

SETSTRING 8 "shak%9" Sets the path and filename for download. In this script, it goes to the Aladdin directory under SHAK%9.

Log onTO "540" Log on to GEnie, page 540 (the Genealogy RT).

If success If an online connection is made, perform the next five lines.

CAPTURE "%8" Turn on capture to the path and file you set earlier.

SENDLINE "6" Tell GEnie option 6.

WAITFORDATA STOP Wait for something.

WAITFORPROMPT Wait for something.

ENDCAPTURE Turn off capture.

ENDIF End of IF function.

Log Off Like it says!

EndScript The end.

When you type the script, replace the # in the first line with the number of the script; just make it next in line after any that came with the program. You might want to make some changes in the script with script edit when you install it. For example, in SETSTRING 9, you might want to change the filename and path, perhaps to put the columns on a floppy disk labeled "Myra's Column." In that case, change shak%9 to A:\shak%9. Or you could set it to something like C:\aladdin \dl\myra\%9.txt. Note that both of these use the date you typed in response to the GETSTRING 9 to name the file. I let it download to the hard drive because it's faster, and move it to a floppy later.

You should use the GEnie front end to retrieve file #6588, which has an Aladdin script to retrieve several useful items on the GRT. Instructions for installing that script are included in the file. Special thanks to online friends Bev (B.Hungerford), SuzQ (S.Ryan), and Joe Meehan (J.Meehan3) for helping me with these!

Arthur C. Clarke said that any technology sufficiently advanced would appear to be magic to someone seeing it for the first time. The GEnie Genealogy RT is not exactly magic, but it's pretty advanced. And with Aladdin, it's a lot of fun.

13

Microsoft Network's Genealogy Forum

I N what was probably the most ballyhooed launch in computing history, Microsoft gave us Windows 95 in September of that year, and with it their very own attempt at an online service. It was a little shaky at first in both software and content, but it's settling down into a nice service, and looks to become a staple in our online cupboard.

The service costs $4.95 a month, which includes three hours of usage per month, and each additional hour is $2.50. If you intend to be a frequent MSN user, you can sign up for a plan that's $19.95/month and includes 20 hours of usage with each additional hour $2.

You get the software free with your copy of Windows 95; it won't run without it. You can get Windows 95 anywhere IBM-compatible PCs are sold. If you bought an IBM compatible in the last year, you probably already have the software for MSN on your machine.

The whole metaphor of the service and the software is the Windows 95 desktop (see Fig. 13-1). You can have many windows open on the service at once; you could, for instance, download a tiny tafel in one window as you read messages in another. It's very easy to use once you get the hang of Windows 95. Still, if you want some detailed help, I highly recommend *Surfing the Microsoft Network by Wallace Wang* (Prentice Hall, ISBN 0-13-241944-0).

In this chapter I'll mainly cover the genealogy areas, but do explore the service. The Encarta Atlas, the History and Archaeology Forum, and the computer support areas, as well as other valuable items, can be a helpful supplement to the genealogy services.

Navigating

You can use MSN for just the service or also as your Internet service provider. If you want just MSN, use it as installed. If you want Internet surfing too, set it up this way:

❶ Double-click on the MSN icon to get the Sign In window.

❷ Click on Settings.

Figure 13-1

MSN opens with a different screen every day. Click on the tab MSN Central to get started.

❸ In the drop-down Service Type box, choose The Internet and Microsoft Network.

❹ Click on the Change buttons for the phone numbers (the Internet service dials up different numbers from the regular service).

❺ Choose the phone numbers, then choose OK. Now you're ready to surf!

Signing on is as simple as clicking the MSN icon on your Windows desktop. You can input your screen name and password each time, or check the box for automatic login. After connecting, as you're reading the MSN Today menu, click on the MSN Central button. This screen, shown in Fig. 13-2, is the window you'll use to go to the different services.

Figure 13-2

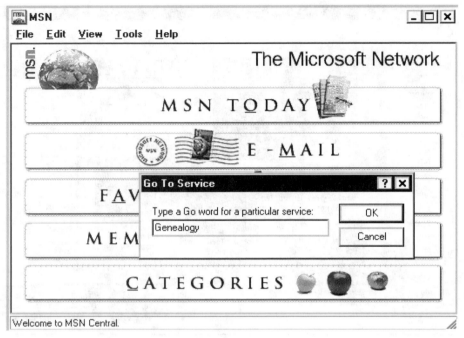

From MSN Central you can click on Edit to get the Go To box. Genealogy will take you to the forum.

Getting around MSN is a matter of clicking the icons. Each leads you to a folder (any window with more than one type of item in it) or a message base, or sometimes a program you can download to your disk and run. When your mouse pointer turns into a little hand, the icon you're pointing to is a text or graphics file that will be viewed with the built-in viewer.

When you're through looking at an MSN offering, you must use File, Up One Level, not Close Window, which is hard to get used to if you've been using Windows a while. If you close the window, you'll close MSN Central, but don't despair. Simply press Alt–Tab until you see the MSN connection again. Then relaunch MSN Central.

To get where we want to go quickly, from the MSN Central window click on Edit, Go To, and Other Location. Type Genealogy in the dialog box. When the Genealogy window appears, click on File and

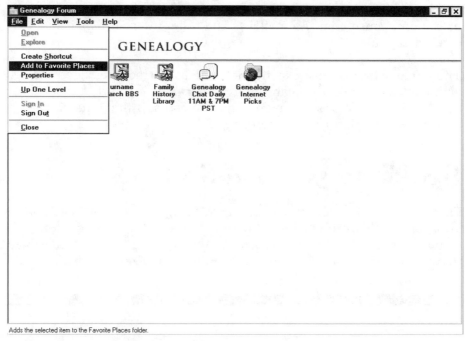

Figure 13-3

Choose File and Add to Favorite Places to save the spot for easy future access.

Add to Favorite Places (see Fig. 13-3). From then on, Genealogy will be in your Favorite Places window, therefore just a couple of clicks away. Indeed, if you really wanted to, you could click on Create Shortcut, and have a desktop icon that launches MSN, dials, and takes you to the Genealogy area.

 # Electronic mail on MSN

Microsoft Network uses Windows 95's Exchange for e-mail. If you click on E-Mail from MSN Central, or the in-box icon on the desktop, Exchange will launch. You set up a profile that includes the MSN service, and you're in business.

MSN e-mail is connected to the Internet. Your Internet address is *user_name*@msn.com. All mail lists and other Internet e-mail services can reach you at MSN.

The e-mail works almost exactly the same as normal message reading, with two exceptions. You can retrieve your mail, sign off, answer the mail, and send the answers later. And you can sort the e-mail into folders to suit you for later reference.

Seek and ye shall find

Find is a wonderful tool to use on MSN. From any window, click on Tools and Find. To find something on MSN, choose On Microsoft Network. In the dialog box, type in genealogy and you'll get a list like the one in Fig. 13-4. Click on a column header to sort the list by that

Figure 13-4

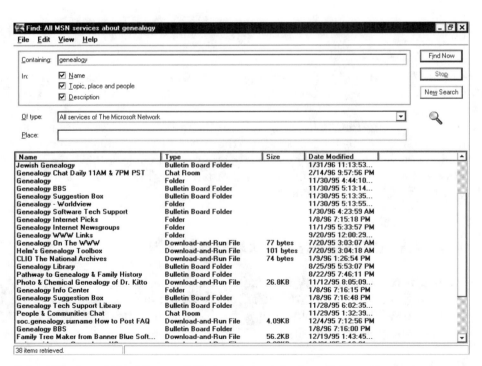

Select Find and On Microsoft Network to get many listings for genealogy. Click on one under the Name column to go there.

column. Double-click on any name listing and you'll go there. If it's a WWW site, it's listed as a download-and-run file. That means the URL will be downloaded and your browser run. If Microsoft's Internet Explorer is your default browser, that's what will run. Mine is Netscape Navigator, so that's what it runs.

Internet Explorer is free and quite a nice little browser. You can find it on MSN; from MSN Central, choose Categories, Internet Center, and you'll find IE in that folder. Version 2.0 loads pictures quickly and has built in support for many multimedia formats. It also allows you to save any site you like to disk, either as a desktop icon that launches the Web browser to that site when clicked or as a full copy of the HTML file. (This last function is useful for those GEDCOM-to-HTML files you find on the WWW.)

The Genealogy Forum

But let's go now to the heart of the matter. Using either the Go menu command or clicking on your Favorite Places list and then on the Genealogy Forum menu, you'll come to the screen shown in Fig. 13-5. The Genealogy Info Center describes what you'll find there, and has the forum's news flashes. At this writing, MSN was in the process of hiring a forum manager for this area and Jody McFadden (e-mail Jody_CatMgr@msn.com) was filling in as category manager. In the Genealogy Forum folder, you'll find the items described in the following sections:

✳ **Genealogy BBS**
A message board that contains general genealogy discussions. Ask beginner questions in this folder or share your research expertise with others. Topics include Adoptions Searches; Genealogy Software; General Help, Hints, and Tools; Getting Started; Introduce Yourself; Resources; and Reunion Announcements.

In the message board, click on a yellow file folder to get the messages in a general topic. By default, they're sorted by date line, oldest first. If you click on Author, Size, or Subject, though, the sort will switch to that column. Messages you haven't read are shown in bold; messages

Figure 13-5

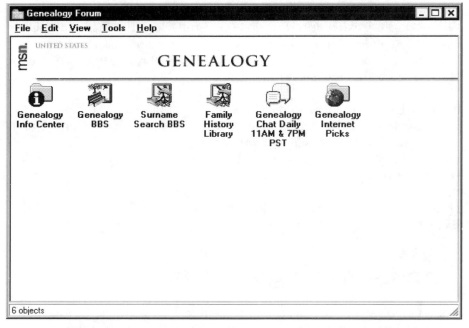

The Genealogy Forum has several offerings; only a year old, it's still growing.

you have read appear in regular type. You can mark them all as read under the Tools menu of the Messages window.

While reading a message (see Fig. 13-6), you can go to the next or previous message with the blue up and down arrows. Note that with MSN messages you can use bold, colors, and different typefaces in your messages; all these are found under the Edit menu.

✳ Surname Search BBS

A message area to exchange information on a specific surname. Post both your research requests and information in the appropriate alphabetical subfolder. Subfolders are arranged both in alphabetical and country order; simply click on the column header to change the sort order.

Tip: The Surname Research BBS and the Family History Library are arranged in alphabetical order. To obtain the messages within the

Figure 13-6

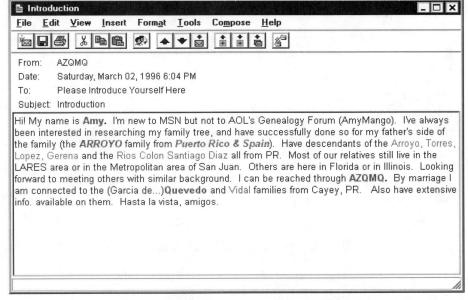

You can specify messages in e-mail and the MSN BBS to have different typefaces, fonts, and even colors.

subfolders in alphabetical order, simply open the folder and click on the subject toolbar.

❋ Family History Library

Here you'll find the latest genealogy and shareware programs. Members upload research data to this library in text, GED, PAF, and TT format.

❋ Genealogy Chat Room

Unmoderated chats are held on the MSN Genealogy Forum twice a day, at 11 A.M. and 7 P.M. Pacific time (see Fig. 13-7). The Chat window has three panes. The upper left one shows the messages being typed by the people in the chat room. The lower right one is where you type your messages and edit them, before you send them by pressing Enter or clicking the Send button. The pane on the right lists who's there. With the tools at the top, you can make each person's type appear in a different color, or make some conversations disappear entirely so you can concentrate on just one conversation.

Figure 13-7

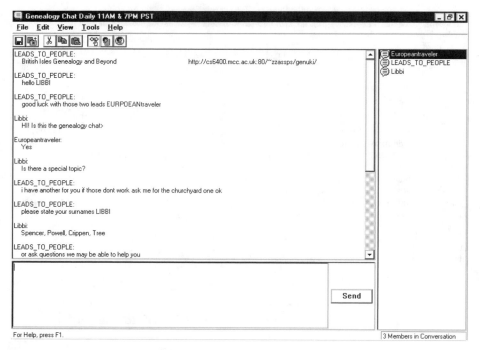

Genealogy chats are held twice a day on MSN.

Chat is a wonderful place to exchange information, according to MSN member Wanda Cowart. "I got my first home computer just about a month ago. I signed up for MSN not knowing what I was getting myself into. It was unreal! Now every night I am on the chat line for genealogy doing what I love best . . . making friends while searching my family tree," she says.

Wanda admits she did a lot of searching the hard way before finding MSN, but microfilm, microfiche, census searches, and so on were not nearly as much fun as she has had online. "It has become addictive and something I do not dread doing or spending a lot of time with."

In less than a month she found some people searching the same surnames, although she has yet to find a perfect match with her lines. But the fun is in the trying, she says.

"I like MSN a whole bunch," Wanda says. "They have great customer service and I am very satisfied. I get immediate responses for immediate questions. They are so kind. I only wish they would have the chat sessions earlier. Mine starts at 10 P.M. and we last until midnight sometimes. That is hard for me because I am enrolled in college full-time and am a mother of three. I also wish they had a chat for Southerners (Dixie)."

Wanda was instrumental in helping to find three people for other members, people who are living but lost relatives (at this time, genealogy shares the chat room with adoption searchers). "The people I searched for and found were called on the telephone . . . thank God for Ma Bell!!!! Later, they would come online and tell me what the info I had given them produced and we would talk for hours . . . about how much more relieved they felt. One man had never met his father. So now he knows how to contact him . . . I am sure that they will meet someday, as they have already talked on the phone. These are wonderful stories to me because I am also searching for lost loved ones who were put up for adoption. . . . We all laugh about going on "Oprah" so we can meet each other in person!

"I love the 'newbies,' as we call them. They remind me of so much that I had to learn when I came online. I only wish they would come online and state their surnames instead of being shy and quiet. MSN chat is no place for people who don't talk . . . it would be a big waste of money for those people. I welcome each one with a glass of lemonade \~/ and ask them to pull up a comfy chair and stay awhile. Part of my southern upbringing I guess." Wanda Cowart is very typical of the people you'll meet on MSN.

✳ **Genealogy Web Links**
An area that is currently mighty sparse. As of this writing, the CLIO server of the National Archives was the only entry, but if you use Find as described previously, you'll find links to Helm's Genealogy Tool Box, Everton's Genealogy on the WWW, the Jewish Genealogy site, and more.

 # Reading Usenet

MSN has a full Usenet newsfeed, but you don't want to search through them all. Instead, from the Genealogy Internet Picks choose Genealogy Internet Newsgroups and soc.genealogy. You'll get the list in Fig. 13-8. Reading newsgroups on MSN is exactly like reading BBS messages, minus the fancy fonts and colors. Unfortunately, all reading and answering must be done online while the meter is ticking.

Figure 13-8

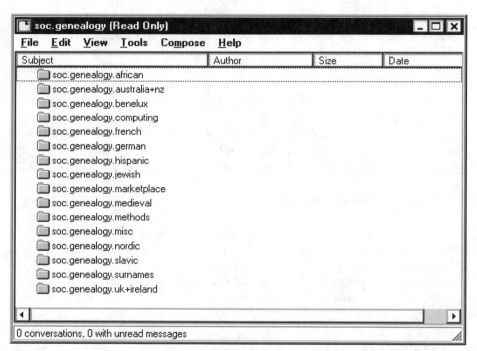

From the Genealogy window, click on Genealogy Internet Picks, then on Genealogy Internet Newsgroups. The genealogy ones are grouped for you here. This, too, can be added to your Favorite Places window.

All in all, MSN's genealogy offerings have come a good way since their launch in September 1995. It's still building, but the members are all helping each other learn genealogy, MSN, and the Internet at the same time. If a "free access for a month" offer is still going on when you read this, try MSN and see if it's what you want in an online service.

14

Prodigy's Genealogy BBS and column

CHAPTER 14

THE basic rate for Prodigy is $9.95 a month for five hours of "core" services, as well as bulletin board and genealogy column use, which are in the "plus" services. It's $2.95 an hour after that. Other packages are available. Prodigy's address, phone number, and e-mail access are as follows:

945 Hamilton Ave.
White Plains, NY 10601
800-776-3449 (voice)
userid@prodigy.com (e-mail)

 # Good news, bad news

A few years back, Prodigy was good news and bad news for the online genealogist. The good news was weekly columns on genealogy by Myra Vanderpool Gormley, several other helpful professional and amateur genealogists on the bulletin board, messages sorted alphabetically by surname, and a real feeling of community and camaraderie—all for a flat monthly fee no matter how much you used the service. In fact, it was one of the best online bargains three years ago. The bad news back then was that Prodigy had no Internet connection at all, screens that looked crayonish, advertisements that took up more than half the screen, and s-s-s-l-l-l-o-o-o-w-w-w front-end software. Plus you had to spend a lot of time online because there was no download and upload function for mail or messages.

Today, Prodigy is mostly good news and only a little bad news. The good news is that the columns and bulletin board are still there, still sorted in that easy-to-use way, and folks from Family History Centers and the New England Historical and Genealogical Society are online and willing to help you. More good news is that Prodigy now has complete Internet access, although the software isn't the best in the world. Still, if you just want to test out the World Wide Web, Prodigy isn't a bad place to start.

On Prodigy, bulletin boards (BBSs) are where you leave messages on a certain subject for others to read and respond to. However, files associated with that topic are available only under Ziffnet for Prodigy, a "custom choice" that adds an extra per-minute charge when you use

it. Core services—which include news, weather, shopping, and other information—come with the basic membership fee. Plus services are the bulletin boards, some online games, etc.

Despite using the term *bulletin board*, Prodigy lacks the file exchange feature most BBSs have. Members can't upload tiny tafels, GEDCOMs, or text files for others to use. They instead have the option to subscribe to Ziffnet for Prodigy, for which separate terms and pricing applies.

The messages on Prodigy are divided into surname searches and geographical topics, with several specialized topics, such as ahnentafels and a beginner's corner. If you read while connected, you can search the message base somewhat by choosing a topic and typing in the beginning of the subject line you want to see. If you decide to use this method, however, remember that Prodigy is still the slowest software around for an online service.

Still, two things Prodigy has that make it worthwhile are the weekly syndicated column and a question-and-answer message area with Myra Vanderpool Gormley, a recognized, certified genealogist. The atmosphere at Prodigy is helpful and friendly, so much so that my mother still swears she gets more done there than anywhere else online, including the Internet.

Prodigy users have access to 28,800-bps connections, at no more hourly cost than the slower speeds. Nowadays, the screens are crisper and neater, and the area for your use has a bigger share of the screen than the advertisements at the bottom. The software is improving month by month; you can download messages, read and answer them offline, and upload your replies almost as easily as you can on Delphi or CompuServe, with a program called Bulletin Board Manager. With the new Internet mail program, you can get Internet mail lists, set mail lists to index, look at headers, and decide whether to spend your nickel to get them. In short, almost all that was good is still there and many improvements have been made.

The bad news is that it's not the bargain it was. To use the Mail Manager (required to send and receive Internet mail) or Bulletin Board Manager, you'll have to pay extra to download the programs so you

can use them with the front-end software. And at this writing they're available only for Windows and DOS. You'll also pay from 10 to 25 cents for receiving an Internet e-mail message.

Unfortunately, the price hikes chased off many people who made Prodigy (*P to the online diehards) such a friendly place. And sometimes those pretty screens take a bit of time to generate (although not near the glacier-like pace of years gone by). There is hope, however, that third-party programs (discussed later in the chapter) will make the chores easier, and Prodigy is still an online place like nowhere else.

The difference

Prodigy has always been a different kind of online community. For one thing, they've long been a leader in the front-end software area for online services. Some think the popularity of their easy-to-understand screens, as opposed to hard-to-remember commands, forced the established, stuffier places like CompuServe to follow their lead with graphical front ends.

At the bottom of each Prodigy screen, you'll find a command bar with "buttons" that execute commands for you. Not all the buttons are there all the time. On the far left of this command bar is an icon that zips you to the main menu, from which you can choose the latest news (updated hourly) or any category of Prodigy service. If a triangle appears in the command bar, then the current screen has more text; clicking the right-pointing triangle will take you forward, and clicking the left-pointing triangle will take you back in that text file. The following are buttons you'll find in the command bar:

Menu Allows you to go to the last set of choices you had before getting to the current screen.

Jump and Path The buttons you'll use most often. Jump allows you to type in a word, or even part of a word, to go somewhere right away. Path will take you through a set of services you choose for yourself.

Web Calls up Prodigy's Web browser for Internet access. You can also connect to the Usenet from the Web.

A-Z and XRef These selections are for finding services and functions according to subject.

Copy Allows you to save what you see right now, either to a file or to the printer.

Tools Allows you to set up Prodigy the way you want it (this is where you choose File or Printer for the Copy button).

? Gets help screens.

Exit Logs you off.

Plus, at the bottom right of the screen is a word to tell you whether you're in a free, core, or plus service. Prodigy allows on-screen advertising—but, please note, not by members in their messages to each other. Almost every screen has a "commercial" at the bottom for some product or service. You click on a button called Look to get the details and order the product or service if you want. (If you take a look and then want to return to where you were, click on Tools and Change Path, and find the previous location.)

Another important difference is terminology. On Prodigy, *bulletin boards* (which it refers to as BBs, instead of the more common BBSs, for *bulletin board system*) are where you leave messages on a certain subject for others to read and respond to. However, files associated with that topic are available only under Ziffnet for Prodigy, a custom, choice that adds an extra per-minute charge when you use it. Core services are included with the basic membership fee; they're things such as news, weather, and shopping. Plus services include the bulletin boards and some online games. Most Prodigy plans allow about two hours of plus and unlimited core use per month. After that, it's six cents per minute for plus and custom choice services. A little box in the lower right-hand corner of the screen shows you where you are at any given moment.

As mentioned earlier, Prodigy lacks the file-exchange feature most BBSs have. Members can't upload tafels, GEDCOMs, or text files. Instead, they have the option of subscribing to Ziffnet for Prodigy, and separate terms and pricing applies, plus a surcharge while logged onto Ziffnet at 9,600 bps.

For comparison, if you use CompuServe's Roots Forum, you're paying a higher hourly rate, just as on Prodigy. But you don't have to use a command to go to a different place on CompuServe's system and pay a surcharge fee to get genealogy files. And on CompuServe, you can leave things for others to use. On CompuServe, however, you pay an extra per-minute fee plus a per-download fee to use some of the databases, such as Computer Database Plus; that sort of system applies to all file downloads on Prodigy.

But the most important difference about Prodigy to its users has been the atmosphere. As one user put it, it's the place for "the rest of us," meaning those who want to use an online service without understanding its every esoteric technical detail—or any of them, for that matter. The "punch-and-go crowd," so to speak. It's a very friendly, popular place.

Steve Larsen, a technical help person from Prodigy, was very excited about launching the download capabilities for the bulletin boards. "You can Jump New Board Look to see a demonstration, and see how to use the new board import function to download all of a subject. Under Bulletin Board Manager, that will be automated. Then you can read all the messages offline with a text editor or word processor. You save your responses to a text-only (ASCII) file. When you're ready to reply, sign on, Jump to the BB, click on the subject, add a new message, import the reply, and you're done. You can Jump BB MGR Prev to see the new BB software in action."

For downloading software, Jump Ziffnet. (Note that Ziffnet is not a core service; a surcharge applies.) Type in the keyword genealogy and you'll find all the popular software shareware packages for genealogy. You can also Jump Genealogy Column (this is a core service), click on Library, and find all the columns Myra Vanderpool Gormley has written for Prodigy, sorted alphabetically by subject.

A Prodigy visit

Let's visit Prodigy on a typical day. One nice thing about Prodigy is its flexibility. When you install the software, it sets the port, speed, and phone numbers to dial to access Prodigy from your computer. You can change any or all of these by clicking on Setup.

Using the Tab key or your mouse, put the cursor in the ID and Password boxes to type these in. Or you can automate this by clicking on the button called Tools and choosing Auto Logon while online. A warning will appear to tell you that completely automating your logon lowers the security of your account. Then you can choose to automate both password and ID, only your ID, or turn off Auto Logon. You'll be told to choose a nickname, which is another password to start the automatic logon. From then on, you need to type only prodigy *nickname* to start the session. For example, if your nickname is cathy, the command to start an Auto Logon session would be prodigy cathy.

Every time you use the Auto Logon option, your first online screen will be the Highlights screen, as shown in Fig. 14-1. If you choose A-Z

Figure 14-1

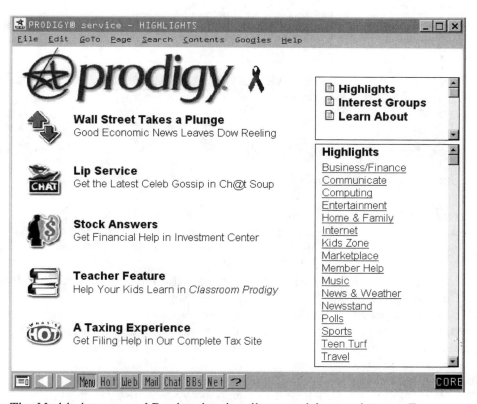

The Highlights page of Prodigy has headlines and featured items. From here you can Jump Genealogy to the BBS area, or go to the A–Z Index and search for "genealogy."

Figure 14-2

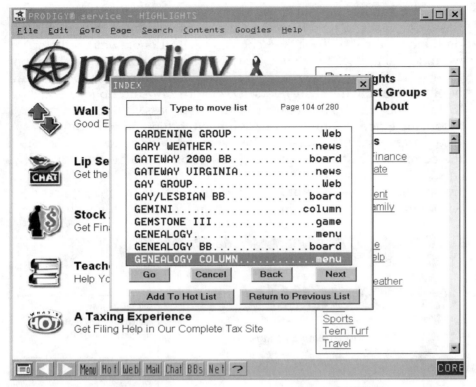

The A–Z Index listing of Genealogy pages on Prodigy.

Index and then type in gene, you'll get the screen in Fig. 14-2. The menu gives you the bulletin board (messages), the weekly column by Myra Vanderpool Gormley, and a Web page of genealogy links.

You can click and go to those choices from the Highlights screen, but if you're going to use Prodigy's genealogy services often, you can make future sessions easier. From this screen, click on GoTo and then on Add to Hot List. This menu item will add any current page to your hot list, or the list of places you like to visit often. If you want to rearrange the hot list, click on GoTo and Hot List. You'll get the screen shown in Fig. 14-3. In this screen, I've already clicked on Add, added the Genealogy BB and Genealogy Column, then clicked on Rearrange to make those my first choices. As I click on the Path menu choice, I'll be taken to the services in that order.

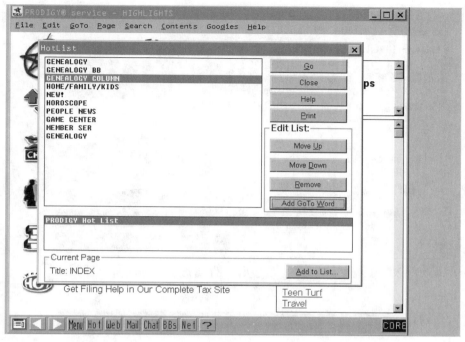

Figure 14-3

Click on GoTo and Hot List, and add Genealogy to the list. Then you'll come to the Genealogy Index page quickly.

Another way to quickly get to the Genealogy BB or Genealogy Column is to click on Jump from the bottom of any screen and type those jump words in the dialog box.

When you get to any BB on Prodigy, the opening menu looks much like the Genealogy one (see Fig. 14-4). You'll find an opening message from the leader, a set of small text files about Prodigy BBs under Guidelines & Info, and your control panel for this session on the right.

The date and time in Read Notes Posted Since defaults to the time of your last logon, but you can change both the time and the date. Select Choose a Topic, then Choose a Subject, then Begin Reading Notes. If you want, however, you can first choose Customize the Board. In Fig. 14-5, I've chosen to have Surnames I-Z as my first topic, and Spencer shown to me first. I can look at the entire board, but this is where I'll go first from now on.

Figure 14-4

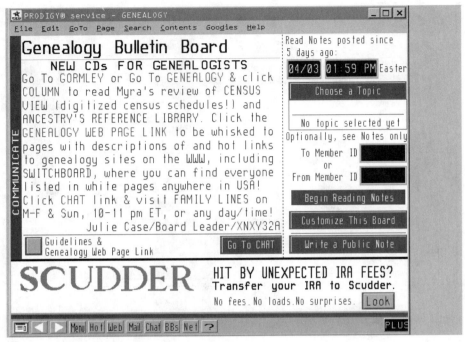

The Genealogy BB (messages) opening screen.

You can also choose how you view messages. At the Choose Topics box, you can choose to see note previews, as shown in Fig. 14-6. Turning Subject Export on means you can export the messages on one subject for reading as a text file later. Turning Selective Export on means you can choose to save only those messages you checked. Be aware, however, that you'll be exporting just a text file, not answerable messages. You have to log back on to answer them.

Under Choose a Topic, the subjects are arranged alphabetically, and you can type in a few letters (for example, spen) to jump through the list to make your selection. You can choose only one topic and one subject at a time. As mentioned before, the topics include surname searches, but there are also headings for adoptions, various countries, and many others. Click on a button to browse through the first lines of the messages by subject or topic.

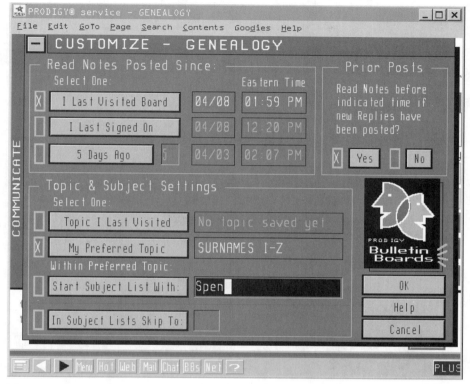

Figure 14-5

You can customize the BB to go to your favorite topics and subjects first.

Under the topic Beginning Genealogy, you'll find the subject Ask Myra. This is where Gormley answers questions from members. For the following session, I exported some notes and replies on this subject. Part of this day's messages went like this (member IDs are deleted):

```
^^^^^^^^^^^^^^     Board:  GENEALOGY   ^^^^^^^^^^^^
^^^^^^^^^^^^^^     Topic:  OTHER   ^^^^^^^^^^^^
===============   Note   1      ==================
Board: GENEALOGY
Topic: OTHER
Subject: ASK MYRA
To: EXPT45B MYRA GORMLEY   Date: 02/27
From:    Time: 12:48 PM

   Dear Myra,
```

Figure 14-6

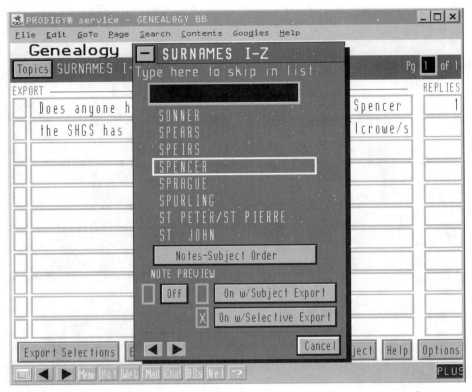

You can tell Prodigy to show you some of the message so you can choose which to download. Without a program such as NavStar, though, you can't answer messages offline.

    Hi. I'm Looking for info. on Panama. My great grandparents met there
and married. He worked building the Panama canal from 1910 to 1923, and
her father owned a commissary ? a hotel and restaurant. They met and
married on an island there in 1914, and all their children were born
there. Where do I look ?

=============== Reply   1 of Note   1 ==================

Board: GENEALOGY
Topic: OTHER
Subject: ASK MYRA
To: Date: 03/01
From: EXPT45B MYRA GORMLEY   Time: 9:26 PM

To obtain birth, marriage, and death certificates for ancestors who lived
in the former Canal Zone (from 1904 to Sept. 30, 1979), send your
requests to: Vital Statistics Unit, Panama Canal Commission, APO Miami
34011-5000. These records cost about $2 each, and you should send money

orders (U.S. currency) made payable to "Treasurer, Panama Canal
Commission." To find your family in the U.S. (federal) 1920 census, use
the Soundex for the Canal Zone—National Archives film No M1599, rolls 1,
2, or 3 (based on sound of surname). For births, marriages, or deaths
that occurred in the Republic of Panama, write to: El Registro Civil,
Apartado 5281, Panama 5, Republic of Panama.
Myra Vanderpool Gormley
PRODIGY service Genealogy Expert

=============== Reply   2 of Note   1 =================

Board: GENEALOGY
Topic: OTHER
Subject: ASK MYRA
To: EXPT45B MYRA GORMLEY   Date: 03/02
From: Time: 2:35 PM

   Myra: Thanks so much for your reply!!

=============== Note   2   =================

Board: GENEALOGY
Topic: OTHER
Subject: ASK MYRA
To: EXPT45B MYRA GORMLEY   Date: 02/27
From: Time: 7:26 PM

MYRA: Perhaps you can tell me what are some good examples of
genealogy/family history books. I am wondering if all genealogy data is
good or some personal information/history interspersed with genealogy is
or may be more interesting. When looking at ads for books by publishers
like the Gen. Helper, Gateway, Gen. Publishing, Clearfield, and others it
seems like most are interested only in attracting the attention of
ancestor record searchers. Are there any that have a combination of
stories and data? I think you would know of some good examples. There are
so many advertised now.

Thanks,
John in SC

=============== Reply   1 of Note   2 =================

Board: GENEALOGY
Topic: OTHER
Subject: ASK MYRA
To: Date: 03/01
From: EXPT45B MYRA GORMLEY   Time: 9:31 PM

John, it is possible to include biographical information as well as
genealogical data in a family history. It is important, however, that a
distinction be made between any unverified "family traditions" and
documented genealogical facts. An outstanding genealogy that incorporates
both an accurate genealogy and reminiscences, anecdotes, and personal
letters is by Virginia Easley DeMarce, titled "Now Living in Boone
County, Missouri: Our Family Genealogies, Vol 1: The Family and
Connections of Edward Everett Easley." This 679-page book is available
from the author (5635 N 25th Rd., Arlington, VA 22207) for about $35. It

was published in 1990. You may wish to obtain a copy of "Guidelines for Genealogical Writing," by Margaret Costello and Jane Fiske. This booklet is available ($3 postpaid) from the New England Historic Genealogical Society (NEHGS), 101 Newbury St., Boston, MA 02116. Also available from NEHGS is Joan Ferris Curran's excellent "Family History: A Legacy for Your Grandchildren." It costs $2.

Myra Vanderpool Gormley
PRODIGY service Genealogy Expert

=============== Note   3   ==================

Board: GENEALOGY
Topic: OTHER
Subject: ASK MYRA
To: EXPT45B MYRA GORMLEY   Date: 02/28
From: Time: 5:21 PM

   Myra: Could you please tell me the address for the U.S. District Court? My grandmother says there might be one U.S. District Court for each state or region . . . If so, I live in Wisconsin.

=============== Reply   1 of Note   3 ==================

Board: GENEALOGY
Topic: OTHER
Subject: ASK MYRA
To: Date: 03/03
From: EXPT45B MYRA GORMLEY   Time: 10:55 PM

   Ryan, the State of Wisconsin is divided into 2 judicial districts, Eastern and Western, for U.S. (federal) District Courts. The Eastern District Court's address is: Room 362, 517 E. Wisconsin Ave., Milwaukee, WI 53202; the Western District Court's address is Room 320, 120 N. Henry, Madison, WI 53703. There are also state district courts. What kind of records are you seeking? Perhaps I can help.

Myra Vanderpool Gormley
PRODIGY service Genealogy Expert

=============== Note   4   ==================

Board: GENEALOGY
Topic: OTHER
Subject: ASK MYRA
To: ALL   Date: 02/28
From: Time: 6:22 PM

   Why is it that I cannot get a note on the surnames for more than a few hours? Each day when I check, my message is gone.
   Please help.

=============== Reply   1 of Note   4 ==================

Board: GENEALOGY
Topic: OTHER
Subject: ASK MYRA
To: Date: 02/28

```
From:   Time: 11:08 PM

   Try entering an earlier date on the Menu screen.
   George in CA

=============== Note     5              =================

Board: GENEALOGY
Topic: OTHER
Subject: ASK MYRA
To: EXPT45B  MYRA GORMLEY   Date: 03/02
From:   Time: 8:19 PM

   Would you please tell me what "instant" refers to in a newspaper death
notice from 1877? At first I thought it meant "suddenly" until I noticed
that all of the notices read that way, i.e., "On the 17th instant" or "On
the 18th instant."

Thank you.
Norine in very snowy Allentown, PA

=============== Reply    1 of Note    5 =================

Board: GENEALOGY
Topic: OTHER
Subject: ASK MYRA
To:    Date: 03/03
From: EXPT45B  MYRA GORMLEY   Time: 11:09 PM

Norine, "instant" was a term used to mean the current
date or month. "On the 17th instant" simply means the 17th
of the current month.

Myra Vanderpool Gormley
PRODIGY service Genealogy Expert
```

This is the sort of friendly, helpful exchange you can expect on Prodigy. The board is very busy, and it could very well take all of your monthly two-hour allotment to keep up with a week's worth of messages!

When you've read and replied to all the messages you want, Jump to Genealogy to get back to the index page of genealogy offerings. (If you put Genealogy Column in your hot list, you can use that to immediately be taken to the next area.) After a brief period, while *working* appears at the top of the screen, you'll see the screen shown in Fig. 14-7. If this were your second visit this week, you could simply click on Path and skip this.

Under Tools, you can set Copy to send text to the printer (the default) or to a file. If you want to save the column to a file, this is a good time

Figure 14-7

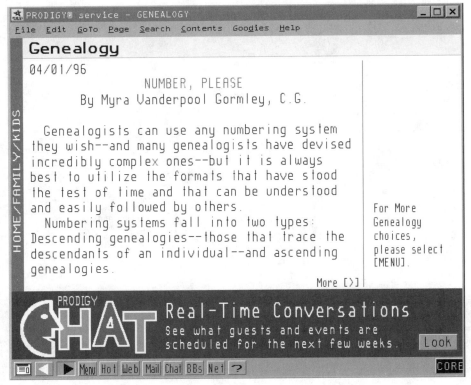

Myra Vanderpool Gormley has a new column each week at Jump Genealogy Column.

to set the toggle, name the file, and copy the whole column to read later.

Gormley has been writing these columns every week for years, and they're online at Prodigy for your reference. There are over 200 columns now. Most of the first 70 are in the topic Reference. You have to backdate at least two months to see copies of those that are there.

From the Genealogy index page, you can access Prodigy's library of Myra's columns. Click on the Archive button and the page in Fig. 14-8 will appear. The columns, in alphabetical order, can all be found here. If you have a topic in mind, type in up to nine letters and the list will scroll to the closest match.

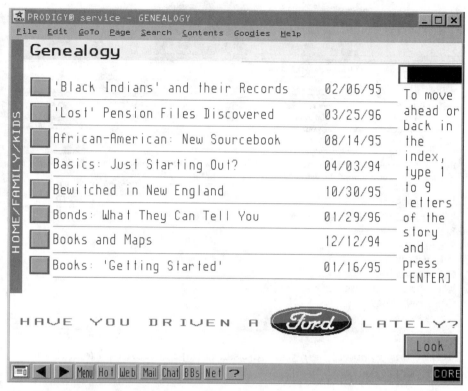

Figure 14-8

The Prodigy library of Myra's columns.

If you select one, when it appears on the screen you can click Copy (which will send it to the printer if you haven't selected File from the Tools button) and read it later. Clicking on Menu will return you to the list of columns. One that I heartily recommend is her discussion about the Black Dutch, which taught me some American history I didn't know.

⇨ Prodigy Internet access

Prodigy's Web browser is slow and clunky, and doesn't handle many of the advanced features of other browsers. Similarly, their Usenet newsreader doesn't allow any offline reading and answering, although

Figure 14-9

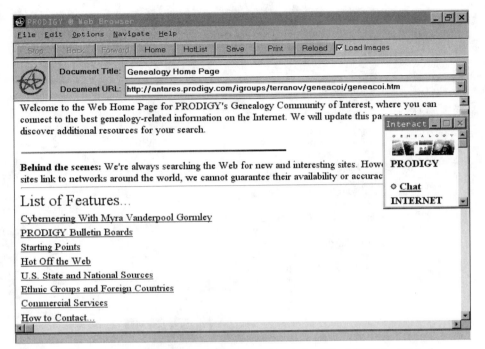

Prodigy has a page to help you start searching the World Wide Web for Genealogy.

it does have a good search capability. Until the software improves greatly, I wouldn't use Prodigy as my ISP.

Prodigy maintains a genealogy Web page (see Fig. 14-9) with some good links to get you started, as well as an explanation of mail lists. But the browser is so slow to load graphics and to connect to sites that it's a really frustrating venture.

To read Usenet articles on Prodigy, Jump Usenet (see Fig. 14-10). You'll have to assign your account names and read some warnings about the service. Then you can choose a button called Find Newsgroups. Type genealogy in the dialog box and you'll be able to subscribe to any of the Usenet genealogy groups by clicking the button Add to Your Newsgroups. Then close out the selection boxes, and your list of subscribed newsgroups will be listed in the window.

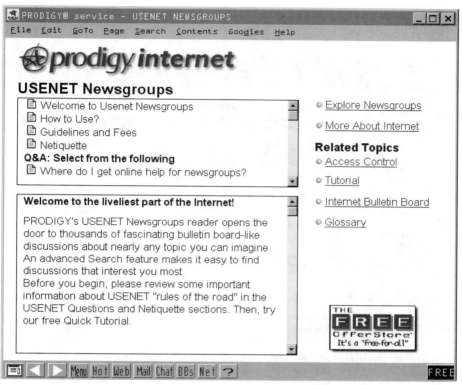

Figure 14-10

You can read Usenet on Prodigy, but only with the meter ticking.

Double-click on any newsgroup to bring up the list of current articles. You can determine how far back your list of articles goes by setting the date in the newsgroup list window. Once you have a list of articles, click on the Search button to search for certain words, which can be very useful in soc.genealogy.surnames (see Fig. 14-11).

Unfortunately, even with the companion software (see the following section), you can't read and reply to Usenet articles offline with Prodigy.

Figure 14-11

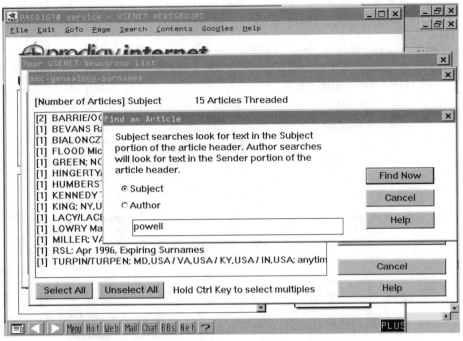

You can search Usenet articles for your surnames, which is a help.

 # Companion software

As much as the Prodigy software has improved over just a couple of years, I still wish it had a few more standard functions. You can have them, but for a fee.

The best news about Prodigy I've seen in a long time is NavStar, for $39.99 (see Fig. 14-12). This program makes the sluggish Prodigy so efficient you might find you save the software's cost in a month! You can Jump NavStar to order it on Prodigy, or you can get a trial version at http://www.dvorak.com. Besides having to have an active Prodigy account, the program requires Windows 3.1 or higher, a minimum 386/40 with 4MB of RAM and 7MB of hard disk space, a mouse, and a VGA or higher-resolution monitor. This front end is a two-pass model. First, for a new session it finds the topics and headlines on your chosen BBS, news, and weather sites. Then, after deciding which

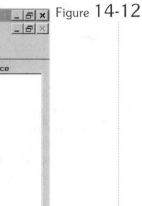

Figure 14-12

NavStar will greatly enhance your use of Prodigy's BB.

ones you want to read, it retrieves the actual text and pictures. It does all this incredibly quickly for Prodigy, and allows you to read and answer all your messages offline. NavStar includes a spell checker, a graphical weather system, graphical threading so you can see the structure of a BB conversation, and the ability to use fancy fonts in e-mail and bulletins. After using NavStar for a few sessions, I was more excited about using Prodigy than I have been for years.

To download a copy, visit their store on Prodigy (Jump NavStar). To have the program mailed to you on disk, e-mail them at 713.3312@compuserve.com (include your name, address, which product you want to buy, and credit card information). For further information, please visit the Web site at http://www.dvorak.com.

An older Prodigy helper is Pro-Util, a DOS-based application. Pro-Util takes about 350K of disk space, but can use less. It also takes 25K to 28K of memory, but only while you run Prodigy. It loads itself before

Prodigy and removes itself from memory when you exit. It changes the working icon to a clock, simplifies uploading and downloading messages, allows you to use a word processor like WordPerfect, includes a spelling checker for your messages, and more.

Pro-Util comes with over 60 pages of documentation on the installation disk, completely rewritten for version 6. You can also get online help with Pro-Util when in Prodigy.

Order Pro-Util by jumping to Royston and selecting option 5, then selecting the complete download. They take Visa and MasterCard on Prodigy, or you can order Pro-Util 6 by mail by sending a check to:

Royston Development
4195 Chino Hills Pkwy. #510
Chino Hills, CA 91709

The price is $24.95 plus sales tax if you're in California, plus $3.50 for shipping and handling. Please include your Prodigy ID so they can contact you with any questions. Also, mention the disk size (3.5-inch or 5.25-inch) you prefer.

15

The Church of Jesus Christ of Latter-Day Saints

A S I've noted before in this book, one of the most frequently asked questions online is "Can I connect to Mormon genealogy information with my modem?" The answer is still "No." So why include this chapter? First, because the Church of Jesus Christ of Latter-Day Saints (often abbreviated as LDS) has many computerized resources and, although most of them are not available in network form, they willingly share them as a public service through their Family History Centers. Second, because those sources are slowly becoming available to libraries, archives, societies, and the general public, it's only a matter of time before this information is available by modem somewhere. And finally, because you simply cannot talk about modern genealogical research and leave out the Mormons.

⇨ Some background

Without trying to explain the theology involved, I'll simply say that Mormons consider it a religious duty to research their family history. The results are archived at the church's headquarters in Salt Lake City and are distributed in microfilm, microfiche, and CD-ROM to their many Family History Centers throughout the world. The data is in several forms, but the most important to the online genealogist are the Ancestral File (AF) and the International Genealogical Index (IGI). Both of these are due to be updated in 1996; not only will new data be inserted in the databases, but new compression techniques will hopefully reduce the number of discs from 7 to 4.

One of the LDS's objectives is to build their copyrighted databases, the Ancestral File and the International Genealogical Index, and continually improve their accuracy and the software used to search them. The IGI is a record of temple work, and the AF offers pedigrees that the IGI doesn't. The IGI and the AF are really unrelated, as data entered in one file doesn't necessarily show up in the other file. Each has a value of its own and both files are worth searching. The advantage of the AF is that you can get pedigrees from it; the advantage of the IGI is that there's more detailed information.

Most non-LDS genealogists see the IGI as the more valuable of the two. While errors turn up in both, the IGI is closer to the original records (data is normally entered into the IGI first) and it has excellent bits and pieces of information, especially references to the primary sources of information. Non-LDS genealogists will always go to the IGI first.

While errors do exist, the percentage seems low; plenty of genealogy books printed in the past 100 years have more errors than these databases. The fact that the data is computerized and compiled by a religious organization is irrelevant.

Treat the AF and IGI the same way you would treat a printed book about a surname—with great caution. Use it as an excellent source of clues, but always cross-check it with primary records. While the computer increases the amount of data you can scan and makes things much easier, it doesn't necessarily improve accuracy. Human beings are still the source of the data.

The LDS apparently wants to make the AF and IGI available to more people. Originally, you had to visit the Family History Library in Salt Lake City, Utah to use the databases. Today, the AF and IGI are on a LAN in that library, which is connected to the Joseph Smith Memorial Building next door and about 200 access terminals scattered about the buildings. But there's still no remote access.

About 15 years ago, the church set up local Family History Centers around the world. In 1988, they started selling the databases on microfiche. In 1991, the church released them on CD-ROM to their local centers, and later to societies and libraries. The New England Historic Genealogical Society has a copy at their library in Boston, as does the California State Sutro Library in San Francisco. More are certain to follow suit. In 1994, the LDS began testing in-home use of the CD-ROMs, but as of yet they're still not available to individuals. Discussion continues about future online access.

The pattern here is more and more access via more and more means. However, the Mormons are very cautious and they take very small steps, one at a time. The church is worried about viruses on the FHC computers and the accuracy of submitted data, of course, but also about having a useful, viable program and database for its members

and the rest of the world. Their main concern is in not turning out a bad product.

In the very near future, for somewhere around $600, you should be able to buy the Ancestral File and the International Genealogical Index. The requirements to run these databases will be at least:

- ➤ 386 SX IBM compatible
- ➤ DOS 5.0 or better (not Windows as of this writing)
- ➤ 2MB of RAM (4MB is better)
- ➤ At least 555K free lower memory
- ➤ 1MB expanded memory with 512K free
- ➤ At least a 40MB hard drive
- ➤ At least one high-density floppy drive
- ➤ A CD-ROM drive with access time of 400 ms
- ➤ A printer with condensed print capability

For information about obtaining the CD-ROMs, write to:

Family Search Support Unit
50 East North Temple
Salt Lake City, UT 84150

 # A visit to an FHC

Terry Morgan, Genealogy Club staff member on America Online (genterry@aol.com), is also a volunteer at the two Family History Centers in Huntsville, Alabama. The setups there are very typical, she says, and she gave me a personal tour of the one closest to our homes.

"The best way to find one near you is to look in the white pages of the phone book for the nearest LDS church," Morgan says. "Call them and find out where the nearest FHC is, and the hours. Honestly, since the hours vary so much from place to place, the best time to call is Sunday morning around 10; everyone's at church then!" If you call any other time, she says, give the staffers lots of rings to answer the phones, which might be on the other side of the church from the FHC. Or, she says, you could write to the LDS main library at the address listed in the last section, and ask for the latest list of FHCs.

All Family History Centers are branches of the main LDS Family History Library in Salt Lake City. The typical FHC is a couple of rooms at the local Mormon church, with anywhere from one to ten computers; a similar number of microfilm and microfiche readers; and a collection of books (usually atlases), manuals, and how-to genealogy books.

The FHC I visited had two IBM compatibles that shared a printer in a room with a small library of about 25 reference books. A room away there were two film readers and two fiche readers. Users are asked to sign in and out, and a cork bulletin board holds the latest genealogical technique brochures from the Salt Lake City Family History Library.

"Some centers offer training on these programs, some insist they train you before you start using the computers, and some just help if you ask," she says. "We offer help if you ask. We've not had much trouble installing ours here. The only tricks were it has to have expanded memory, and you can have some TSRs [terminate-and-stay-resident programs, which sometimes cause conflicts] running, but few enough to have low memory and expanded memory as well." The programs as of this writing won't run under Windows, but Morgan says that could be in the future.

In the typical FHC setup, you must reserve a computer and you get a certain block of time to use it. Printouts to paper of what you find are usually a nickel a page. Some centers allow you to bring your own disk to record the information, but others insist you buy certified virus-free disks from the FHC at a nominal fee.

Database searches

The computers are set up to run Family Search, a program that allows you to search the CD-ROM databases (including the AF and IGI).

When you begin, you have an opening screen with these eight choices:

> ➤ Tutorial

> ➤ Ancestral File

> ➤ International Genealogical Index

> ➤ United States Social Security Index

> ➤ Military Index

> ➤ Family History Library Catalog

> ➤ Temple Ready

> ➤ Personal Ancestral File

The first six choices are the ones you'll use most often, and in a moment I'll describe them. First, however, let's look briefly at the last two.

Temple Ready is a program of interest only to church members; it helps you prepare genealogical records for Mormon religious rites. Personal Ancestral File is the popular LDS program for personal genealogical data. GEDCOMs and family groups are its greatest strengths. If you've ever considered buying this venerable program for yourself, you can come to an FHC to test-drive it. The Family Search tutorial has helpful text files about using this program.

The first six selections are arranged in the order most people want to use them. They are as follows:

Tutorial

The tutorial takes you step by step through the various databases, showing you how to access information on them using the Family Search program. It's worth 15 minutes of your time to explore this. When you're through, you'll be ready to investigate the databases.

Ancestral File and International Genealogical Index

The AF is a good place to begin your search. This database has pedigree charts of family groups sheets, donated by people from all over the world, usually in GEDCOM format. "It's important to remember," says Terry Morgan, "that this information is not verified. It's best to consider it an opinion file. The Salt Lake City FHL can't check out each of the millions of submissions, but they will try to find and merge duplicate pedigree lines and they accept corrections that you choose to submit." All are invited to donate their data, so you're likely to get good clues on where to start looking from this database.

The Ancestral File searches are slightly different from those on the IGI. In the Ancestral File, you don't have to have a place reference for a search; IGI allows that variable. The AF search is conducted on the basis of a name, which is required, and an event date, which isn't required but narrows the results.

You select a record from a menu of "hits." In the IGI, the documentation for that record is shown; for the AF, the submitter's name and address at the time of submission is shown. (This will change in the future, as the LDS plans to release an upgrade with more documentation for AF entries from donators.)

You need to check both the AF and the IGI, but the IGI is mainly submitted by church members. It isn't in pedigree format, but there are more names overall in the IGI. You can search by name, event, and location, and print or save the results to disk. Call numbers of documentation will also come from the IGI. The CD-ROMs of the IGI cover the entire world; Remember, Morgan says, that if you order a microfilm of a record that came from France, it will be in French!

The IGI record screen will show you what documentation was entered for that person: an original document, a book, a microfilm of a courthouse record, whatever. To the left is a set of numbers—the call number. If it's microfilm, you can rent the source material. For $3 you can examine the material at your local FHC for up to three weeks. It

takes about three weeks, on average, for the material to arrive after you fill out the request form. Books cannot be circulated this way unless they've been microfilmed, Morgan says.

You can print out the results of an AF search (F2) or save them to a diskette. You can also use this program to produce family group sheets. The IGI results can also be printed or saved to disk.

Morgan also points out that if you find an error or omission, you're invited to submit your data to the library in Salt Lake City. Expect to see your data reflected in the CD-ROMs in a year or two, she says.

United States Social Security Index

The United States government made these records public domain; the LDS put them on CD-ROM, indexed them, and wrote a search program for the data. It contains very good death records for the period from 1962 to 1994, and some records back to 1937. But for any record to be on this disk, the death had to have been reported to the Social Security office.

The data includes birth and death dates, the last place of residence, where the death payment was sent; the state of residence when the Social Security number was issued, and the Social Security number itself. It's searchable by name.

Military Index

This is another set of public-domain records that the Mormons made into a usable database, and covers U.S. citizens who died in the wars in Korea and Vietnam. It has birth and death dates, rank and serial numbers, and vital statistics as far as the military knew them: marriage status, state of residence, etc.

Family History Library Catalog

This CD-ROM contains the entire contents of the main Family History Library in Salt Lake City, which is updated yearly. It's also available in every FHC as a microfiche. The search choices are:

Search Locality You can enter a country, state, county, city, or township, and get a list of everything the library has that mentions that locality. The record will show the author, date, format of the item, and call number. To search on a subject (say Mayflower or Land Grant), type the term in the Search Locality field.

Browse Locality This is more open, and will result in more hits. "I do recommend using the microfiche only to 'browse' through a subject," says Morgan. "If you just want to see what was filmed from a particular state or country, you could pull out the Nebraska fiche and read it all in perhaps an easier way than using the computer, but only in that one instance do I think the fiche are easier to use than the computer."

Surname Search This allows you to not only search for surnames, but add keywords. After the initial results, you can hit F6 to add a locality, related family name, and so on. You can also search by author and title with this function.

Film/Fiche Number If you have the call number of a microfilm or fiche and want to know what else is included on that roll, this search will tell you. Sometimes widely diverse items are included in one roll; sometimes very closely related items are.

Computer Number Search If you know the computer index number to a certain record, you can retrieve the rest of the information with this search.

Tutorial This is a guided tour of the catalog search system.

Other resources

Other valuable resources are available at FHCs. "A very good resource are the research outlines," Morgan says. "Each Family History Center has a full set, like this one we keep in a three-ring binder here. They're also available for sale if you write to the main library in Salt Lake City."

The outlines, for every state, Canadian province, and dozens of other countries, are guides with ideas of how to research in those localities. It includes addresses of genealogical societies, government addresses such as courthouses and archives, maps, and short histories—in short, any resource that particular location might have. It also points out tips and techniques for research in a particular place that might be different. "When you're stuck and don't know what to do next," Morgan says, "these research outlines are just wonderful."

Another resource are the word lists. As mentioned previously, if you find that a microfilm you ordered is in French, these short booklets have the translations of the terms genealogists care about most: birth, death, baptism, marriage, wills, deeds, land transfers, and so on, for several dozen languages. They're available for sale, and every FHC has a reference set.

In fact, most FHCs can help you order microfiches, books, and other materials the LDS sells. Some even offer regular courses on genealogical research.

 # The connection

Right now, you have to go to your nearest FHC to access these resources. If your local FHC has a staff of knowledgeable volunteers like Terry Morgan, it's well worth your time to leave the modem behind for a while to investigate these resources. Another reason to try out your local FHC is that someday, if time, money, and security issues permit, you might be able to dial into the FHCs. If that happens, you'll want to be familiar with the programs and ready to go!

16

Online library card catalogs

CHAPTER 16

ONE of the most wonderful things about the online world is the variety of libraries switching over to electronic card catalogs. This speeds up the search when you're physically present, of course. With an online card catalog and many terminals scattered throughout the building, you don't have to look up your subject, author, or title on one floor and then go to another to actually find the reference source. If your local library hasn't computerized its card catalog, it probably will soon.

But oh, the joy of looking in the card catalog before you actually visit the library. You know immediately whether that library owns the title you're looking for. You can find out with a few more keystrokes whether a title is on the shelf, on reserve, on loan to someone else, or lost without a trace. If the title in question isn't at that library or branch, you can find out if it's available on interlibrary loan. Some, more advanced systems will even let you enter your library card number, in effect checking the book out to yourself before you get there. All before you leave home.

Let's take a sample walk through a typical system. This one is in my hometown, at the Huntsville Public Library. At the main desk they have a little folder explaining the log-on parameters and commands. If your local library is online, they probably have something similar for you to go by.

Once you have your trusty communications package up and running, you have to set the parameters. First of all, set your terminal emulation to VT100. Most card catalog programs assume that's what you're using. Those that ask what you're using and give you choices still work best in VT100.

The modems at HPL go only as high as 2,400, so set that as your speed. Choose 8 data bits, no parity, and one stop bit (8-N-1). (If you're using a package like ProComm Plus, which captures your session for a later script, you might want to turn that option on.) When you connect, you'll get an opening screen. Press Return to get past it.

Now you can move onto the main menu. If you choose the first menu option, you'll get some information on this system. Then it gives you

the menu to search the catalog. This menu actually takes up two screens. In practice, the first one is usually the one you'll want.

From this screen, type in S=GENEALOGY. Note that there are more hits than appear in the first screen; you can move backwards and forwards through this selection as much as you like. As the system tells you often, those that are actually at Huntsville Public Library are in bold; other titles are available through interlibrary loan.

Say you're interested in genealogical materials from Alabama. Simply type ST (start over) and S=ALABAMA GENEALOGY. If you choose the last book, by Kathleen Jones, the screen will tell you how many copies the library has, where it's located, and whether it's available right now.

To get out of this system, type ST (start over) and then type QUIT. When you've returned to the original menu, type 5 to exit. The system will thank you and hang up.

Now let's go to a different system. This one, the University of Alabama in Huntsville Library, runs a typical card catalog program called Project for Automated Library Systems, or PALS. The modems at UAH go only up to 2,400, so set that as your speed. Choose 8 data bits, no parity, and one stop bit (8-N-1). This program was originally written at Mankato State University for Unisys 1100 and 2200 computers. Many universities have such models, and use PALS.

Now dial the modem pool at UAH: 205-895-6792. When the computer lets you know it's connected, hit the Enter key a few times (two will usually do). When asked for a login name, just enter your initials. At the Local> prompt, type:

```
CONNECT UAH1100
```

and press the Enter key. This command tells the first computer to log you onto another computer. It does, and once again asks you for a user ID and password. It provides a string of @ symbols after the prompt to cover up your entry if you have an account on that computer. If not, you're just here for the public access part. The

commands for that part start with $$. The command for the library system is:

```
$$Open library
```

Once you enter the command and press Enter, you should see something like this:

```
SESSION PATH CLOSED SESSION PATH OPEN TO: LIBRARY
```

Finally you're in the PALS system. Don't be discouraged; many systems are like this. If you turned on the capture feature, you could use that file to write a script to take care of all this business for you next time. The opening screen awaits your command, but it has to be the right command. The most commonly used ones are listed in Table 16-1. To search for books on a specific subject, enter SU and the subject heading. For example:

```
SU learning disabilities
```

Table 16-1   **PALS Commands**

Command	Description
BE	Begin
AU	Author
TI	Title
CO	Author/title
SU	Subject heading
BR	Browse
EN	End
TE	Term
TT	Title term
AT	Author term
ST	Subject term
CA	Call number

PALS uses only Library of Congress subject headings when conducting a subject search (SU), so check the Library of Congress list of subject headings to verify the correct terms. Many PALS commands can be used with Boolean logic. To combine terms in a TE, ST, TT, or AT search, use the following Boolean terms:

AND All records containing both terms.

OR All records containing either term.

NOT Records that don't contain the term following the word NOT.

When you're through, type the command END. The PALS display screen will come up again, you'll type $$SOFF, you'll get a prompt that says Local>, and then you'll type LO.

You can telnet to this library from the Internet, and the commands are much the same once you're logged in. So let's look at another system, this time telnetting there with a gopher. You'll be using Delphi for this example, but it should be similar to whatever system you use. After logging in and going to the Internet gopher (see the chapter on Delphi), you'll get the following:

```
Internet SIG Gopher
Page 1 of 1


1    PERSONAL FAVORITES                                    Menu
[items deleted for space]
15   LIBRARIES, GUIDES, AND RESEARCH                       Menu
16   MATHEMATICS, SCIENCE, AND TECHNOLOGY                  Menu
17   SCHOOLHOUSE (K-12)                                    Menu
18   SOCIAL SCIENCES, HISTORY, AND EDUCATION               Menu
19   THE GRAB BAG (WITH 'NEW THIS WEEK 11/29')             Menu

Enter Item Number, ?, or EXIT: 15
```

Libraries are what you want, so type in 15. The next menu looks like this:

```
LIBRARIES, GUIDES, AND RESEARCH
Page 1 of 4


1    *** SUBJECT MATTER GUIDES ***                         Text
```

```
2     Information by Subject Area (from RiceInfo, Rice Univ.)    Menu
3     Resources by Subject (from Univ. of California)            Menu
4     Clearinghouse of Subject-Oriented Internet Resource Guides Menu
5     Gophers_Arranged by Subject (SUnet)                        Menu
6     Subject Tree from Library of Congress (Marvel)             Menu
7     _____     Text
8     ALL the INTERNET Libraries                                 Menu

Enter Item Number, MORE, ?, or BACK:
```

Let's be adventurous and try all the libraries on the Internet. Remember, at this point you're using a gopher, which searches through the Internet for your choices:

```
ALL the INTERNET Libraries
Page 1 of 1

1     About Library Catalogs                                          Text
2     Catalogs Listed by Location                                     Menu
3     Catalogs Search by Keyword                                      Search
4     Instructions for different catalog types                        Menu
5     Library Bulletin Boards                                         Menu
6     Manuscript and Archives Repositories - at Johns Hopkins Menu
7     Paper List (BBarrons' Accessing Online Bib Dbases)              Menu
8     Updates made recently to the list of libraries                  Text
Enter Item Number, SAVE, ?, or BACK: 2
```

Each one of these items is interesting, but let's try to find a library in Ohio. Select 2, on the next menu choose the Americas, on the next menu choose the United States, and then choose 34, Ohio. You'll get three pages of menus, allowing you to choose from the libraries this gopher found in Ohio. Part of this is as follows:

```
Ohio
Page 2 of 3

35   Ohio Northern University                                   Telnet
36   Ohio Northern University                                   Text
37   Ohio State University at Columbus                          Telnet
38   Ohio State University at Columbus                          Text
Enter Item Number, MORE, PREV, SAVE, ?, or BACK: 35
```

These locations have a Text choice and a Telnet choice. Text will describe the library in question, sometimes what the holdings are, sometimes what the library card catalog software is like, and sometimes just the rules of using it. The Telnet choice will actually take

you there, as long as the connection isn't too busy. If it is, you'll see a long pause, and then some message to the effect that you should try again later. Let's try selection number 35 and see what's there:

```
Enter Item Number, PREV, SAVE, ?, or BACK: 35
Please log in as: library
Trying POLAR.ONU.EDU,telnet (140.228.25.1,23) ...
Escape (attention) character is "^\"
login: library
library
What kind of Terminal are you using?
   V > VT100
   W > WYSE emulating TVI925
   Choose one (V,W) v
Please confirm: are you using a VT100 or compatible terminal? (y/n)y
```

This system uses another card catalog program called Polar, which has menus to help you along:

```
Loading program you requested


Welcome to the POLAR System,
a catalog of material held in
Heterick Memorial Library and Taggart Law Library


   A > AUTHOR
   T > TITLE
   S > SUBJECT
   K > KEYWORDS
   X > Other Searches
   I > Library INFORMATION
   R > Reserve Lists
   V > VIEW your circulation record
   Q > QUIT


PLEASE NOTE: This catalog includes records for all titles in HML and for
all titles in LAW cataloged after 1979. Please consult the card catalog
in the Taggart Law Library for titles cataloged before 1980.


Ohio Northern University
Choose one (A,T,S,K,X,I,R,V,Q) s


The Thesaurus that is used for subject headings in this catalog is the
Library of Congress Subject Headings. If you are unfamiliar with this
thesaurus, try searching by a noun.


   for example __-> Sports
        or     __-> Twain, Mark
```

```
     or      __-> New England
```

```
For names, type the last name first.
.... then press the RETURN key
```

```
Ohio Northern University
```

You're here for genealogy, so that's your subject range. However, be aware that you can search for wills, deeds, and personal papers—anything a library might have. But for now, type in genealogy:

```
SUBJECT : genealogy
```

```
************** searching **************
— Hit 's' to stop searching at any time —
Total entries found so far =
```

At this point there will be a pause while the catalog is searched. Don't get impatient; let the program do the work. Eventually you'll get the results:

```
Ohio Northern University
```

```
You searched for the SUBJECT: genealogy
```

```
31 SUBJECTS found, with 49 entries; SUBJECTS 1-8 are:
```

```
1   Genealogy _> See Related Subjects  .................. 6 entries
2   Genealogy ......................................... 5 entries
3   Genealogy Africans Fiction  ........................ 1 entry
4   Genealogy Afro Americans Connecticut  .............. 1 entry
5   Genealogy Afro Americans Handbooks Manuals Etc.  ..... 1 entry
6   Genealogy Bibliography Catalogs  .................... 1 entry
7   Genealogy Connecticut  ............................. 1 entry
8   Genealogy Eskimos Greenland  ....................... 1 entry
```

As with other systems, you choose from this menu and find out what's under the heading, where it is, and so on. That should be enough to give you an idea of what's at this library.

Remember that you connected to Delphi, which connected you to a gopher, which connected you to this library's computer in Ohio, so you're connected to this system through a chain of computers. You must log out of each one in turn to leave. To get out, return to the

previous menus (the gopher command is Back) until you're back at your home menu, in this case the Delphi prompt Internet Gopher>. Then log out of Delphi as usual.

These are just three examples of the many systems out there. Some are menu-driven and easy to use; some give you only a prompt and expect you to know what to type.

Fine, you're saying, lots of libraries are online. But how do I know where to look for them? Well, the gopher in this last example is a good route. Another source is the Internet-Accessible Library Catalogs file, available from anonymous FTP at yaleinfo.yale.edu, port 7000. Then use the FTP command CD to get to /LIBRARIES. Or you can use the host at gopher.utdallas.edu, port 70, and go to the directory /LIBRARIES, or the host gopher.sunet.se, port 70 and the directory /LIBRARIES/YALEINFO. Also, look for a file called LIBRARY .INSTRUCTIONS at ftp.unt.edu, under /PUBS/LIBRARIES. This file explains how to use many of the programs you'll come across in dialing up library card catalogs, and would be handy to print out and keep by your side. It's updated periodically by the authors. Also, the program discussed in chapter 1 in this book, Hytelnet, has lists of online libraries.

Finally, be sure to ask at your local library whether they're connected to other systems; they might have an up-to-the-minute list.

17

The Library of Congress online

CHAPTER 17

THE Library of Congress has an extraordinary amount of information for genealogists, but until very recently you had to go to Washington, D.C. and rummage in dusty confusion and frustration to find the treasures. Now, several research aids and services are available, some in print and some online.

Over 26 million Library of Congress records in 35 different files became available to the general public on the Internet in 1992. Previously, such access had been available only to researchers at the library, library staff, congressional offices, and selected institutions and agencies involved in cooperative programs with the Library of Congress. The Library of Congress requires no fee to search its files, but many Internet access providers do charge fees to connect to the Internet.

The host address for telnet access to the Library of Congress Information System (LOCIS) is locis.loc.gov (140.147.254.3). You can also connect via the World Wide Web at http://lcweb.loc.gov/.

LOCIS includes more than 15 million catalog records for books, microforms, music, audiovisuals, manuscripts, microcomputer software, serials, maps, name-and-subject references, and in-process items. LOCIS also contains citations to federal legislation (1973–), copyright registrations and legal documents (1978–), Braille and recorded materials for those unable to read print, selected foreign legislation (1976–), foreign legal references (1989–), and a listing of 13,000 organizations that provide information arranged by subject.

Except for national holidays, LOCIS is available for searching at the following times (EST): Monday to Friday 6:30 A.M. to 9:30 P.M., Saturday 8 A.M. to 5 P.M., and Sunday 1 P.M. to 5 P.M.

Complete instructions for searching LOCIS and obtaining the LOCIS Quick Search Guide and LOCIS Reference Manual are available on the initial screens presented to users upon connecting to LOCIS. The manual, in searchable form, is at gopher://lcweb.loc.gov/11/locis/guides.

The availability of selected Library of Congress computer files over the Internet is a major step toward the creation of an electronic "library without walls," as outlined in the library's strategic plan for the year 2000, which was delivered to Congress last year.

You can receive a recorded message containing instructions for connecting to the Library of Congress Information System (LOCIS) over the Internet by calling 202-707-3656.

Although documentation for searching Library of Congress files is available for free downloading over the Internet, you can also purchase it in a packaged, easy-to-use format (described in the following sections). Use this documentation to understand the content of the databases available for searching and learn how to formulate search queries. Instructions for signing onto the Library of Congress Information System (LOCIS) over the Internet are also available.

LOCIS Reference Manual, 1993

This printed reference manual, available for $30 including postage, describes how to gain access to the Library of Congress Information System (LOCIS), which includes more than 26 million Library of Congress records in 35 different files. File descriptions include MARC (machine-readable cataloging) files; copyright files, 1978 to present; and federal bill status files. Commands for searching both the Library of Congress technical processing/cataloging system (MUMS) and the reference/retrieval system (SCORPIO) are also described. The manual includes instructions for signing onto the system over the Internet and conducting searches. Approximately 200 pages long and measuring 8.5 × 11 inches, the manual is spiral-bound for easy reference. A handy index to the files, commands, and search points is also included.

LOCIS Quick Search Guide, 1993

Available for $15, including postage, this is a handy, quick-reference guide for searching the Library of Congress Information System (LOCIS) over the Internet. Spiral-bound for easy use at your workstation, the guide features approximately 30 pages of brief, clearly formatted instructions for searching Library of Congress files.

For each file, a brief description of the content is followed by concise instructions for formulating search queries, and selecting and displaying records. User tips, examples, and instructions for limiting searches are also included. The guide is also 8.5 × 11 inches. To order, use your Visa or MasterCard and call 800-255-3666 (toll-free, U.S. only) or 202-707-6100, or send a fax to 202-707-1334.

Let's look at a Web session with LOCIS. Figure 17-1 shows the opening Web page, which tells you about the following offerings:

General Information and Publications
    Find out about the Library and its mission, information for visitors, publications (including Library Associates and *Civilization Magazine*), employment opportunities, and other general information.

Government, Congress, and Law
    Search THOMAS (legislative information), access services of the Law Library of Congress (including the Global Legal Information Network), or locate government information.

Research and Collections Services
    Browse historical collections for the National Digital Library (American Memory), visit Library Reading Rooms, access special services for persons with disabilities, and read about Library of Congress cataloging, acquisitions, and preservation operations and policy.

Copyright
    Learn about the U.S. Copyright Office and the registration process, access copyright information circulars and form letters, and read about many other copyright-related topics.

Library of Congress Online Services
    Search Library of Congress databases and online catalog (including LOCIS) or connect to the Library's Gopher (LC MARVEL).

Events and Exhibits
    Read about Library events, conferences and seminars or view electronic versions of major exhibits.

Explore the Internet
    Search the Internet, browse topical collections of Internet resources organized by Library of Congress subject specialists, and learn more about the Internet and the World Wide Web.

At the top of the page, you'll notice the "search" link. This is a text search based on topics (not a full-text search) of the offerings at

Figure 17-1

Use any browser, including those you find in commercial online services, to go to http://lcweb.loc.gov to access the Library of Congress, National Archives, and other government resources.

LOCIS. If you click on the word *search*, you'll get to the page in Fig. 17-2. You can type in just one very general word, such as genealogy, and get very general results, as shown in Fig. 17-3. Or you can add words to get more specific results.

From here you can also use Marvel, the gopher of the Library of Congress. Searching Marvel for *genealogy* will provide the results in Fig. 17-4. From here you can go to the index of the U.S. 1790 census, at the following address:

```
gopher://gopher.nara.gov:70/00/genealog/holdings/catalogs/census/
  1790/1790pt1.txt
```

or you can access information about interlibrary loans, or dozens of other text, pictures, and even sound files. To use Locis from a telnet program, tell your browser the location of the telnet. (For example, if

Figure 17-2

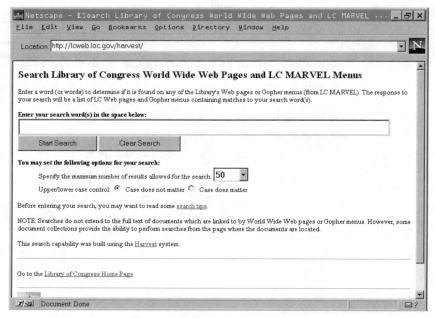

You can search the entire site for "genealogy," any surname or state, or a combination of these.

Figure 17-3

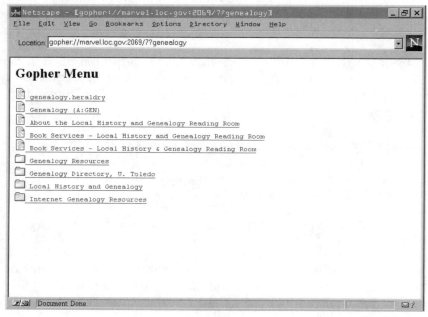

A simple search, such as "genealogy," will get you very general results.

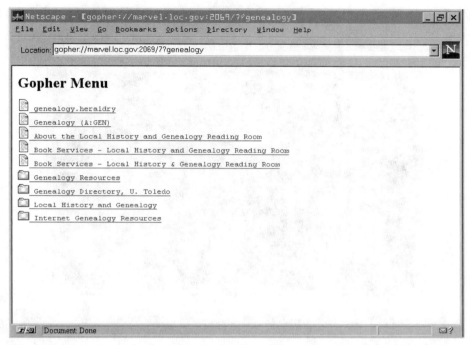

Figure 17-4

Marvel is a gopher of text information files. There are several on genealogy.

you use Qmodem Pro for your telnet and Netscape Navigator for your browser, click on Options, General, and then Apps, and tell Netscape that your telnet program is D:\QMODEMPRO\QMWIN.EXE.) Click on the telnet link on the Web page http://lcweb.loc.gov/homepage/online.html, and you'll get something like Fig. 17-5, although your telnet might look a little different. To find out if there are books in the Library of Congress that interest you, choose 1 from the opening menu. Then choose 1 at the next menu to search for books. From here, use the Browse command. You could type in browse genealogy ohio spencer and see whether any books in that subject come up. The information you get there can help you place an interlibrary loan request.

You'll also want to visit the Library of Congress' ftp site. Here you'll find:

Figure 17-5

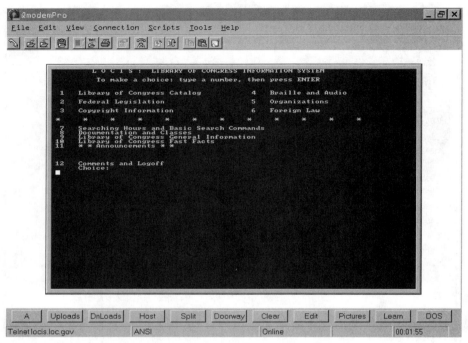

LOCIS via telnet, this happens to be Qmodem Pro's telnet function. Simply input 1 to search for books you might want via interlibrary loan.

/pub/american.memory This directory contains various reports and papers written about the American Memory Project at the Library of Congress.

pub/exhibit.images This directory contains images and text from various Library of Congress exhibitions, with a separate directory for each one.

/pub/folklife This directory contains the text of Folkline, a weekly cooperative information service of the American Folklife Center at the Library of Congress and the American Folklore Society. Folkline information is subdivided into three categories: professional opportunities, training opportunities, and conference calls for papers.

/pub/reference.guides This directory contains the full text of various reference guides, finding aids, and bibliographies produced by

Library of Congress reference staff. You'll find both large and binary files in this directory, and smaller text files through LC MARVEL.

Explore the Library of Congress online often, as the offerings are large and always changing.

A

The GenServ project

The Genealogical GEDCOM Server system (GenServ) has an extensive collection of GEDCOM databases that contain basic genealogical information such as names, dates of birth, marriages, details of family relationships, and often the sources of this information and other descriptive text.

Once you're a registered user, you can access GenServ via the World Wide Web at http://soback.kornet.nm.kr/~cmanis/ and, using the forms there, submit your queries. You can also request automated searches of this information by sending commands to GenServ by electronic mail, and the system will send you the results by e-mail as well. You don't have to have full Internet connectivity in order to use GenServ—just an e-mail box somewhere.

You can perform one sample search, for free, before you submit or pay anything by going to http://soback.kornet.nm.kr/~cmanis// and clicking on One-Time Search for Any Surname. Read the instructions carefully, because you'll get only one try.

GenServ was set up and is managed by Cliff Manis. It was implemented by Ron McDowell, based on the use of the LifeLines genealogical program and database, written by Thomas Trask Wetmore, and incorporates a search program written by John Smith.

GenServ was edited by Brian Randell, Cliff Manis, and Nancy Bruce. Jon Rees serves as a point of contact for European users submitting databases. John Chandler has written and modified several of the GenServ reports used on this system. All the databases and reports are being maintained using LifeLines, version 3.0.2.

The GenServ database has been collected from people who donated their own family data for this project. The administrators are interested in any genealogical databases, large or small.

The data is accessible through commands sent to the system via a regular e-mail message. The system then formats the request and e-mails a report back to the user who sent the request. The system runs on a 150-MHz Pentium with 64 megabytes of memory and 10 gigabytes of hard disk space, and is online 24 hours a day to support your requests. Starting in April 1996, GenServ will have an ISDN 128K connection to the Internet.

The most efficient way to use GenServ, in terms of connect time, is to use your e-mail Internet access, whether that's through a commercial online service or an Internet service provider.

You can provide up to six GEDCOM databases to GenServ, including ones on behalf of other genealogists who don't themselves have the necessary computer and networking facilities. However, only people who have themselves submitted one or more GEDCOM databases can make queries, though these can also be on behalf of others.

There are over 3,300,000 names in the system, although the administrators admit there are duplications. This number has been growing rapidly.

 # Signing up

For the first three years, GenServ was free. But as costs and the time necessary to run the system rose, the administrators found they had to start charging, although they've attempted to keep it as reasonable as possible. The various costs are listed in Table A-1. To become a user,

you must follow the sign up procedure carefully. First, create and send a GEDCOM, as detailed in the following section, and send it to:

Cliff Manis
HHC, 18th MEDCOM
P.O. Box 579
APO AP 96205
USA
cmanis@soback.kornet.nm.kr (e-mail)

If you live in Europe, you can send your disk to:

Jon Rees
Church Cottage
Ringsfield, Beccles
Suffolk NR34 8JU
UK
AEP3 DFR J.M.REES@DFR.MAFF.GOV.UK (e-mail)

Then send a check for the level of service you want. Make it payable to GenServ and send it to:

Cliff Manis
Attn: GenServ System
P.O. Box 33937
San Antonio, TX 78265-3937

GenServ Costs

Table A-1

Yearly cost	Type	Gives you
$12	Regular sponsor	A maximum of 12 requests per hour. More than one message per hour is possible, but only 12 requests total.
$6	Over 60 and students	For those users over 60 years old, and students attending school (verification will not be attempted)
$35+	Prime sponsor	For any company, group, or individual who is willing to contribute support at a higher level. Up to 50 requests per hour.

 # Preparing your GEDCOM

A GEDCOM file is required for access to GenServ, but don't send off your disk willy-nilly! Have your genealogical software compile a database with all the genealogical data you've accumulated and analyzed in your researches, including not only basic data such as names and dates, but also any Notes fields. Be sure the database is the results of your own researches, not simply one produced by automatic extraction from some other system such as the IGI CD-ROM system. (The database remains the property of the original submitter, and won't be provided in GEDCOM format to anyone else.)

When GenServ searches, it does so on the entire set of databases that have been submitted to it, but each database remains separate and associated with the name of its author. So if you find new or better data in the future, you can withdraw a database that you submitted previously and replace it with an updated one. This has another implication, however: no effort is made to eliminate or merge duplicate individuals found in more than one database, and many duplicates are, in fact, known to exist.

In theory, a GEDCOM database exported from any genealogical database management system should be acceptable to any system that claims to be able to import GEDCOM. In practice, so many differences exist between the GEDCOM formats used by various systems that a GEDCOM database produced by one system might not load correctly or at all into some other systems.

So once you've generated your GEDCOM and before you send it to GenServ, run a test to be sure the database can be successfully imported by one of the following systems:

➤ PAF (LDS), version 2.1 or later

➤ GIM (Genealogical Information Manager), version 2 or later

➤ Brothers Keeper, any version 1992 or later

➤ LifeLines, the UNIX genealogical program, any version

Three of the above programs are available via ftp.cac.psu.edu (128.118.2.23) from the Genealogy area. Also, it's wise to check the database with the GIM_312.ZIP program and Brother's Keeper.

If you use Family Tree Maker, be sure to save your GEDCOM as a PAF file (version 4 or 5, using the IBM PC character set), with no indent and with abbreviated tags before checking that it can be successfully imported into one of these systems.

If you use Roots IV, be sure to save it as a Roots 3 GEDCOM file (Roots IV GEDCOMs can't be read by GenServ). Having performed such a check, send your GEDCOM database on a 3.5-inch floppy disk (in a diskette mailer) as either an ASCII file or a DOS file compressed with PkZip to the previously listed postal address for Cliff Manis (who is currently living in Seoul, Korea). The address for Cliff will be valid through at least August 1996 and maybe 1997.

Finally, with the disk you must include a piece of paper on which you've typed your e-mail address, postal street address, city, state, zip, country, and telephone number. Cliff will get your disk in less than three weeks, and will process it and give you an access code within another seven days. In all, give him about 30 days to send you a user code; if you don't get it by then, contact him by e-mail. Some special tips on submitting your GEDCOM:

➤ Apple Macintosh users should use Apple File Exchange or an equivalent utility to produce IBM-compatible floppy disks.

➤ If you have a database with over 30,000 surnames, please contact Cliff for special instructions for sending your large GEDCOM file to the GenServ system. The system has databases containing over 50,000 names each, but such GEDCOMs need special handling. You can e-mail Cliff about your large database at cmanis@Soback.Kornet.nm.kr.

➤ GenServ is very interested in the complete GEDCOM file, with all note lines and other tags.

➤ The data and documents on the system are the responsibility of the individual authors of the GEDCOM files. The files aren't edited or judged for content by the operators of the GenServ system. The data belongs to the author of the GEDCOM file,

and it's the responsibility of individual data providers to comply with all applicable laws and standards of what should or should not be published in their own GEDCOM files.

➤ Cliff Manis will not attempt to locate your e-mail address if you send a diskette without a valid e-mail address. If you don't include it, he can't help you.

➤ Updates to GEDCOM files on the system can be sent in only at six-month intervals. Don't send updates more frequently than this.

➤ Read the documents of the GenServ system carefully in full before you try sending in a file. You can get it several ways: by ftp download from ftp.cac.psu.edu or flattop.fc.net, or by sending an e-mail message to genserv-doc@progcons.com.

➤ If you find any discrepancies among duplicate entries in GEDCOM databases on GenServ, bring them to the attention of the submitters of those databases.

➤ The day you send the disk by mail, e-mail Cliff Manis to tell him it's coming! This gives him another chance to see whether your e-mail address is valid. He will also use this e-mail address to send a message confirming that your database has been loaded and tested, or to notify you that the database can't be loaded. (No attempt will be made to edit the database in order to get it to load.)

➤ To update, do the same thing you did for the first submission, but label the diskette "update to *database_name*."

⇨ **Using GenServ**

When your database is accepted into the GenServ system, Cliff will send you the user name, access code, and e-mail address that GenServ associates with your database(s). You have to include your user name and access code in any later request you make to GenServ. The e-mail address is the address to which GenServ will send its responses to any messages from you, no matter how you actually send them. It's therefore very important that you notify Cliff Manis (cmanis @progcons.com) of any changes to your e-mail address.

GenServ commands

The GenServ commands are as follows:

USER Identifies and authenticates the person submitting an inquiry to GenServ.

SPLIT Controls how GenServ divides up long reports into a set of messages before sending them to you. Useful if your mailbox has a size limit for messages.

SEND Requests one of a small set of standard information files.

EXCLUDE Controls which of GenServ's databases are to be searched.

SEARCH Performs an index search, i.e., requests a listing of all the individuals with a given name occurring in the currently-selected set of databases held by GenServ.

SOUNDEX Like SEARCH, but specifies the Soundex encoding of the surname of interest.

SEARCHCOUNT Calculates and returns a count of all the individuals with a given name occurring in the currently-selected set of databases held by GenServ.

SOUNDEXCOUNT Like SEARCHCOUNT, but specifies the Soundex encoding of the surname of interest.

MATCH Provides a convenient way of checking whether any of the individuals with given surnames in a particular database are a likely match to any of the individuals recorded in any of the other databases.

REPORT Requests a detailed report (of one of a number of different types) on an identified individual—typically found by means of the SEARCH or SOUNDEX commands.

To issue a command or commands, send a regular e-mail message to genserv@progcons.com. The server ignores the Subject line; it looks only at the body of the message to discover what you want and what to send back to you. Upper and lowercase don't matter. Multiple commands can be sent in one message, with one command per line (except REPORT commands, which require three lines). All command lines start with a keyword. The server will respond separately to each command. (Depending on the length of the response, it might be sent by GenServ as one or more messages.)

The server is entirely automatic. It tries to give error messages for certain kinds of incorrectly formatted user messages. If your User line is correct but one of your requests is wrong, you'll get an error message. If your User line is wrong or invalid, the server simply won't respond. If the surname isn't found in the database but the commands and the User line are correct, the server will respond. So if you don't eventually receive a reply, assume that the format of your request message was incorrect.

All GenServ commands are processed as they're received, but there might be a small delay before the resulting reports are sent by e-mail. All valid user requests are usually processed within an hour, but the system will process only up to six requests in 30 minutes for any one user. Remember that the response can also be delayed, perhaps for hours, by network outages.

Send your requests in batches, no more than six at a time. You don't have to try to get everything in one day; this system will also be available for use next week and next year!

 # A sample command message

The following example message:

```
USER: MANIS, CLIFF 60101AAA0001
SPLIT: 20
EXCLUDE: MB5 CHAR4X
SEARCH: manis
```

would produce a listing similar to the following:

```
This Index of Surnames has been generated by GenServ

INDEX OF SURNAMES FOUND
====================================================================
LAST, First     INDI# Spouse name      SNDX Birthdate   Deathdate Dbase
----------      ----  ------------      ----  ----------   ---------- -----
MANIS, Alda C   171   OWENS, Joyce F   M520 11 Mar 1939             mb5
MANIS, Amos     1443  FRANCIS, Mary E  M520         1805       1840 mb5
MANIS, Annas    12572 JONES, John      M520 14 Mar 1791  2 Nov 1874 mb5
MANIS, Annas    486   JONES, John      M520 14 Mar 1791  2 Nov 1874 char4x
MANIS, Arnold M 1459                   M520 18 Jun 1893 19 Jul 1893 mb5
MANIS, Arthur M 866   MOORE, Ollie L   M520  8 Sep 1886 27 Mar 1950 mb5
----------      ----  ------------      ----  ----------   ---------- 
```

The second column is an identification number that—until the relevant database is modified—you can use with REPORT commands in order to obtain detailed reports on an individual as an alternative to giving the individual's name. The third column gives the name of the individual's spouse, if one is listed in the database. The fourth column gives the Soundex encoding of the individual's last name. You can use the SOUNDEX command to request that searches be performed using such a Soundex code, and avoid having to make a whole set of separate searches based on many different similar-sounding versions of an individual's surname.

A complete example

The following example:

```
USER: Manis, cliff 60101AAA0001
SPLIT: 64
REPORT: Rv2
DATABASE: mB5
NAME: Manis, Alda c

Exclude: mb5
search: D'Anjou
search: MANIS
search: harris

send: Datadate
send: datatot
```

```
send: fileset
SEND: HELP
```

uses a shorter form of the access code, which is acceptable; sets a
64K message-length limit; requests an Rv2 report on Alda C Manis in
database mb5; searches the entire set of databases except database
mb5 for individuals with the surnames D'Anjou, Manis, Harris, and
Peters; and finally requests several information files, including finally
(perhaps rather belatedly) this manual. (It also illustrates the ability to
use either upper or lowercase letters, interpose separator lines, and
have leading spaces.) One of your first messages as a user to GenServ
should be:

```
USER your-id
SEND FILESET
```

This describes the set of files currently available for you to request by
means of the SEND command. You should make a habit of getting this
and reading it regularly, as it contains the latest information about
GenServ, and is updated with the command USER NEWS on a regular
basis. It has the most current information about what's happening on
the system. Sometimes it's updated two or three times a week, and it's
the file with which Cliff keeps users informed about new things on the
system. If you aren't reading this file, you're missing the latest
information about the system. The new reports and new information
will always be listed in the FILESET file. Other files you can get are:

HELP The official manual, describing the capabilities of GenServ.
This is the documentation for users.

INFO The same file as HELP.

RPTSAMP A file consisting of examples of all the types of reports
currently available.

DATADATE A complete listing of the databases in GenServ and the
date and time that each database was loaded. By using this and the
DATATOT file, you can determine which databases have been loaded
since your last request.

DATATOT A listing of the last few databases to be loaded, giving the date and time that each was loaded.

 # Conclusion

There's much more GenServ can do, and the administrators are tweaking and engineering all the time to improve it. For details on the reports and latest features, get the documentation as described in the last section. This is one great project; do try to support it!

B

Tiny tafel matching system

Like a GEDCOM, a tiny tafel is a way of expressing what data you have to share. Unlike a GEDCOM, however, its primary use is not to exchange that data, but to alert people to its existence and show how to reach you to exchange data. A tiny tafel allows you to indicate interest, to let people know what you have and what you need in a quick, standardized way. Though computers read tiny tafels to make these matches, once you learn the format, you too can read and understand what the TT has to say.

Paul Andereck, editor of a now-defunct magazine called *Genealogical Computing*, proposed the tiny-tafel format in 1986, as an alternative to the numerical ahentafel. It would be a shorthand for the data: instead of listing every known ancestor in a particular surname line, the TT would instead show a range for the surname, in dates, locations, and Soundex codes. An entire surname line would be summarized by one line in a tiny tafel. The top of the file would have contact information for exchanging the actual data. The data fields in a TT would be fixed, making it easy for various computer programs to read the files, and making matches easier.

The standard format for tiny tafels was first used in Commsoft's Roots program, but now several genealogical data programs either have built-in or add-on utilities to output a tiny tafel from your data. As the

format is very rigid and unforgiving of typos, you should probably have a program prepare your tiny tafel rather than try to do one "by hand." You should be able to read them, however, and know what each column and line means.

Computers can easily read tiny tafels and build databases of them, looking for matching entries. Many bulletin boards carrying the National Genealogy Conference have such databases, and the Fidonet itself has a program to look at such databases all over the world and report the matches back to you. This is the tiny tafel matching system (TTMS).

The word *tafel* is German for *table*, so a tiny tafel is a small table of data pointers. Each line and column has a specific meaning.

 # Anatomy of a tiny tafel

The first few lines in a tiny tafel contain information about the TT's originator. N starts the line with the name of the person. As many A lines as necessary can be used for the surface mail address of the person. T is the line for voice phone contact. B is the line for the BBS the person uses, and C for the communications setup of that board. The S line lists commercial online services, with user ID, for e-mail contact; there can be up to five of these lines. The D line describes what sort of floppy disk this person can use to exchange data: 3.5, for instance. F, the format line, describes the software the person uses. Several R lines might follow with remarks such as "I could have some erroneous data." Of these introductory lines, only the N line, the first one, is mandatory. The other mandatory line is the last one of this introductory section, the Z line. This line has the total number of data items (lines). If the number of lines doesn't match the number in the Z line, the TTMS program assumes an error has been introduced into the file. This is one reason why it's best to let the computer create your TT; if you add or delete lines between the Z and the terminator line (W), but forget to change the number in the Z line, your TT will be rejected by the system. So the top of a typical TT will look like this:

```
N Elizabeth P. Crowe
A 619 Mountain Gap Road
```

```
A Huntsville, AL 35803
T (205) 555-5555
S etravel@delphi.com
S LibbiC@aol.com
S lcrowe@iquest.com
C 28.8K/O/Zmodem
D 3/1.4M/DSDD
F BK for Windows
R I also can exchange data via fax
Z ********
```

The Z line will hold the final count of the data lines. Now comes the fun part—the description of the data. Here, each column in each line is significant. Each line is considered a record, and fields of different but usually specific lengths are assigned to the columns of the line. The data is divided as follows:

Columns 1 to 4 Soundex code for the name with the highest interest level.

Column 5 A blank space.

Columns 6 to 9 Birth year of the earliest ancestor.

Column 10 Interest flag for the ancestor line, which are one character each: a space for no interest, a period for low interest, a colon for moderate interest, and an asterisk for the highest interest level.

Columns 11 to 14 Latest descendant's birth year.

Column 15 Interest flag for the descendant end of the family line.

Columns 16 to 16+ The surname string area, which can be variable. You can add up to five surnames per line from 16 on, but you want to save some room for the place names, too.

Columns 16+ to PL Place names for the birth of the earliest ancestor and latest descendant. A backslash indicates the ancestor place and a forward slash the descendant place.

So a typical TT line could be:

```
K530 1770*1996 Kennedy\IR/Boston MA/St. Louis MO/San Francisco CA
```

The soundex code is K530. The submitter is very interested in this line in the 1770s, but not interested in the present generation. The Kennedy came from Ireland to Boston, and the family migrated through St. Louis to San Francisco. Once you get used to it, it's very easy to read.

Some tips and rules: you must enter valid dates, and dates are required. The matching system cannot work without dates. If listing the first and last of a line hides some migration, you can break the surname into two lines. Remember that this is a shorthand version of your research, so you render the information as best you can. If you aren't sure about the exact location of a place, put something there, even if it's just a continent. The more information you give, the better chance you have of finding someone with similar interests. If you have to edit a program-generated tiny tafel, remember to change the Z line if your total number of data lines changes.

⇨ Using tiny tafels

There are lots of places and ways to share tiny tafels. The first thing many people do with them is post them to the Usenet newsgroup rec.genealogy.gendata (the corresponding Fidonet group is GENDATA). These are for posting only; discussion of the tiny tafels takes place in other newsgroups and echoes or by private e-mail. On the Internet at http://emecee.com, you'll find Michael Cooley's archive of tiny tafels. You can submit yours and search the ones that are there. The Roots-L archive (at the moment residing at http://infobases.wia.net/roots-l/) also has information in a format very similar to a tiny tafel.

But the most fun thing to do is to find a bulletin board system near you that participates in the tiny tafel matching system. This task isn't as daunting as it sounds; the National Genealogy Society's list of genealogical BBSs is a good place to start. Look for boards that list

DA as one of their echoes. You can also ask around at local computer user groups and genealogy clubs for the nearest one.

TTMS is free. Any BBS offering the TTMS service must provide it for free, although many sysops require that you first post a tiny tafel of your own to qualify for the free access. Submitting tiny tafels is just one of the three main functions of the TTMS software. The other two are instant searches, where you search only those tiny tafels on the BBS you're using, and the offline search, where you submit a query and receive a report on the results several days later. The query will be sent to all the other TTMS boards before the report is generated. This is a way to do a nation-wide search with just a few keystrokes.

Generally, this is done through a "door" program (a program that takes over while the BBS software steps aside, except for communications). An example is shown in Fig. B-1. This is the screen

Figure B-1

```
QmodemPro                                                    _ □ ×
File  Edit  View  Connection  Scripts  Tools  Help

B>lue Wave Mail
Select:


Commsoft Tiny-Tafel Query System V1.25
                            Copyright 1986, 1987 , 1990 by Commsoft, I
nc.
Welcome to COMMSOFT's Tafel Matching System (TMS). There are 1435
Tiny-Tafel files containing 56628 lines here in San Francisco.
TMS has 70,000+ nationwide.

If you contribute your tafel, you get access to the U.S.
data and a new menu.

I    S.F. search
E    Upload  Tiny-Tafel file
Q    Quit TMS and return to BB System

Enter choice (i e q): I


INSTANT MATCH. Search for family names in this TMS database.
Enter surname or soundex code to match: Spencer
There are 76 entries with soundex code S152 in this database.


Line  Count    Surname
0       1      SAEBENS
3       3      SAPPINGTON
4       1      SEBYNS
5       1      SEVENOAK
6       1      SHOPFNOSKY
7       1      SIBENS
8       1      SKOBINSKY
9       1      SPANG
10      1      SPANGLE
14      4      SPANGLER
-- MORE --

  A    Uploads  DnLoads   Host   Split  Doorway  Clear   Edit   Pictures  Learn   DOS

Roots SF at 14400          ANSI                  Online                  00:03:14
```

In Instant Match, you can check tiny tafels on just one BBS. Simply enter the surname and close or exact matches will be listed.

from Genealogy SF in California, profiled in chapter 2. After logging on, as described in chapter 2, you can do an instant match. This isn't very efficient because you must do it while online and because you can search only one board at a time, but it will do for practice. As the illustration shows, you answer a few questions and then matching lines from tiny tafels are shown. If one looks close enough to be interesting, you can get the contact information by typing the line number of the entry (see Fig. B-2).

Figure B-2

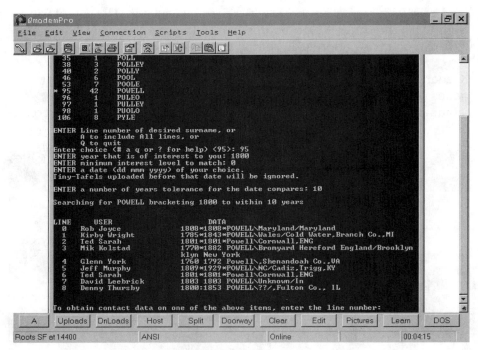

If you find a match, the tiny tafel line matching your search will be displayed. You can get contact information by entering the line number of the one that interests you.

Once you enter your tiny tafel into TTMS (and remember, do it only once!) you'll be able to choose the Match option. Just as with Instant Match, the software will ask you questions and you specify name (or soundex code), dates, places, and interest levels. You can also limit the search by the date of the tiny tafel, thus searching only those files new since your last search.

In a few days, you'll start getting reports from other TTMS BBSs. To retrieve the reports, go back to the TTMS and it will tell you which reports are waiting. You can read the reports online or download them to your computer to read offline. I recommend the latter; these reports have much more information than instant searches, and can run up to 100 pages.

The TTMS reports will first remind you of the criteria, and then list the matches by BBS. Names, contact information, and the TT line that matched will be listed for each hit.

 # Submitting a tiny tafel

You can submit a tiny tafel by calling a TTMS BBS directly. You can also e-mail your TT to Brian Mavrogeorge at mavrogeorge@sfo.com. With your TT, include four surnames and other information for your search (dates, interest level, locations) and Brian will get the results back to you. You can also post your TT onto the Fidonet National Genealogy Conference, in soc.genealogy.surnames, or in alt.genealogy.

Glossary

Terms

ahentafel The word means *ancestor table* in German, and the format is more than a century old. It lists all known ancestors of an individual, and includes the full name of each ancestor as well as dates and places of births, marriages, and deaths. It organizes this information along a strict numbering scheme.

anonymous FTP (file transfer protocol) The procedure of connecting to a remote computer as an anonymous or guest user in order to transfer public files back to your local computer. Anonymous FTP is usually read-only access; you often cannot contribute files. *See also* file transfer protocol and protocol.

Archie An Internet program for finding files available by anonymous FTP to the general public.

baud A measure of speed for data transmission across a wire. It is not equivalent to bits per second, but to changes of state per second. Several bits might go across the wire with each change of state, so bits per second can be higher than the baud rate.

backbone A set of connections comprising the main channels of communication across a network.

Bitnet A cooperative computer network interconnecting over 2,300 academic and research institutions in 32 countries. Originally based on IBM's RSCS networking protocol, Bitnet supports mail, mailing lists, and file transfer. Now merging with CSNet and running the RSCS protocol over TCP/IP protocol (Bitnet II), the

network will be called Computer Research and Education Network (CREN).

bulletin board system (BBS) A combination of hardware and software into which you can enter information for other users to read or download. Many bulletin boards are set up according to general topics and are accessible throughout a network.

chat When people type messages to each other across a host or network, live and in real time. On some commercial online services this is called a *conference*.

client-server interface A program that provides an interface to remote programs (called *clients*), most commonly across a network, in order to provide these clients with access to some service, such as databases and printing. In general, the clients act on behalf of a human end-user (perhaps indirectly).

compression A method of making a file, whether text or code, smaller by various methods so it will take up less disk space and/or take less time to transmit. Sometimes the compression is completed by the modem; sometimes the file is stored that way. The various methods to do this go by names (followed by the system that used it), such as uuencode (UNIX), PkZip (DOS), Arc (DOS), tar (UNIX), and StuffIt (Macintosh).

conference A live, online chat, a forum, or an echo of e-mail messages.

CREN Computer Research and Education Network is the new name for the merged computer networks Bitnet and Computer Science Network (CSNet). It supports electronic mail and file transfer.

database Information organized for computer storage, search, retrieval, and insertion.

domain name system (DNS) The Internet naming scheme that consists of a hierarchical sequence of names, from the most specific to the most general (left to right), separated by dots, for example nic.ddn.mil. *See also* IP address.

door A program on a BBS that allows you to perform specific functions, e.g., download mail, play a game, or scan the files. The BBS software shuts down while you're in a door and the door's commands are in effect.

downloading The electronic transfer of information from one computer to another, generally from a larger computer to a smaller one, such as a microcomputer.

echo A set of messages on a specific subject sent to specific BBS that has requested those messages.

e-mail An electronic message, text or data, sent from one computer to another computer.

flame A message or series of messages containing an argument or insults, not allowed on most systems. If you receive a flame, ignore the message and all other messages from that person in the future.

forum A set of messages on a subject, usually with a corresponding set of files. It can be on an open network such as ILINK, or can be restricted to a commercial system such as CompuServe.

File transfer protocol (FTP) Allows Internet users to transfer files electronically from remote computers back to their own computer. Part of the TCP/IP/Telnet software suite.

gateway Used in different senses (e.g., mail gateway, IP gateway), but most generally for a computer that forwards and routes data between two or more networks of any size or origin. An electronic gateway, however, is never as straightforward as a regular gate; the process of getting the proper addresses in the proper sequence is more like a labyrinth. Use with care!

GEDCOM The standard for computerized genealogical information that's a combination of tags for data and pointers to related data.

gopher An Internet program that searches for resources, presents them to you in a menu, and performs whatever Internet program

(telnet, FTP, etc.) is necessary to get the resource. See Veronica and Jughead; all three are read-only access.

host computer In the context of networks, a computer that directly provides service to a user—in contrast to a network server, which provides services through an intermediary host computer.

hotkey When a BBS system responds to one-keystroke commands without requiring you to hit the Enter key, that option is called a hotkey. Some BBS software enables it with no option to turn it off; others let you set it either on or off in your user configuration.

hub A BBS that collects e-mail regionally and distributes it up the next level; it also collects the e-mail from that level to distribute it back down the chain.

Internet The backbone of a series of interconnected networks that includes local area, regional, and national backbone networks. Networks in the Internet use the same telecommunications protocol (TCP/IP) and provide electronic mail, remote login, and file transfer services.

Jughead An Internet program that helps gopher build menus of resources by limiting the search to one computer and a text string.

IP (Internet protocol) The Internet standard protocol that provides a common layer over dissimilar networks; it moves packets among host computers and through gateways if necessary.

IP address The alphanumeric address of a computer connected to the Internet, also called the Internet address. The format is usually *user@someplace.domain*.

listserv An electronically transmitted discussion of technical and nontechnical issues. It comes to you by electronic mail over the Internet using listserv commands. Similar lists, often using the UNIX readnews or rnfacilty commands, are available exclusively on the Usenet. Internet users can subscribe to Bitnet listservers. Participants subscribe via a central service, and lists often have a moderator who supervises the information flow and content.

lurk To read a list or echo without posting messages yourself. It's sort of like sitting in the corner at a party without introducing yourself, except it's not considered rude online; in fact, some places expect you to lurk until you get the feel for how things are done.

modem A device to modulate computer data into sound signals and to demodulate those signals into computer data.

moderator The person who takes care of an echo, list, or forum. This person takes out messages that are off-topic, chastises flamers, and sometimes maintains a database of old messages and handles the mechanics of distributing the messages.

MNP Data compression standard for modems.

NIC (network information center) An NIC provides administrative and user support, and information services for a network.

NREN The National Research and Education Network is a proposed national computer network to be built upon the foundation of the NSF backbone network, NSFnet. NREN would provide high-speed interconnection between other national and regional networks. SB 1067 is the legislative bill proposing NREN.

offline The state of not being connected to a remote host.

online Being connected to a remote host.

OPAC Stands for online public access catalog, a term used to describe any type of computerized library catalog.

OSI (Open Systems Interconnection) This is the evolving international standard under development at ISO (International Standards Organization) for the interconnection of cooperative computer systems. An open system is one that conforms to OSI standards in its communications with other systems. As more and more genealogical data becomes available online, this standard will become increasingly important.

PPP Point-to-point protocol. An improvement on SLIP, this protocol allows any computer to use Internet protocols and become a full-fledged member of the Internet with a high-speed modem. The advantage of SLIP and PPP accounts is that you can usually achieve faster connections this way than through a service such as Delphi.

protocol A mutually determined set of formats and procedures governing the exchange of information between systems.

remote access The ability to access a computer from outside a building in which it's housed. Remote access requires communications hardware, software, and actual physical links, although this can be as simple as common carrier (telephone) lines or as complex as telnet login to another computer across the Internet.

shareware Try-before-you-buy concept in microcomputer software, where the program is distributed through public-domain channels and the author expects to receive compensation after a trial period. Brother's Keeper, for example, is shareware.

signature A stored text file that contains your name and some information, such as names you're searching for or your mailing address, to be appended to the end of your messages. It should contain only ASCII characters and no graphics.

SLIP Serial line Internet protocol, allows a computer to use Internet protocols with a standard telephone line and a high-speed modem, becoming a full-fledged Internet member. Several commercial companies now offer PPP or SLIP accounts for a monthly or yearly fee.

sysop The system operator of a BBS, forum, or echo. The sysop sets the rules, maintains the peace and operability of the system, and sometimes moderates the messages.

tagline A short, pithy statement added to the end of a BBS e-mail message. Taglines are rarely seen on commercial networks such as Prodigy, Delphi, and CompuServe.

tiny tafel A table of contact information, surnames, dates, and places. Meant for indicating interest, not for exchanging information. A TT provides a standard way of describing a family database so the information can be scanned visually or by computer. All data fields are of fixed length, with the obvious exceptions of surnames and optional places. Many TTs are extracted from GEDCOMs.

TCP/IP Transmission control protocol/Internet protocol is a combined set of protocols that performs the transfer of data between two computers. TCP monitors and ensures the correct transfer of data. IP receives the data from TCP, breaks it up into packets, and ships it off to a network within the Internet. TCP/IP is also a name for a protocol suite that incorporates these and other functions.

telnet A portion of the TCP/IP suite of software protocols that handles terminals. Among other functions, it allows a user to log onto a remote computer from their local computer. On many commercial systems, you use it as a command, e.g., telnet ftp.cac.psu.edu. Once there, you're using programs, and therefore commands, from that remote computer.

terminal emulation Most communications software packages allow your personal computer or workstation to communicate with another computer or network as if it were a specific type of terminal directly connected to that computer or network. Your terminal emulation should be set to VT100 for most online card catalog programs.

terminal server A machine that connects terminals to a network by providing a host telnet service.

thread Discussion made up of a set of messages in answer to a certain message and to each other. Sometimes very worthwhile threads are saved into a text file, as on CompuServe's Roots Forum. Some offline mail readers will sort by thread, that is, according to subject line.

TN3270 A version of telnet providing IBM full-screen support, as opposed to VT100 or some other emulation.

upload To send a file or message from one computer to another. *See* download.

Usenet A set of messages and the software for sending and receiving them on the Internet. The difference between Usenet and a mail list lies in the software and the way you connect to them.

V.32 A data compression standard for modems.

Veronica An Internet program to help gopher find resources based on a search string.

Z39.50 protocol Name of the national standard developed by the National Information Standards Organization (NISO) that defines the level protocol by which one computer can query another computer and transfer result records using a canonical format. This protocol provides the framework for OPAC users to search remote catalogs on the Internet using the commands of their own local systems. Projects are now in development to provide Z39.50 support for catalogs on the Internet. SR (search and retrieval) ISO Draft International Standard 10162/10163 is the international version of the Z39.50 protocol.

Smileys (emoticons)

Because we can't hear voice inflection over e-mail, a code for imparting emotion has emerged. These punctuation marks take the place of facial expressions, and are called smileys or emoticons. Different systems will have variations of these symbols. Two versions of this "unofficial smiley dictionary" were sent to me by Cliff Manis (the Roots-L mailing list administrator; Internet address cmanis@csf.com), and I've edited and combined them. Several versions are floating around, but I think this one sums up the ones you're most likely to see.

:-) Your basic smiley. This smiley indicates pleasure or a sarcastic or joking statement.

;-) Winky smiley. The user just made a flirtatious and/or sarcastic remark. Somewhat of a "don't hit me for what I just said" smiley.

:-(Frowning smiley. The user didn't like that last statement or is upset or depressed about something.

:-I Indifferent smiley. Better than a frowning smiley, but not quite as good as a happy smiley.

:-> The user just made a really biting sarcastic remark. Worse than a :-).

>:-> The user just made a really devilish remark.

>;-> Winky and devil combined. A very lewd remark was just made.

- -:-) Smiley is a punk rocker.

- -:-((Real punk rockers don't smile.)

=:-) Smiley punk rocker.

=:-((Real punk rockers don't smile).

=:-) Smiley is a hosehead.

;-) Wink.

,-} Wry and winking.

:,(Crying.

:-: Mutant smiley.

.-) Smiley has only one eye.

,-) Ditto . . . but he's winking.

353

:-? Smiley smoking a pipe.

:-/ Skepticism, consternation, or puzzlement.

:- Ditto.

:-` Smiley spitting out its chewing tobacco.

:-~) Smiley has a cold.

:-)-8 Smiley is a big girl.

:-)~ Smiley drools.

:-[Unsmiley blockhead.

:-[Smiley is a vampire.

:-] Smiley blockhead.

:-{ Mustache.

:-} Smiley variation on a theme.

:-{) Smiley has a mustache.

:-{} Smiley wears lipstick.

:-} Wry smile or beard.

:-@ Smiley face screaming.

:-$ Smiley face with its mouth wired shut.

:-* Smiley after eating something bitter or sour.

:-& Smiley is tongue tied.

:-# braces.

:-# | Smiley face with bushy mustache.

:-% Smiley banker.

:-< mad or real sad smiley.

:-=) older smiley with mustache.

:-> hey hey.

:- | "have an ordinary day" smiley.

:-0 Smiley orator.

:-0 No Yelling! (Quiet Lab).

:-1 Smiley bland face.

:-! ".

:-6 Smiley after eating something sour.

:-7 Smiley after a wry statement.

:-8(condescending stare.

:-9 Smiley is licking his/her lips.

:-a lefty smiley touching tongue to nose.

:-b left-pointing tongue smiley.

:-c bummed out smiley.

:-C Smiley is reaally bummed.

:-d lefty smiley razzing you.

:-D Smiley is laughing (at you!).

:-e disappointed smiley.

:-E Bucktoothed vampire.

:-F Bucktoothed vampire with one tooth missing.

:-I hmm.

:-i semi-smiley.

:-j left smiling smiley.

:-o Smiley singing national anthem.

:-O Uh oh.

:-o Uh oh!.

:-P Disgusted or nyah nyah.

:-p Smiley sticking its tongue out (at you!).

:-q Smiley trying to touch its tongue to its nose.

:-Q smoker.

:-s Smiley after a BIZARRE comment.

:-S Smiley just made an incoherent statement.

:-t cross smiley.

:-v talking head smiley.

:-x "my lips are sealed" smiley.

:-X bow tie.

:-X Smiley's lips are sealed.

::-) Smiley wears normal glasses.

:'-(Smiley is crying.

:'-) Smiley is so happy, she/he is crying.

:^) Smiley with pointy nose (righty). Sometimes used to denote a lie, myth or misconception.

:^) Smiley has a broken nose.

:(Sad Midget smiley.

:) Midget smiley.

:[Real Downer.

:] Gleep . . . a friendly midget smiley who will gladly be your friend.

:* Kisses.

:*) Smiley is drunk.

:< midget unsmiley.

:<) Smiley is from an Ivy League School.

:=) Smiley has two noses.

:> midget smiley.

:D Laughter.

:I Hmmm . . .

:n) Smiley with funny-looking right nose.

:O Yelling.

:u) Smiley with funny-looking left nose.

:v) left-pointing nose smiley.

:v) Smiley has a broken nose.

`:-) Smiley shaved one of his eyebrows off this morning.

,:-) Same thing, other side.

~~:-(net.flame.

(-: Smiley is left handed.

(:-(unsmiley frowning.

(:-) Smiley big-face.

):-) ".

(:I egghead.

(8-o It's Mr. Bill!.

):-(unsmiley big-face.

)8-) scuba smiley big-face.

[:-) Smiley is wearing a walkman.

[:] Smiley is a robot.

[] Hugs.

{:-) Smiley with its hair parted in the middle.

{:-) Smiley wears a toupee.

}:-(Toupee in an updraft.

@:-) Smiley is wearing a turban.

@:I turban variation.

@= Smiley is pro-nuclear war.

***:o)** Bozo the Clown!.

%-) Smiley has been staring at a green screen for 15 hours straight.

%-6 Smiley is braindead.

+-:-) Smiley is the Pope or holds some other religious office.

+:-) Smiley priest.

<:-I Smiley is a dunce.

<:I Midget dunce.

<¦-(Smiley is Chinese and doesn't like these kind of jokes.

<¦-) Smiley is Chinese.

=) Variation on a theme . . .

>:-I net.startrek.

¦-) hee hee.

¦-D ho ho.

¦-I Smiley is asleep.

¦-O Smiley is yawning/snoring.

¦-P yuk.

¦^o Snoring.

¦I Asleep.

0-) Smiley cyclops (scuba diver?).

3:[Mean Pet smiley.

3:] Pet smiley.

3:o[net.pets.

8 :-) Smiley is a wizard.

8 :-I net.unix-wizards.

8-) glasses.

8-) Smiley swimmer.

8-) Smiley is wearing sunglasses.

8:-) glasses on forehead.

8:-) Smiley is a little girl.

B-) horn-rims.

B:-) Sunglasses on head.

C=:-) Smiley is a chef.

C=}>;*()) Mega-smiley . . . A drunk, devilish chef with a toupee in an updraft, a mustache, and a double chin.

E-:-) Smiley is a Ham radio operator.

E-:-I net.ham-radio.

g-) Smiley with ponce-nez glasses.

K:P Smiley is a little kid with a propeller beenie.

O :-) Smiley is an angel (at heart, at least).

O :-) net.religion.

O-) Megaton Man On Patrol! (or else the user is a scuba diver).

X-(Smiley just died.

Index